THE FINE ART OF

GRIEVING

JANE EDBERG

Published by Linen Press, London 2024

8 Maltings Lodge
Corney Reach Way
London W4 2TT
www.linen-press.com

A CIP catalogue record for this book is available from the British Library.
United States Library of Congress Registration Number: TXu 2-348-601 December 21, 2022

Cover art: Jane Edberg
Cover Design: Jane Edberg
Typeset by Zebedee
Printed and bound by Lightning Source
ISBN: 978-1-7394431-2-2

About the Author

After the death of her son, Jane Edberg read every grief book she could get her eyes on, from memoirs to self-help books, only to find that her experience of grief and the impact of processing loss through art were not well represented, if at all. What was missing compelled her to write a memoir about her unconventional path through grief using the profound transformative power of art.

Jane holds a Master of Fine Arts from the University of California, Davis with an emphasis in performance art and fine art photography. She has been teaching creatives for over thirty-five years and offers writing workshops and private coaching. She serves as a contributing editor at *The Journal of Radical Wonder*. Her most recent writing is featured in the book, *Death, and its Terrible, Horrible, No Good, Very Beautiful Lessons: Field Notes from The Death Dialogues Project*, Motina Books, 2022; and in the flash anthology, *BAM 42 Stories*, BAMWrites, to be released in 2024; recent journal publications include *Cholla Needles, Gyroscope Review,* and *MacQueen's Quinterly*. Her etymphrastic artwork is showcased in the poetry book, *My Dead*, Kelsey Books, 2023.

Jane was born in Windsor, England but has lived most of her life in the United States. She resides with her husband and their poodle near the beautiful Monterey Bay National Marine Sanctuary in California.

Praise for The Fine Art of Grieving

'I cannot find the words to match this artist's, mother's riveting memoir. I have served fifty years researching and writing about the arts and humanities to promote death education for medical personnel and the general public. Jane's memoir says so much more about grief than all my "colleague experts." Even for the most experienced therapists among us, her memoir should be required reading for professionals in the field of dying, death, and bereavement. More importantly, her book is a must read for anyone, as we will all, at some point, experience traumatic loss and grief. Jane's words and images offer us hope as she leads us through a transformative healing process.'
— Dr. Sandra Bertman, PhD, Fellow in Thanatology, author of *Facing Death: images, Insights, and Interventions*; *Grief and the Healing Arts: Creativity as Therapy*

'The Fine Art of Grieving is unique in the world of books. Its deep and brilliant exploration of loss and recovery is heightened in beauty and illumination by wondrous, accompanying photographs.'
— Marion Roach Smith, author of *The Memoir Project: A Thoroughly Non-Standardized Text for Writing & Life*

'The Fine Art of Grieving is a strong brave book about the hell a person can go through and survive. I am deeply impressed and inspired by Jane Edberg's writing and her actions and her determination and her art.'
— Abigail Thomas, author of *Still Life at Eighty: The Next Interesting Thing*

'The Fine Art of Grieving is a literary force that will change the way you look at grief, at art, and what it means to be human. Edberg's depiction of the pain and despair of grief in equal balance with the exquisite beauty of showing up fully to the human experience is a stunning accomplishment. Jane Edberg is the writer that all of us weirdos have needed our whole lives.'
— Roxan McDonald, author of *Spiritual AF Activity Book and Guided Journal*, social media influencer @spiritual_af

'Grief is not just an emotion, but a rupture in life that never fully heals and yet creates positive transformations. You can't reason it away, and yet art can take it to a place where you can reflect on it in your heart. Jane Edberg shows you in beautiful language and visual art how to apply a healing alchemy when tragedy visits you. Reading her story may help you live through and beyond whatever challenges life offers you.'
— Thomas Moore, author of *Care of the Soul,* and *Soul Therapy*

'Jane's approach to processing grief, both through her art and writing, is beautiful and harrowing. The rawness of emotion and the intentionality of how this story is told provides the reader a unique experience that all stories of grief should strive for: a chance for us to sit with sadness that also confronts the strangely personal ways grief consumes us.'
—Nathan Shuherk, BookTok – social media influencer @schitzophrenicreads

'With shocking courage and creativity, Edberg unveils the power of grief to transform life. Shaman, artist, drowning woman, moon-hostage, pyromaniac, unlikely Viking priestess: she reveals every last bit of her participatory magic to teach us the mercy of grief.'
— Shelly Eyre Graham, PhD, Clinical Psychologist & Author

Author's Notes

The Fine Art of Grieving is a creative non-fiction narrative, a work of art, a memoir based on what I remember to be true. My recollection of experiences over time may not reflect what others remember. Memory is subjective and mine has its own story to tell.

*

Some names have been changed to respect the privacy of those individuals. Some events have been compressed. Dialogue has been recreated from memory consistent with the nature of the content and the person speaking.

*

This memoir includes sensitive topics, including but not limited to trauma, loss, grief, death, suicide, mental illness, and graphic language. Readers are encouraged to assess their own comfort levels and exercise discretion.

Remembering Nanda.
Dedicated to my family, and the transformative
power of loss, grief, love, and art.

What's Art Got to Do With It?

Facing Ashes

Grief is an unstoppable train.

December 1, 1999.

The box sat undisturbed on a shelf in a shadowy corner of my art studio, a room I had avoided for almost a year.

The box weighed two and a half pounds. It measured six-by-six-by-four inches. An envelope taped to the lid secured documents detailing its contents and proper disposal. Inside the box was a clear plastic bag packed to the brim, sealed tight by a pinched metal clasp. Attached with wire, a stamped stainless-steel tag no larger than a quarter read CR-79 13550.

Anticipating the first anniversary of my son's death, I brought the box into the living room where sympathy cards and dried roses still hung from ribbons tacked across the entryway. A photograph of his smiling face lay flat in a silver frame on an otherwise empty wall. No one is home.

Light coming through a picture window from an unchanged colourless day cast a square of illumination onto the coffee table. I knelt on the floor next to the table, draped white satin across its surface and placed a wide bowl on the fabric, dead centre. A view camera, the size of a birdhouse, sat next to me on a tripod, lens tilted down, aimed directly into the bowl.

With a knife, I split open the box. Fingers sore, nails chewed raw, I removed the bag, pried off the clasp, twisted the wire and released the tag. Squeezed the numbered coin into the middle of my palm until warmed and placed it against my cheek before setting it on the table. I cradled the sack by its belly and poured out the greyest of greys through a mesh sieve to sift the fine grains into the bowl. Tumbled the remaining shards onto cloth. Listened to the decibel of crushed bone.

I scooped handfuls of Nanda's ashes and let them fall through my fingers. Nineteen years of life pulverised. I pressed my palms into his ashes and lifted them to reveal two handprints, detailed fingerprints and my clearly defined lifeline. No trace of him. I shook the bowl to dissolve the impression.

Holding my breath, I lowered my face and hovered over the basin of my son's remains. My skull, a clapperless bell. His empty landscape, the surface of the moon, pits and fissures, offered no sign of existence. I dipped in my tongue. No taste. Eyed the wet spot as it dried, faded, hardened. Exhaled. Grit against the roof of my mouth, chalk between teeth, I used my sleeve to brush porous bits of him from my tongue.

A trickle of tears rolled off my chin into the bowl. Blood-grey clusters formed. Not a glimmer of hope, but a wish that everything could forge back to the way it was. Hands went under, clumps crumbled. Over and over, I tried to resuscitate what was not there. Deep breath in, I buried my face.

As I raised my head, I heard the click of the front door and turned to see my daughter, Rachel, walk in. I had lost track of time, forgotten about my sixteen-year-old and where she had been. She stood with a fixed gaze on my face powdered with ash. Pale grey specks scattered over my black shirt, constellations across black leggings.

Rachel closed the door slowly, eyes locked to mine, her forehead creased over one arched eyebrow. I saw my kid dressed in a hoodie, blue jeans and her graffitied tennis shoes. I also saw her future woman self—wise, empathic, full of grace.

My eyes shifted to the window through to the backyard, to a honeysuckle-covered fence that hid railroad tracks where trains rumbled past our house like clockwork. Twice a day, horns bellowed. She slid her backpack off her shoulder to the floor.

'Mom? Do you need help?'

I turned to face her. She tipped her head to one side. Soft light caught the curve of her cheek. My knees burned into the carpet.

'Yeah.'

Rachel walked to my side, leaned over and examined the composition on the coffee table. She held her breath and squinted to see my faceprint embossed in a bowl of her brother's ashes. A grimace pushed deep into the sand of him.

Hands and Face in Nanda's Ashes

Rachel touched the metal tag with one finger, picked up the empty remains container and glanced at the plastic bag, then observed the ripped-open boxes of film. Her eyes landed on the camera, its shutter release cable dangling.

'What are you trying to do?' She rolled her sleeves to her elbows.

Chin to chest, I idled. 'I don't know.' Hands lead-heavy in my lap, I rested on my heels.

'This looks like art, Mom. You're making art.'

She reached into her sweatshirt pocket for a hair tie and gathered waves of auburn hair into a messy bun. Rosy-cheeked, chocolate almonds for eyes, she smiled, eyebrows curved high, hands rested on her hips.

'Tell me what to do.'

I taught my three kids how to use cameras when they were old enough to hold them, but never the view camera, the heavy beast and its methodical steps. I loosened the tripod head to swivel and adjust the camera upright. She scooted closer and cranked the handle to position the ground glass to frame my face. As she draped a focusing cloth over her head, I looked into the dark eye of the lens.

'Can you see me?' I asked.

'Yes.'

'Now turn the knob on the bellows to focus,' I instructed, as ash fell from my face.

'Got it.'

Rachel pulled the cloth from her head and adjusted the controls using her pointer finger and thumb, pinkie in the air.

'Slow shutter, full-open aperture?' She knew I loved murky-dark portraits.

'Exactly. Flip the lever and slip in the film holder.'

'K.' She pushed in the holder, cocked the shutter, pulled out the slide and reached for the cable release. 'Hold still.'

My nerves twisted as she followed the steps for each exposure. I tried to hold still. I could not find myself to be myself. Like shaking a bowl of ashes, I had dissolved. Reset. Everything erased as I knew it.

A slow shutter speed held the camera's curtain open and blurred my writhing onto the film. Between shots, I covered my face with my hands, imagined what grief looked like, then rubbed my eyes free of ash to see her cherub face.

'I used to make art.'

Rachel sighed. 'You've never stopped making art.' She pointed towards the front yard. 'You know, like the images you made of Nanda's blanket in the garden.' Her eyes cut into mine as I teetered. 'And his blanket in the river.'

'I'm just documenting.'

'It's more than that,' she said.

'Do you think the photo I created at the railroad tracks is art?'

'Yeah.' She studied me, her eyes full of worry. 'Those are cool images, Mom.'

'I am making art?'

Without Nanda, I felt like a one-year-old stumbling into a new life. Rachel nodded.

I heaved myself from the floor to stand in front of a six-foot square of black velvet fabric pinned to a wall, a backdrop I had used since Nanda's death to document changes in my face.

Rachel, her bottom lip sucked in, dragged the camera into position and took a series of photographs of me as I shook my head. Ashlettes sprinkled like confetti. I wiped the ash from my face across the velvet surface, leaving behind a ghost image.

Through the floor, a distant quaking of steel rolling across rails announced an approaching train. We both stopped silent as a thump-clatter trembled the house. Outside the window, above the fence line, a blur of boxcars sped by, screeching. A horn blasted. We looked at each other, shoulders to our ears. The horn blasted again. I shut my eyes and threw my head side to side.

Can art be made after losing a child? Will art save me from this grief?

Rachel released the shutter and the gate I had locked shut, the creative portal I had walled off, hijacked by loss, opened.

What Grief Looks Like

Discovering the Art-Self

Art is essential.

When I was four, while getting dressed for some special occasion, for some unknown reason, possibly the removal of tight curlers or getting ringlets brushed and hair-sprayed into curls, I went into a rage, held my breath, turned blue and passed out.

'High strung and bloody spoiled,' Dad said, exaggerating his Londoner's accent.

When I came to, Mum asked me, 'Are you the Queen of England?'

I'd heard her comment to mean, 'There is nothing special about you.'

Soon after, in the backyard, I screamed, 'Yes, I am the Queen of England.'

Barefooted, in a pink chiffon dress, I squeezed dirt pudding between my toes and swung a stick through wet ground to let loose some fury. Little me slung sludge onto the house walls. Blobs of earth meandered down stucco. I whacked black mud into Mum's flower garden and slayed hollyhocks and tiger lilies till they drooped and dripped brown.

I'll never forget the slam of the screen door and Mum's cheeks, beet red, wildcat green eyes, teeth bared. Her aproned waist and impractical shoes. Stiff bouffant hair. I can still feel her wrangling my arm, smacking my legs.

My art-self emerged when I beat the earth and withstood the slap. The wild mud swackery became my first art-making or mark-making or, more precisely, art awakening, the autonomy of self-expression. The power of art-self enabled me to make someone feel how I felt, to change the look on Mum's face. A creative portal opened wide. Worth getting smacked, or what—back in the '60s—a British mother would call a good hiding.

As a quiet child, an observer, I was often misinterpreted as shy. Or seen as anxious, given that I bit my fingernails to the quick. Curious, experimental, perceived as mischievous. My imagination often considered weird and crazy. I personified the word misfit. Although extra sensitive, I had learned to be strong-willed yet patient. Often referred to as a tomboy. High strung and spoiled? Not really.

Learning how to harness creativity, I continued to express my insides outwardly, visually; that is how I processed everything in my world. Art, the making and unmaking, creating, imagining, and dreaming, helped me to investigate, to problem solve while developing, sustaining, and honouring my authentic self.

Jane 1960

December Never Happened

Grief steals time.

Tired of trying to make it in a small bubble of a town in Davis, California, with no job prospects, I convinced my husband, Roger, stepdad to my three kids, to open a map to broaden our career search. We were lucky. By midyear, both of us secured positions. Early September, Roger, Rachel, and I moved to Santa Cruz. Arian, age twenty-one, and Nanda, eighteen, almost nineteen, stayed in Davis. They rented a house with friends and were committed to work and school.

While setting up a new household and art studio, I worked sixty to eighty hours a week at a community college. In addition to teaching, I chaired the school's technology committee and curated the art gallery where I designed and hung an art exhibition every month. Overwhelmed, with no opportunity to visit Davis, I missed the boys.

Our family planned to celebrate November and December birthdays, Roger's, Nanda's, and mine, in Santa Cruz during the Christmas holiday.

Plans changed.

On December 2, 1998, Nanda was pronounced dead on the railroad tracks.

Shocked into standby, autopilot, essential functions only, barely, I slept through my birthday and spent most of December semiconscious. Like a robot, I handed in Nanda's work keys and house keys, paid his bills, closed his bank accounts, collected his personal effects, and ordered his body to be cremated. I thought if I waited, none of those tasks would ever get done.

Arian, ravaged with grief and not keen on large group get-togethers, opted to spend the holidays with his girlfriend. Roger, Rachel, and I went to Los Angeles to visit relatives until New Year's Eve.

I sat at the in-laws' kitchen table for days oblivious to my husband

and daughter. Christmas uncelebrated. Listless, I dipped a paintbrush into a jar of black ink, dragged it onto watercolour paper and watched it bleed, pool up in dimples of paper pulp, then soak into the fibres. I tried to draw salt and pepper shakers, bowls, cups, spoons, forks and knives, apples, bananas, a table and chairs, and the leafless trees I could see through a kitchen window. I slogged through the motions believing none of it was art. With a dripping brush, most of the illustrations morphed into inky clouds, some pages smothered in black, a reflection of my art-mind. Blank.

Nanda in the Ink

Not Making Art

Creativity doesn't care if you are broken.

Happy Fucking New Year! January 1, 1999. Time abbreviated. Stuck. Twenty-nine days had elapsed since I received the call. *Nanda, still gone.*

A friend of Nanda's sent me a video. I sat close to a TV screen to watch my son walk across a grassy field. No sound. He smiled into the camera as if smiling at me. Muscular as a middleweight boxer but walking like a ballet dancer. His face aglow as if painted by the Dutch master, Vermeer. I watched as he tossed his keys twenty feet into the air, spun around, then caught them behind his back into one hand without looking. When the screen turned to snow, I stared into the pixels and imagined Nanda as dissipating light. *Where did all that energy go?* I remembered his fierce side and how he seemed fearless in the face of injustice. He once punched an older guy bloody for calling his girlfriend, Carmen, a racial slur. With the same hand, he had written in a journal about his worries of becoming an adult next to a pencilled in self-portrait as a superhero. Nanda would drop everything to give undivided attention to someone in trouble, to anyone in need. *I wish he could have saved himself.*

In that immeasurable moment upon hearing about Nanda's death, my art-self hard drive crashed to zero, and the creative portal vanished. Nothing sparked creativity which meant I had no way to process grief. Art-making had been my salvation until a switch flipped from my child alive to my child dead.

Thinking had to be sucked hard through a nano-sized straw. In a dread point of view, I looked at a bottle of ink and instead of yearning to draw pictures to express loss, I wanted to smother everything black until everything disappeared to prove to myself, he was really gone, as in dead gone.

Later that morning, alone in the studio at the far end of our house, I wrestled with paint on a canvas for an hour, hypnotic brushstroke after brushstroke. Colours muted until I slathered the surface into a flat field of grey. I heard wind moaning and gazed out the window at a blustery sky, a cadaverous front garden where skeletal plants shook against a white picket fence, and beyond the fence, an empty street and a tidy row of suburban houses. I opened the window, welcomed in a rush of misty ocean air and spun in the cave of my head.

Roger walked in and asked me, 'Honey, what are you working on?'

'Huh?' I responded, with no energy to look at him.

'I'm asking you if you've started any drawings.'

'What drawings?'

'Maybe you should start a drawing.' He waited for an answer that didn't come. 'Okay, then, maybe not,' he said, and left the room.

Before Nanda died, I made art about a complicated childhood. What once seemed urgent, healing past trauma, was cancelled by death.

Resisting an internal riptide, I rested my hands on the sill and tightened my knees. Window curtains undulated over my head. Winter school break, four weeks off, would offer me some relief.

The studio, full and hollow, transformed into a puzzle, two lives, mine and Nanda's, both of us vying for attention, both of us missing. A mountain of boxes and bags occupied the middle of the room where, five days after his death, I had left his things. I hoped to cram his possessions into the closet to preserve them for a time when I felt ready to ponder his clothing, drawings, journals and collections, but when I rolled the closet door open, I had forgotten about the neat rows of shipping containers stacked floor to ceiling. I hadn't even unpacked most of my boxes since our move to Santa Cruz. I never landed.

My toes clenched the carpet. The thought of emptying studio boxes seemed dreadful, but I got to work. I piled art against studio walls, organised folders, papers and magazines into file cabinets, books into bookcases, and anything without a logical spot I stashed under my work table.

At the bottom of a container, I discovered calendar planners, 1970s, '80s and most of the '90s. I slid down against a couple of Nanda's bags, sat crossed-legged on the carpet and placed the planners next to me. A stack of life.

In my lap, I opened the 1979 calendar to November and spotted the number 23 square with bright-red-inked letters: *Baby Due*. That was the year my connection to my first husband, Billy, eroded. I had been struggling with depression. Also, that year, we had sex once and directly after, I had calculated the number of days it took for a human to gestate and marked it into the calendar. Nanda was born precisely on that date. I slapped the calendar closed and made a separate pile.

Shuffling through planners, I skimmed through 1985 and found the square which was hand-printed with a broad black marker: *D-Day*. Billy and I signed our no-contest divorce paperwork at an attorney's office after spending years trying not to come to that final agreement.

Thumbing through 1986, '87, and '88, bittersweetness set in as I opened the 1989 calendar to June, to a metallic red heart sticker on the day I earned both Bachelor and Master of Fine Arts degrees. Through extra hard work, I completed them in four years instead of six. I had redeemed my attitude towards education, having never graduated high school. I survived homelessness instead, but that is another story.

In the same calendar, I found dried orchids pressed between the pages of July. That's when I married Roger.

I hauled myself off the Nanda bundles and retrieved the 1998 calendar from my work table. Every square had been crossed off with a customary X to show that I had made it through each day until Nanda's tragic event. After his death, I couldn't bear to look at a calendar, much less mark each day as done, each day an indication of having been robbed of him. Day to day, impossibly long. No one made planners for moment to moment. A 1999 calendar was never purchased.

Crouched on the floor, I pulled aside the calendar years of Nanda's life, '79 to '98. His short life embodied in a shallow stack of nineteen years of planners. I feared my memory of him would shrink in proportion. I stashed them into an empty storage container and wrote *Nineteen Years of Nanda* in black marker across the side, then reclined into a bag of his clothes, shut my eyes and fell asleep.

We lived in Santa Cruz for less than three months before the call. In loss there is before and after. No present. Everything had changed. Roger's face became a shrunken head like something seen through the wrong end of a telescope. Rachel disappeared. Well, in truth, I disappeared. Me, mother, wife, teacher, artist, person. Undone. Unable.

My sense of purpose sucked away. Unrecoverable. Reduced to no one. No desire, not even an inkling. Unsound.

*

One evening while eating dinner with Rachel and Roger, I looked up from staring at my food to see their minds buried in their plates of macaroni and cheese. No words spoken. Our breathing inaudible. Not even eating sounds. The three of us in separate worlds.

'I'm in my own cubicle,' I said.

Roger and Rachel glanced upward, paused, looked down and returned to their food.

*

By late afternoon, low sun poked through lace curtains stencilling paisley patterns over my face and I woke up. Damp air chilled me to goosebumps but, too numb to care, I sorted through boxes, trying to consolidate my world with Nanda's. *Oh God, I am not storing his things for him; I am safekeeping them for me.*

Funny how I thought life could never get worse. Before Nanda died, my behaviour was weirdly functional when it came to work or family. An overachiever. Still, I spent considerable time trapped on a fucked-up-childhood merry-go-round and made mournful art to bring meaning to hard-wired trauma. I'd fallen to the cave-of-despair bottom, what I thought qualified as lowest of low. Dropped in regularly, anxious, on the cusp of devastation, readied to assume a foetal position or surrender to a fatal leap.

I ripped an ink drawing from the studio wall—a narrative about abuse. *What is this trite self-absorption?* The room greyed as sunlight faded. When I switched on an overhead light, the window framed a carbon sky. Under the influence of self-doubt, I remembered a professor back in grad school who told me my art was brilliant but soon after called me a sob sister. My artwork had depicted a sad childhood. They told me the best thing I could do was, 'Stop making art.' They laughed and said, 'Go home. Be a mom. Bake a cake.' That message stung, but it didn't stick, as most of the Master of Fine Arts seminars seemed like bootcamp. However, a seed was planted. After stripping the studio walls naked, I leafed through a collection of drawings. *Sentimental artifice. Self-pity. Indulgence.* I ripped my art to shreds and tossed it to the floor. *Sob sister. Sob sister. Sob sister.*

Art meaningless, I packed away palettes of watercolours, bottles of ink, boxes of acrylic paints, cups of brushes and jars of stones, shells, bones and butterfly wings. Random thoughts tangled, impossible to organise.

On my work table, I readied camera gear and film along with paper and pens to conduct an inventory, to document everything I deemed essential from that moment on. All I had to do was hold a camera to my eye and press the shutter release button. *Easy. Illustrate quick observations. Jot down notes to decipher someday.*

I heard a faint knock and turned to see Roger, his waist-length dreadlocks cushioned between the door jam and his head. His eyes, chameleonic, appeared greenish-gold, matching his T-shirt.

'I'm just checking in again. What are you doing?' he asked.

'I am putting away all of this shit I don't want.'

He walked into the room, reached for one of my art journals and flipped through the pages.

'Why are you putting all your stuff away? Don't do that.'

He bent down, gathered a handful of drawing scraps and shook them at me.

'This is your work.'

My eyes met the floor.

'Wow! How can you do this? You'll be sorry.'

I scanned the mound of drawing bits and art materials. Head still slumped, I raised my eyelids to see him. 'I can't compete with death.'

'Come on.' He snorted and wagged a finger at me.

'None of this shit is important.' My cement head fell back, eyes stuck to the ceiling. 'I can't make art anymore.'

'Wow!' He placed the journal along with the drawing bits on my work table and creased a knot between his eyes.

'I can't see the point,' I said.

With both hands, he lifted my face and kissed my forehead. 'Just wait. You will.'

The Map

Grief is the space your loved one occupies and does not occupy.

Two days after Nanda's death, numb to the core, I sat in a sterile office in front of the coroner. Short bangs framed her immovable face. Under bright lights at a bare desk, I didn't take my eyes off her. She had my son.

From her lab coat pocket, she removed a sandwich-sized plastic bag packed full and bound with an official label, Nanda's full name typed across it. She placed the package on the desktop and squared it with both hands.

'Here are the personal belongings,' she said with pursed lips and eyes low.

'Where are his clothes? His jacket?' I asked.

'They are soiled.'

'His shoes?'

'You won't want them.'

I did want them.

I wanted everything of his.

Tongue-tied, I thought I'd committed a crime and didn't deserve his belongings.

I'm a terrible mother.

'What about his hat?' I asked.

'I don't know about a hat.'

I wanted Nanda's jacket and his new blue shirt, but my throat seized. I wanted his shoes.

Where's his damn hat?

'I want to see my son.'

'First of all, I am going to recommend against a viewing. Do you understand that your son has been hit by a train?'

'That doesn't matter. I want to see my son.'

I shouldn't have left him in Davis.

My cheeks started to burn. I couldn't leave until seeing him was possible.

In a lowered voice she said, 'This office is not designed to accommodate an in-person viewing. You can sign a release, but we still have a problem.' She reached into a drawer for a form.

'Problem?' I asked, as I signed the release.

'I need the father to sign. I need both signatures. Until then, your son is a ward of the court. We can hold your son for another day. After that, you'll be charged if we continue to store his body.'

Store his body?

As she listed preliminary findings, my ears rang.

'Well-nourished young man. Well-groomed. Nineteen years of age matches his general appearance. Good teeth. Muscular. An arrow tattoo on his right shoulder.'

She had not interviewed any witnesses yet, had not completed the autopsy report, and was still waiting for drug test results.

'Cause of death, accident or suicide, still under investigation.'

She mentioned the train's speed and how long Nanda stood on the tracks. Without much consoling, she stood to let me know she was done.

'Where exactly did my son stand?'

Hand in the air, she signalled to hold on and removed a café receipt from her coat. She flipped it to examine both sides, then set it on the desk, print side up. From her lapel pocket she pulled out a red fine-tipped marker and a mechanical pencil.

Using the rows of numbers on the receipt as a guide, she pencilled in four lines to represent four sets of train tracks. She pointed, fingernail short and clean, to the middle lines.

'These are tracks one and two.'

She then drew curved lines to join the outer tracks to those middle tracks.

'This is where trains switch rails.'

Next, she made a red dot in the triangle where an outer track merged to meet track two.

'This is where he stopped.'

A half inch from the red dot, she drew a micro red line on track one, no longer than an ant, to represent Nanda's body lying across the track twenty-seven feet from where he originally stopped.

'You can find the spot by locating the 46.7 railroad marker.'

She returned the pens to her pocket and handed the receipt to me, nodded and left the room. Dazed, I slid the map into my pocket.

'Thank you,' I said.

*

Once inside the car, I cradled the map like a wounded hummingbird in my palm.

A map, two by three inches, the size of the universe. Small enough to be eaten but can never be swallowed. The map that revealed my biggest story.

The map, too much and not enough.

I hated the map. A map that can never be revised. So perfect, there is no mistaking it for anything else. So cruel and inflexible, no incantation could change its meaning. Nanda's death impossible to deny.

A map of logistics: his trajectory and his end. The map told me it was simple. Here to there. Alive to dead.

I focused on the red dot in the triangle, then on the red line, the exact length of Nanda's body scaled to the tracks. What I could not see was the invisible dot, me, anchored to train tracks for the rest of my days.

The map said, 'You have absolutely no control.'

'What have I done? What sort of mother am I?' I asked.

The unforgiving map did not answer.

I wanted to erase the red dot, cut away the red line, bring it in close, nurse it to life. *Wake up, red line, come home.*

Maybe I could love the map. A map that made all train tracks personal. So beautifully pained, I could kiss the spot, the rails where my old-self ended and my new-self began. My new place of birth.

I wanted to transform the map, read it until it disintegrated. But the map, even if destroyed, would live inside me. I could redraw the map. A complex composition. A piece to perform. A dance. Basic choreography. His short journey. A performance—done once. The map of the forever Nanda Junction. Art.

The Nanda Junction

Grief has its place.

Every time I drove through town, I was doomed to pass the Nanda Junction. But after my visit with the coroner, I summoned up the nerve to visit the railroad tracks. At night. Alone. I had been a couple times before but this was different—I had the map.

The sky flushed indigo and wind stirred as I drove onto Olive Drive, a lumpy road parallel to the railroad tracks, edged with trees as old as the city of Davis. Nanda routinely walked over those rails to get from the side of town where he worked to the other side where he lived. I rolled onto a shoulder and idled, waiting for an 8:00 p.m. Union Pacific. When the train came into view with its headlamps beaming, I stepped on the gas pedal. Steady with the locomotive, I clocked it travelling at sixty-seven miles per hour. I had heard that thirty-five miles per hour was the speed limit for freight trains passing through town.

At the end of Olive Drive, I slowed to an acceptable speed and turned to drive over a railroad crossing to reach the other side of the tracks, then made my way to Second Street. I parked the car and walked into the wind. A full moon spotlight followed me.

On a slope of ballast, I caught sight of the mound of remembrance, the memorial that had been made for Nanda. I had seen it before, the day after Nanda died, when I agreed to meet a newspaper reporter at the accident site. The judge-faced reporter asked me questions while a photographer, masked behind a black lens, circled me. I squatted to take a closer look at a photo of Nanda wedged into earth. The reporter told me she wanted to capture a story from a grieving mother, an artist who had lost her artist son but the next day, a front-page headline read 'Man Faces Train.' A colour photo of me crouching next to the memorial covered half the page and the story ran with a text that insinuated suicide. The reporter had turned him into a daredevil who lived on the edge. Nanda didn't purposely set out to do dangerous things. Sometimes he made impulsive decisions like scrambling up a steep cliff without thinking how to get back down with his friend taking two hours to talk him through a safe descent, or spending more money than he had because he'd found a deal he couldn't resist on a sporty pair of Michael Jordan shoes. The reporter's story wasn't a fair representation of Nanda.

Less than two days after Nanda's death, the memorial had quadrupled in size. Half a graffitied skateboard jammed into gravel stood like a tombstone. A framed photograph of Nanda with his girlfriend, Carmen, sat upright among unbound photos of Nanda with his friends. Candles fluttered in wax-drizzled jars. Love notes and sympathy cards flapped. Smoke from incense swirled. Across the ground was a scattering of stones, shells, sequins, glitter and pretty twigs. Pink and blue satin ribbons snaked over a pack of cigarettes, a bong and a bottle of Jack Daniels. Bundles of flowers, some fresh, some wilted, amassed at the periphery. My eyes followed as loose leaves and petals tumbled along the tracks. I swayed, ready to topple.

Someone had flowed fountains of candle wax down the front of the skateboard. Dripped, dribbled, and splattered wax over photos. Wax lines drawn across everything. I imagined a river of wax flooding the railroad tracks, cascading over me, streaming through L Street, burying the town, spilling down highways, rapids of wax pouring into the ocean.

Washed in moon glow and ambient light from street lamps, I ambled further up the tracks along Second Street. I found a man dumping water from a plastic milk carton onto an unmanaged triangle of earth located between the street curb, railway, and maintenance road. The mound was filled with a mishmash of grasses and flowers. Nearby, a tattered blue tarp draped over a shopping cart and bicycle snapped in the wind.

In a baggy army jacket, soiled elbows and torn collar, cargo trousers, cuffs folded over boots too big for his feet, a hoodie and ratty scarf covering his head, the man hoisted two pails of water and unloaded them into his garden. I sensed him harmless and stepped to the curb.

'Hey. What are you doing?' I asked.

He stooped to press dirt around a bunch of slumping primroses. I wasn't sure he heard me. I continued to watch him push plants into wet soil. *Am I dreaming?*

'Ah, some guy died on the tracks Wednesday night,' he replied. 'I thought I'd make him a garden. Found some plants in the hardware store dumpster.' He punched wet soil with his fist. Stringy hair waved from the hoodie, his face hidden.

I felt faint and squatted, cupped my hands to my face and pressed my fingers into my eye sockets, hoping to reset. *Is this real?*

Rows of meagre plants sagged in the dirt like mourners at a funeral.

'They'll perk up.' He lumbered to his camp, straddled his clunker bike and rode off towards downtown.

I walked the slope of gravel to the train tracks to observe glimmer on the rails. *Moonlight.* Distant car sounds, a plane overhead, then a baby crying. It took me a minute to see where the crying was coming from until I noticed a little girl, seven or eight years old, pushing a stroller, the cheap, simple, collapsible kind with wiggly wheels that spun in all directions. That rickety stroller carried a frantic baby, legs kicking. The girl was headed my way from L Street, pushing the stroller, laughing while it jiggled along the worn road. She bucked the stroller over the curb, across the sidewalk and up the gravelled slope onto the tracks.

I wanted to ask her, 'Where are your parents?' And tell her, 'You can die on these tracks.' But instead, dumbstruck, I kept quiet as she meandered.

The girl and the baby went clickety-clackety, tipped up and over, sometimes sideways to navigate the rails. Each jerky movement paused the baby's crying. After crossing, they disappeared into an apartment building on the other side of Olive Drive.

The tracks darkened beyond streetlight falloff, but I could still see. I analysed the map, found the 46.7 marker and headed to the red dot spot. The Nanda Junction.

Miles down the track, a light bounced on the horizon. I couldn't hear it, but another train was coming. I crossed the tracks, balanced on a rail, walked one foot in front of the other until I spotted a triangle Y-shape where the outer track connected to track two. *Right here. This is where he stood.* With arms wide open, I pivoted on my toes to face the direction of the train. I stepped down and wedged my feet into the track's triangle, then pulled my 35mm Instamatic camera from my fanny pack, aimed at my booted feet framed in the Y and took a photograph. I imagined being run over by the train, body air-cushioned, bouncing beneath the locomotive then bobbing upright like a child's blow-up-clown punching bag, wobbling, feet never leaving the ties. I returned the camera to my pack.

The engine's pulse drew closer, its light grew brighter, but I couldn't determine which track the train was on. I stared ahead and waited for a horn to blow. My lungs expanded; shoulders lifted. I felt the wood tie and gravel through the bottoms of my boots. Hand in pocket, I clenched the thin receipt, the map, the ticket, and waited for the hurricane train.

A few hundred feet in front of me, a flash melted across the field of view and dispersed beneath the railway signal towers. The train drew near but I still couldn't be sure on which track. The headlight was so bright the back of my eyes ached.

I didn't want to move. I wanted to feel the barrelling steel scoop me into the air. I wanted to fly like Nanda. Every cell of me vibrated. *Stay!* The light expanded, intensified. The face of the train caught the shine of the moon. A rumble started at my feet and travelled into my chest. *Just stay.* The train pounded towards me, coming down track two, the same track I was standing on. I lost sense of where I was, but when the train's shadow engulfed me, I jumped. My boots caught in the rail, and I catapult-stumbled, long rhythmic strides, crunched across rocks, lost my balance, then fell into ballast. The horn wailed through me and screamed off into the distance as boxcars chattered, squealed and stirred the air, leaving a metal aftertaste on my tongue. The air smelt of oil.

Sprawled like a killed deer, knees and palms dug into gravel, my heart throbbed in my throat. *Where's the map?* I lifted my head, scanned the tracks, flipped over and plunged a grazed hand into a pocket to find the map still inside.

I rolled over, worm-crawled to rest an ear to a rail, pressed to suction onto cold steel and listened to aftersounds of locomotion. Teeth chattering. Ears ringing. Twenty minutes must have passed before my heart pulsed into a normal rhythm.

My hand cramped as I pressed the receipt flat to my thigh trying not to wrinkle the Nanda map. In the other pocket, I fumbled five coins. I had been jostling them all day, listening to the jingle without thought. I sat up, freed my hands, and positioned the coins in a neat row onto a rail, readied for the next train.

In my periphery, a small beetle scurried across a wood tie. A life lived beneath trains. I pictured the creature dodging boulders flung from train tornadoes, hunting for roadkill, then grease-stuck to the rail. Short-lived. I imagined Nanda riddled with beetles, carried off by thousands, like a cartoon, promenaded across the tracks, squeezed down a dime-sized hole into the ground, never to be seen again.

'What were you thinking, Nanda?' I yelled and hauled myself to stand, a stack of bones, ankles to knees to hips to neck, swaying, no cartilage, tendons or ligaments, muscles ready to slump off. Jaw unhinged. I yelled it again, louder at the sky and dropped to my knees. 'Why? Why? Why?' Chin to chest, a couple of tears fell to the shiny surface of the rail. I sat on my heels and smeared the wetness with my fingertips till dry. *I'm so sorry.*

Like Nanda, who often took off his shoes to feel a place, I unlaced my boots and kicked them off into gravel. Rolled the socks off my feet and perched on a rail. *What am I supposed to do?*

Beneath a radiant moon, I reviewed the map. Stood and searched for the red line, the map's undotted exclamation mark, the spot where Nanda lay dead across track one. I arched my spine over that rung and gazed at a starless sky. 'Where is my son?' The full moon stared back at me.

As the night air cooled, dampness crept into my clothes. Full-body shivering, I pushed my feet into the boots, jammed socks into pockets and recycled through the information the coroner had shared. She told me the train's engineer had noted the train speed being thirty-five miles an hour. *No way!* He had sounded the horn twice and clocked thirty seconds from the time he noticed Nanda on those tracks to the moment of impact.

Waiting for the Train at the Nanda Junction

Learning Time

Thirty Seconds

Grief warps time.
   I counted,
one thousand one
one thousand two
one thousand three
one thousand four
one thousand five
one thousand six
one thousand seven
one thousand eight
one thousand nine
one thousand ten
one thousand eleven
one thousand twelve
one thousand thirteen
one thousand fourteen
one thousand fifteen
one thousand sixteen
one thousand seventeen
one thousand eighteen
one thousand nineteen
one thousand twenty
one thousand twenty-one
one thousand twenty-two
one thousand twenty-three
one thousand twenty-four
one thousand twenty-five
one thousand twenty-six
one thousand twenty-seven

one thousand twenty-eight
one thousand twenty-nine
one thousand thirty.

Thirty seconds is a long time.

Feet spread, planted firm against rails, I set the timer on my wristwatch for thirty seconds and pressed the start button. Barely breathing, with my eyes stuck open, I counted as seconds flashed, one to two, two to three, three to four, four to five, five to six. I tried to cram thirty seconds into my scrambled brain as the numbers fuzzed in and out. Poised like a drooping tulip, I held the watch inches from my face, weighing the seconds. Clenched my teeth and squeezed my toes. Those racing digits would not move faster.

The watch sounded, dit-dit-dit dit-dit-dit. I hit the stop button to silence the timer and started again. Shook my head to accelerate time. Each beat noted. My jaw tightened. I expected thirty seconds to be fleeting. Dit-dit-dit. *Thirty seconds lasts forever.*

My eyeballs bumped along the repetition of railroad ties. I tapped the stop button and hit start again. Frozen, I thought about the adage 'Time stands still for no one.' There is a theory, the faster you move through space, the slower you move through time. Nanda stayed still and might have accelerated a trillionth of a nanosecond. Not enough. *Why did you just stand there?* Dit-dit-dit.

'Fuck! Fuck! Fuck! Why the fuck did you stand there for thirty seconds? Thirty fucking seconds.' With a jacket sleeve, I blotted tears and snot from my face.

You had to have seen the train. 'Didn't you hear the horn?'

Dit-dit-dit dit-dit-dit dit-dit-dit dit-dit-dit dit-dit-dit dit-dit-dit dit-dit-dit dit-dit-dit dit-dit-dit dit-dit-dit dit-dit-dit. 'Why didn't you move?'

Stop. Start. Thirty seconds. Dit-dit-dit. Stop. Start. Another thirty seconds. Thirty seconds after thirty seconds after thirty seconds. Dit-dit-dit dit-dit-dit.

Nanda's last thirty seconds. He must have argued with that train. Too slow. Too late. Nanda's time ended. An epoch. An exact moment. December 2, 1998. Time of death: 8:05 p.m.

After another round of beeps, I silenced the alarm and set it to zero. I dropped my arms to my sides, but seconds kept rolling, and I kept counting. Untimely.

Time is relative. In grief, time is distorted. I chewed on thirty seconds repeatedly. Thirty seconds could not be devoured, only choked on, and still, like a curse, the repetition of time looped through me. I learned the real time it took to count to thirty.

Decades of memory, forty-two years, almost half of which included Nanda, nineteen years alive, flickered like film reeling through a projector. I rewound to my early childhood, cranked through my teens, my young adult years, the births of my kids, midlife. The times of life. Lifetimes. So many moons.

In a rush of recollection, I caught glimpses of how I grew to be quiet, invisible and suicidal. Saw myself die. I tried to picture Nanda standing on those railroad tracks. Counted again. Thirty seconds. Time and place. A place in time. Timing is everything. I begged the cyclone of memory-frames to slow down long enough for me to piece together what happened.

One thousand one ...

First Steps

In the year of my birth, 1956, I immigrated with my parents and my grandmum, Bibby, Dad's mother, from England to Canada, part of the British Commonwealth at the time. Dad joined the Canadian army and transferred as a police officer, with a better income and an opportunity to purchase a home. I was six months old.

*

I grew up next to railroad tracks in the rural countryside of Transcona, Manitoba. The train yard and quarry were located a couple of miles north. Railways sprawled in all directions across Manitoba, through Canada and beyond. A line ran two blocks away from our house. The tracks provided me solitude away from troublesome parents and bratty neighbourhood kids. I remember my first steps onto the tracks. I was four.

Late summer, under a vast sky and miles of prairie, I followed the rails. An only child. A four-year-old alone. I bounced barefooted in a starched cotton dress looking like a daffodil.

Decades have passed, and I can still hear a clickety-clickety-clickety-clack of a stick I dragged behind me over ties. I rhythmically hummed as trains drummed along rails and stood close enough to feel the vibration in my chest, the rush of wind in my face. I counted boxcars. Lumbering repetition calmed me.

Halfway to the train yard, prairie side of the tracks, goldenrod waved bright yellow tassels. Bees buzzed. I wove myself into overhead-high blooms. Hidden, I pretended to be lost. In the distance, meadowlarks chattered and trilled. Oo-oo-swoodle-oodle-dee oo-oo swoodle-oodle thrrrip-thrrrip-thrrrip.

I leaned back against the spring of goldenrod stalks to sway and hover over cool ground; to feel the tickle of leafhoppers as they popped and crawled over me, some stuck to my sweaty brow. Above me, a brilliant blue sky painted with yellow brushes. *I see the sky, and the sky sees me.*

A couple of years later and still fearless, I discovered a quarry near the train yard. Slopes of gravel twenty feet and higher. Kids had left behind pieces of battered cardboard boxes to use as sleds. I climbed the ballast pile dragging a sheet behind me. At the top, I sat on the board, clutched the sides, and tobogganed the steep bank of gravel. On first descent, I used my feet to decelerate, and instead of slowing, I tumbled. The outcome: bloodied knees and knuckles but with enough dirt and gravel dust to keep blood from dripping down my legs.

At the pit bottom, I checked to see if the sun met the horizon of the mound of crushed rock. Watched for dust to lift as wind quickened by dusk. That's when I knew to return home.

I skipped along a rail and stopped at a cast iron water pump, my landmark for flattening coins. With a jump, I heaved the pump lever up and let my weight hang to bring it down. Up and down until water gurgled from the spout. I cupped my hands and drank. I plucked a coin from the side of my underwear, five cents of milk money I had saved, and centred the coin on the rail next to the pump. Kids in the neighbourhood had cans full of flat and distorted pennies. A Canadian nickel at that time was hard-earned cash.

The next day I returned to retrieve the artefact. Against grey rocks, the shiny silver gleamed, easy to find. On one side, a beaver smashed into a cartoon; on the other side, the Queen of England's face compressed into a faint ghost.

One thousand two ...

Out of Sight

Mum nicknamed me Mouse.

'Quiet as a mouse,' she said.

And rarely seen.

Bibby once explained that Mum, horrified and bewildered, took me to a doctor hoping to find a cure for her overly sensitive, too fidgety, dreadfully anxious five-year-old.

'What was she supposed to do with a child who didn't eat, didn't talk, and was prone to fits?' Bibby asked me. She told me that instead of crying because crying wasn't allowed, I held my breath.

By the time I was thirty and had three children of my own, Mum explained why I was an only child. She told me she had been overwhelmed, starting at the age of fifteen, helping to raise her two brothers and four sisters while her mother resided at a sanatorium for tuberculosis and nerves.

'My mother was a very strict Victorian but she took good care of us when she could,' Mum said. 'When she fell ill, I was the mother.'

Mum kept me clean, well dressed and fed. Dad liked to remind me that they provided a proper upbringing: attention to etiquette, a good education, a tidy room, early to bed, early to rise. What he didn't admit to or maybe didn't consider was his tendency to drink and rage. I grew up in an era that glamorised a daily consumption of cocktails and cigarettes—even Valium and amphetamine were considered mainstream.

At the age of four, I could go anywhere I wanted if I returned home before sundown. Missed meals were no big deal; there were plenty of mothers handing out snacks. If I wasn't playing in my room, in the basement, or outdoors on the loose, feral, I'd spend time with Bibby.

We'd cuddle on her chesterfield to watch *The Ed Sullivan Show* and *Lawrence Welk* way past my bedtime. She gave me two sweets a day—Licorice Allsorts. We played Find the Thimble and chess. She read me Shakespeare as we listened to classical music. Bibby bought me my first camera when I was eight.

Dad usually worked late, and Mum, she liked to be left alone to cook, do housework, tend her garden, or visit with her friends.

Mum, sucking on a cigarette with little puff-bursts of smoke, would say, 'Go on then. Keep out of my sight.'

And I did.

One thousand three …

My First Full Moon

The air felt warm, and even though the sun sank below the horizon, the sky blazed full of colour. No older than six, headed home through grassy yards, I spotted a giant moon floating above a neighbour's doghouse, a classic red house shape that peaked above the fence with three steps to a dog hole. I don't remember a dog.

I climbed onto the doghouse roof and straddled the ridge. The full moon slid into the dimming sky. I could see the man in the moon, but I felt akin to the witch carrying firewood—a story told by Bibby. She joked we came from a long line of witches.

'Or was it bitches?' she asked. Grinning, wickedly laughing. 'Hur-hur-hur-hur-hur.'

Mum sometimes called me a bitch. Depending on her mood, that could be a compliment or a sign of disapproval. I discovered in a baby diary years later, the one where my parents recorded milestones, Dad had neatly printed, 'Good Lord! First word out of the child's mouth, BITCH!'

The notion of casting spells made me want to be a witch. The witch in the moon, I imagined her walking towards me. Close to tears, I trembled, like the first time I heard a live orchestra. The magnet moon lifted the hairs on my arms. Earth swelled and rotated. I tightened my body and rode the crest.

'Susan.'

I heard Dad call my name. My first name. I had insisted everyone refer to me by my middle name, Jane, like Jane Goodall, Jane and Tarzan, and especially Jane Eyre, which rhymed with Jane Ware, Ware being my maiden name. His voice boomed. I could hear him a block away, sounding off like the commanding officer he was.

'Susan.'

He couldn't see me.

'Susan.'

When the moon got sucked into the sky and looked like an ordinary white button, the witch disappeared.

'Susan.'

Everything turned blue-grey. I stretched towards the stars as his tone deepened.

'Susan.'

He bellowed in baritone.

'Susan.'

I shrank, slid off the doghouse and ran home.

One thousand four …

Learning to Draw

As soon as I could hold a writing implement, and maybe even before that, Dad would sit me on his lap at the kitchen table, place a newly sharpened pencil between my fingers, grasp my hand in his, and draw.

Warm with a firm grip, his hand guided mine, quick lines across a sheet of paper until a cartoon of a policeman, horse, or schoolgirl appeared on the page. He whistled, trilled a few notes of the *Blue Danube* waltz, and songs from the movie *South Pacific*.

I swayed as his hand guided mine to sketch a caricature of me in a pirate's hat. His face close to mine, fragrant with Old Spice, warped into a salty swashbuckler.

'Arrrrrrr, matey,' he said, peering through one eye.

With a flexing of muscular arm, his staccato marks shook me while he blackened an eye patch on the pirate face.

'All right then, luv. Down you go.' He slid me to the floor and swatted my bottom.

I turned around, and he handed me the drawings. For safe-keeping, I hid them behind a dresser in my bedroom, but somehow, those drawings disappeared. Later, I found them crumpled, mixed with food scraps inside the rubbish bin in the kitchen.

One thousand five ...

Maps I Drew

My second-grade teacher had a pointy face beneath a black beehive hairdo, wore red-orange lipstick and spoke French. She glared through cat-eye spectacles, mud puddles for eyes. Erect in clickety high heels, her slim body sleeved in a slate-grey dress, she strutted towards me. And because I never paid attention, because I was a daydreamer, a scared mouse, I could not interpret what she yelled as she yanked me from my chair. My classmates kept their heads down and remained quiet as they peeked sideways at us.

From the cubby beneath the desk, she extracted, sheet by sheet, my drawings: maps scrawled across maths book pages, cartoons over English lessons, diagrams of secret passages of escape on blank pages ripped out of school workbooks. I knew it was bad. Especially the one I drew on the inside cover of a French language book, an image of her holding a thick leather strap over her head and a cowering child beneath her. I most definitely knew better.

All my daily scribblings, half a school year of crumpled illustrations of the wrongdoings of adults, of an imagined life, and plans for escape, I had stuffed as far back as I could hide them into the cove of the desk. She dug deep into that cubby. Her knees turned white against taut stockings. Between French words were words I understood.

'Disgraceful. Look at this filthy mess.'

She dumped the drawings on the floor and insisted I throw them into the garbage bin.

'Dégoûtant,' she said.

I stared at her mouth; her baby-sized teeth reminded me of chewing gum, sharp white Chiclets. The veins in her pale face bulged blue; I daydreamed of them bursting. I wanted to cry, but I laughed. She clutched the collar of my seersucker dress and dragged me into the cloakroom at the rear of the classroom, grabbed the thick leather strap off its hook and told me in English to hold out my hands. I can still feel and hear the slap of braided leather over bare palms. Five whacks each. Before that last strike, I flinched and the strap landed across my knuckles.

I knew she would call my parents. I knew the punishment at home would be worse. But their efforts were futile. My need to create outweighed the flogging.

One thousand six …

Rampage

One early grey morning, lying in bed, I heard arguing through a heater grate. The floor rumbled. Dad's voice muffled. I jumped out of bed, pressed an ear to the door. Our house sounded like a sinking ship full of wild horses.

'Why can't you bloody well do as you are told?' he bellowed.

Floorboards creaked. I heard Mum sob and her slippered feet scuff through the hall. She stopped at my door. I didn't move. The handle turned, so I leaned on the door to prevent it from opening more than a couple of inches. Her teary green eyes spied through the crack. She smelled of night cream, and her pale face glistened, eyes puffy pink, cheeks and forehead mottled.

'Your father is on the rampage,' she whispered.

I was almost eight and understood. Whenever she used the word rampage, she and Dad were having a row. Dressed in a sheer pink nightgown, head crowned with rows of tight curlers under a hairnet dotted with satin roses, her face stretched with worry. I wanted to save her, but I didn't want Dad to come into my room. We both loved him, but sometimes he scared us to death.

Peeking around the door, I watched as she continued down the hall and disappeared into Bibby's room, the fabric of her nightgown almost catching as she closed the door behind her. Barefooted, Dad thudded after her. My chest fluttered. I hurried to close the door. He stopped, saw me through the gap and gripped the door handle. Both of us clung tight until I let go. The door opened. I stiffened. Greasy black hair hung over his brow. His eyes blazed in a stubbled face. Most mornings, an early riser, he'd be dressed sharp, even on a weekend day. His Jekyll side had flared. Wrapped in a black and brown striped terry robe, belt

50

tied tight around his waist—usually worn when he had dirty work to do—with folded arms, chest expanded, a noisy breath escaped him, smelling of booze and cigarettes. I stepped back. His forehead dented over his eyes as he clapped his hands. My insides jumped.

'Get yourself dressed.'

Dad could clap louder than anyone I knew. Two lightning-bolt, tongue-biting cracks. I didn't give him eye contact. Instead, I fixated on a silver Saint Christopher pendant hung from a chain around his neck that bobbed on a carpet of black hair on his chest. I don't know how he acquired the pendant, the one he had worn as a boy, the one he said saved his life, the one that would appear in every war story he ever told, and he told a lot. Saint Christopher carried an orphaned child, Jesus, across a river. *Jesus*. Dad didn't believe in God. But he did feel like an orphan. His father died before he was three.

Dad wanted to name me Christopher until I was born—not a boy. He told me he wished for a boy. He favoured boys. Boys, much better than girls. Boys had nerve, muscle and brains. He wanted a boy to love because he never had a father to love him.

'Right then, let's get a move on. Chop! Chop!' He smacked his hands together again.

I monitored him so intently my face hurt. He balanced his cigarette stub upright on top of my bookcase and unloaded my books to the floor. From the dresser top, he collected a brush, comb and hand mirror, a musical jewellery box which opened to a spinning ballerina and a porcelain bouquet of roses, and he laid them on the bed. I scanned the items, curious why he placed them there. One after another, he emptied dresser drawers, dumping clothing to the floor.

Dad cursed, bloody hell this and bloody hell that. I chewed on fingernails, careful to pull my fingers out of my mouth before he noticed. Almost caught. He halted, glared at me, then continued marauding. I kept quiet with crossed legs squeezed so hard my bones almost touched. He snatched my cowboy hat from the closet shelf, a match to the hat worn by Roy Rogers, and tossed it to the floor.

My trumpet was next. Dad brought it to his mouth and gave it a blow, only producing a sad sound. I can't recall where I got the trumpet, but I could fake 'Reveille' which made the neighbourhood boys holler and run to me. But there it was, in Dad's hands, headed for a pile.

I inched off the bed to a rug on the floor, hugged knees to chest and hung my chin over folded arms. Tried to disappear. No crying. Crying would get me smacked.

He paced about the room, pulled pillows off the bed, and snatched Tebby.

Please, not Tebby.

Tebby, a stuffed toy tiger, was the size of a real baby tiger. Bibby bought him for me before I turned one. She helped me name him. Not a teddy bear or a tabby cat, so he became a combo, a Tebby. I slept with him every night as a stand-in security blanket.

Dad swung the tiger into the air by one paw. I shot up from the floor.

'Don't you dare!' he said.

He eyed the tiger, turned it upside down, right side up, then gave it a shake. I could have tried to rescue my stuffed animal, but a tug-of-war with Dad, he'd win, and that would have been the end of Tebby. He almost wrung the plush animal in half while glaring into its glass eyes. I tightened my fists. Dad narrowed his eyes at me, Tebby twisted in his grip. He smiled. A bully smile. I stared through him, expressionless. He pressed his teeth into his bottom lip and swung Tebby in one hand.

'Go on then,' he said.

I yanked Tebby free, climbed onto the bed and curled around the stuffed animal.

Beneath the dresser, Dad discovered a box of assorted pens, broken crayons and coloured pencils and a bundle of my drawings. Images of bodies squashed into boxes, pages of rows and rows of people stacked on top of each other, two-headed people, three-headed, four-headed people. Most kids my age drew houses with sunshine, flowers and ponies. Two things no one could control: my imagination and biting my nails. Pen and paper were easy to come by, and fingernails grew back. But the threat of being sent away loomed if I kept generating weird art. He tossed the box into the wastebasket along with the pictures.

I squashed Tebby to my chest and tucked the tiger's head under my chin. Dad left the room in a rush. Too scared to move, I waited. A few minutes later, Dad returned with a roll of tape on his wrist, and a fat marker between his teeth, and a pad of paper in hand. Sweat trickled down his face as he tore the paper lengthwise in strips. He handprinted the name Danny, the boy who lived next door, on a strip and taped it to the Stetson. Then wrote Cody on another strip, Danny's brother, and stuck it to my rock tumbler. Dad labelled most of my things.

Dad had previously arranged for the neighbourhood boys to come meet at our house. There must have been seven or eight boys in the bedroom when he handed out my toys and books.

'Wait!' I said, trapped in a bubble where no one could hear me.

Dad gave away my phonograph and records, a motorised toy police car, toy guns and belt, a bag full of plastic bullets and my Tonka truck. The room vibrated with energy. I crawled under the bed covers with Tebby listening as the boys oooed and aaahed.

'Thank you, Mr. Ware.'

'You are the best, Mr. Ware.'

'I wish you were my dad, Mr. Ware.'

After relinquishing my belongings, Dad herded the boys out of the room.

'Your mother will sort your clothing,' he said as he followed them, closing the door behind him.

The chatter of boys could be heard as they left through the front door. I lay on the bed with Tebby and tried to fall asleep, but instead, worried about what Mum might do with my clothes.

A few days later, I sat on the bricked edge of the flowerbed near the front steps of our house as our furniture, beds and boxes were loaded into a truck and hauled away. Our car, parked near the front yard on the street, was packed tight to the ceiling. Dad, fresh-shaven, in a crisp, starched shirt and pressed trousers, hopped in the driver's seat, gave the car door a slam, rolled the window down, and waved.

'Ta-ta for now,' he said and drove off.

Not much later, Bibby, after a quick good-bye, left in a taxi.

Dazed, I went into the near-empty house, tiptoed across wood floors into my bedroom and noticed the clean squares on the walls where framed pictures of ballerinas once hung. I sat on the floor and moaned.

Dad gone.

Bibby gone.

One thousand and seven ...

The Bead Tin

Bibby moved into a basement apartment of a four-story brick building in downtown Winnipeg. Mum and I were granted permission to stay with her. I thought that meant forever, but unbeknownst to me, there was a plan for us to join Dad later in Los Angeles.

The main room couldn't have been much bigger than 200 square feet and served as a bedroom and living room. A Murphy bed, which Bibby and Mum shared, flipped down from a wall. There were two windows at street level; I could see feet walking by. One side of the room had a kitchenette, the other side had a walk-in closet where I slept on a pad of folded blankets on the floor across from a teeny bathroom.

Living in the city reduced my play area to exploring our building. I ran up and down the stairwells, used the fire escapes as a jungle gym, hid to read and sing in the boiler room—lovely reverberation— and played in the alley at the rear of the complex.

On the top floor, in a tinier apartment, lived Bibby's friend, Vivienne, a woman in her late sixties, who often wore black turtleneck sweaters and black trousers. I loved her waxy red lips but coveted her ebony hair. She kept it tightly braided, bobby-pinned into a bun at the back of her head. When she smiled, her shrivelled-apple face creased around blue twinkle eyes.

One afternoon, I ran upstairs to her apartment to show her how I looked in the figure skating outfit she had given to me earlier, a perfect fit. It had been her daughter's years before. It was made of gold satin, cut like a swimsuit, with a short bit of frilled skirt around the hips, heavy with gold beads and sequins. I shimmied so the skirt, trimmed in layers of gold-beaded fringe, swung and whooshed with a rhythmic bead tinkling.

'Smashing,' she said. 'Aren't you cold with your bare arms and legs?'

'Yes, but I love it like this.' I rubbed my hands over the bead strings to make them swing.

'And your feet. No shoes?'

I smiled.

'Well, of course. You can't wear your skates inside,' she said. 'Come on, let's braid your hair and make a bun so you really look the part. You can braid mine to practice.'

Vivienne sat on a cushioned stool in front of the mirror of her vanity. I stood at her side and observed as she pulled bobby pins out of her woven bun to loosen the braid. She ran her fingers through until the strands fell in waves past her bottom to the floor.

'You can help me brush. Start at the top and gently make your way down.'

She collected a brush from her vanity and handed it to me. I hesitated.

'You don't have to,' she said.

I took the brush and examined the bristles. I had never groomed someone else's hair or touched anyone, other than wrestling boys, cuddling with Bibby or holding Dad's hand. I feared I would hurt her. Vivienne squinted, tipped her head to one side and smiled.

'I'm tough. Go ahead, dear.'

Brush in hand, I studied Vivienne's river of hair.

'It's okay, brush gently and slowly. Long strokes.'

I started at the top of her head, pushed the bristles in and glided them through her tame satin threads. Not like my hair, which consisted of stringy knots. The brush wiggled over curves as I guided it through her mane down her back. I combed my fingers under to gather her slippery silk into a ponytail and looked at her in the mirror.

'Let's braid my hair.' She put her hands together to her lips like a prayer.

'Bibby calls it plaiting. Do you want me to plait your hair?'

'That's right.'

I combed my fingers beneath her tresses, gathered and separated three parts, and interwove them the way Bibby had shown me. Vivienne helped me secure a rubber band to its end. I gripped her thick braid, the weight of rope, thought of Black Beauty and snapped her braid like a rein. She squeezed her shoulder blades together. I let go.

'Oh, I'm sorry. Pardon me,' I said.

She glanced over her shoulder and gave me a wink.

I spiralled her braid onto her scalp, slid each pin in, trying not to poke her, and admired a firm hair basket of a bun the size of a soup bowl.

'See? Now let me fix your hair.'

We traded places. She lifted my waist-length hair, fluttered her fingers through to the straggled ends, and with soft hands, untangled each twisted wisp.

I'd let Bibby, who was reluctant, brush my hair, but she wasn't good at getting the tangles undone. Mum could undo a tangle, lifting me from my seat while raking knotted masses out by the roots. I'd suppress squirming and screaming through the whole ordeal to avoid a swat from the flat side of the brush. Either way, grooming of any kind threw me into an anxious nail biting.

Dad told me, 'You'll never get married with those disgusting digits.'

Frantic to get me to stop, they tried everything: wrapped my fingers with tape, tied gloves to my hands, painted my nails with bitter aloes; they even sewed my pyjama sleeves shut. Although I connected the chastisement to nail biting, nail biting proved to be of higher value—my personal renewable resource for coping. But also enjoyable. I loved chewing cuticles and peeling away slivers of nail when I drew pictures, read books, and especially to unwind before falling asleep at night. Pure ecstasy. I would never stop biting my nails.

One time, when Bibby saw me gnawing, she pulled my hand away from my mouth and scrunched her brow.

'Stop nibbling at your fingers or you'll find yourself with stumps for arms.'

She had told me there once was a young man who enjoyed eating his fingernails so much that he imagined eating a banana and ate all the way to his elbow. She winked, grabbed my shoulders and cackled.

I watched in the mirror as Vivienne feathered my hair across my back, tangles untied. When she lifted the brush, I wedged a fingernail to a tooth. She looked in the mirror at me, then soft-stroked, holding strands as she brushed. I never bit down. Her thumbs slid along the nape of my neck as she sectioned hair to weave into a braid. I relaxed and clasped my hands into my lap. She pinned and circled the braid into a mini version of the Vivienne bun. No hairspray. No pain. I rolled my shoulders back, held my chin high and smiled. When she smiled, her earrings sparkled.

'Oooh, your earrings are lovely.'

She had holes in her earlobes; my first time seeing pierced ears in real life. Her gold filigree orbs swung when she moved her head. Danglies, that's what I called them, the kind movie stars wore.

Earlier, I had asked Mum if I could have pierced ears.

'Only tarts and gipsies do that sort of thing. Absolutely not,' she replied.

Vivienne didn't seem like a tart. I believed at the time a tart referred to a young girl or woman who hung around with men. No men in Vivienne's apartment. I asked her if she was a gipsy.

'Oh, heavens no, but wouldn't that be fun. Caravans and long colourful garments.' She pretended to swish a skirt. 'Bangles.' And stroked her arms as if covered in bracelets. 'Freeeeeeee to go wherever I desire.' She chuckled. 'Do I look like a gipsy?'

I laughed nervously.

'Aren't you sweet?' She scooped my chin into her warm hand for a second. In the vanity, she opened a jewellery box and lifted a pair of gold earrings set with heart-shaped, blood-red garnets. Danglies.

'These are for you.'

'I'm not allowed to have my ears pierced.'

'Save them. Some day, dear one.' She held them next to my cheek and tilted her head back to get a better view. 'Beautiful. Hold out your hand.' She released the danglies into my palm. 'Oh, before I forget. Your grandmother told me you love beads and buttons and that the two of you have been making necklaces. I have an old tin full of beads. Would you like them?'

'Yes, please.'

So excited, I thought I'd float to the ceiling. She went to her china cabinet, opened a drawer and lifted out a round metal container. I recognised the red tartan and white Scottie dog on the lid, Walker's Scottish shortbread. The kind Bibby bought.

'Are you English?' I asked.

'I'm French-Canadian.'

My stomach churned. I had heard the English loathed the French. But I adored Vivienne.

She opened the tin to reveal pearls, shell buttons, gem beads, strings of glass seed beads, crystal beads and beads made of brass and silver.

'Well, what a mess. But you're a smart girl. You'll have it organised in no time.'

She replaced the lid and handed the container to me. Heavy as a fruit cake. Excited to ogle and sort what I thought were jewels for a queen, I said goodbye, kissed each of her cheeks Euro-style and sprinted to my favourite secluded spot. Behind the brick-walled apartment building, in an alley overgrown with grass and weeds, littered with garbage and discarded appliances, rested a bench next to a potholed-gravel road, two tyre-worn ruts through its centre. The occasional tenant ventured there to empty their trash, or a delivery person would come through the back door. I rarely saw a soul. That's how I liked it. I'd skip rope on a flat bit of concrete near the trash bins or bounce a ball against the apartment walls. I spent hours on the bench drawing. So much quieter than the bustling at the front of the building, a city sidewalk full of pedestrians, and a busy road full of exhaust from cars and trucks motoring by. That's why Bibby never opened the windows.

Dressed in the skating outfit, I sat cross-legged on the bench in the shadow of our building with the tin in my lap. I didn't mind the cold. Excited to make an inventory of the contents, I held the tin steady, pried off the lid and placed it upside down on the bench to hold strings of beads as I pulled them out of the container.

I heard laughter. Two girls, strangers, a few years older than me, bounded in my direction. One had ginger hair, the other sported a bowl cut. They stopped when they saw me, and both started to giggle. I stared at the ground, tried to be invisible and hoped they would pass quickly. They came closer and squealed.

'What are you doing? Who gave you permission to be here?' questioned the girl with ginger hair.

Doll-like, in a red shirt with a bow tied under her chin, she roared and grimaced. In her blue, pleated skirt, she bent her legs askew like a silly clown, inches away from me. Like a detective, like Dad, I examined her. *That's a uniform she's wearing.* Her shoes, clean and polished. Lace-ups, a type of shoe girls at private schools wore. I had just turned eight. I guessed they were teenagers. *Hooligans.* Cross-eyed, she sucked her lips in, swung her head like a hyena and leaned her forehead against mine. *Watch out. She's bonkers.* Chin to chest, shoulders squeezed to my ears, I grunted. She stepped back.

'She's a freak, a freak show freak. What are you wearing?' asked the girl with the bowl cut.

The bowl cut girl jumped towards me, arms waving over her head like a broken ballerina. She poked out her tongue, stuck her smirky face into mine, then stood beside the ginger-haired girl, her arms folded.

'Well. What do we have here?' the ginger-haired girl asked as she eyed the tin of beads.

I didn't answer. I picked up the lid.

'Did you hear me?' she yelled.

I couldn't move.

'Can't talk?' asked the bowl cut girl shaking her head.

'Is that your freak show outfit?' asked the ginger-haired girl.

Still no words.

They both started chanting. 'Freak. Freak. She's a freak. Freak. Freak. She's a freak.'

I couldn't cry, but I wanted to. I also wanted to bash those bullies in the face to break their noses. Rip the ginger frizz from the ginger-haired girl's head. Kick the bowl cut girl's perfect teeth in. But mostly, I wanted to run.

The girl with the ginger hair reached down, nabbed the bead tin, heaved it into the air, and as it spun, beads and buttons sprayed in all directions. Beads pinged and tumbled over the bench into the dirt. Beads rolled over my lap, settled between my thighs, in the bend of my knees. The clang of metal hitting the ground, the echo of undulating tin, a reverberation of wobbles until it stopped. I droned a guttural sound. Stood to brush away beads stuck to skin. Gazed at the gem-sparkled ground. Then got on my hands and knees and sobbed.

Both girls snorted.

'Look what you've done,' I groaned.

Knees pressed into dirt, hands in mud and gravel, my eyes blurred with tears. I grovelled searching for beads, buttons and gems only to clutch a few. I crawled to retrieve the tin. A hand slapped my back and grabbed an edge of the skating outfit. I heard a rip. Sequins and fringe beads sprinkled to the ground.

'Leave me alone!'

Wet-faced, strands of mucus streaming from my nose, I showed them my fist. They stopped, burst into laughter and ran down the alley out of sight.

The sun sank behind the tall buildings and the temperature dropped. In that twilight, I grasped handfuls of dirt, hoping to collect strings of beads. Instead, my knees buried beads deeper. I cupped both dirty hands to my face and rested my forehead on the ground.

'I don't want to be in trouble.'

I didn't want Vivienne to be mad. My breath steamed, arms and legs mottled red with cold. Gold glitter fell from the skating suit. Feet, hands, knees, coated in mud. Face smeared with dirt. In the tin, I managed to save some beads, buttons and gems, along with tiny pebbles and grit. Night fell into the alley and the sky disappeared.

Inside the building, in a dim hallway, under a glary wall sconce, I opened the door to Bibby's apartment. Inside smelled of stuffed cabbage and cigarette smoke. Bibby and Mum were nestled in dainty armchairs sipping glasses of sherry. I closed the door, looked at my hands, then knees and feet, then at Mum.

'Bloody hell. Look at the sight of you,' Mum said as she flashed the whites of her eyes. She sucked on her cigarette and blew a line of smoke away from me.

I held the bead tin for them to see.

'Aw. Let's have a look,' Bibby said and took a sip of sherry.

'Go run the bathwater, that's a good Mouse,' Mum said.

'Vivienne gave me this bead tin. Two stupid girls outside bashed it to the ground,' I said, making sad eyes.

Mum waved her cigarette and said, 'How dare they! I'll wring those wicked cows' necks. Never mind. I'll have it sorted.'

Bibby winked. 'Chin up, luv. We'll get more beads.'

*

A month later, Mum and I headed for the United States, a 2000-mile journey by train. I had no idea we were moving away forever.

Mum's varicosed legs swelled to the size of elephant limbs and turned red as blue veins bulged beneath her skin. Most of the time, she stayed horizontal in the train cabin with bags of ice bound to her legs with towels. I roamed the train and spent lengthy periods in the near to last compartment, the panorama viewing carriage—a glass house on wheels. Canada slid past me: prairies, steep Rocky Mountains, farmlands, and towns. I bit my nails and used a complimentary Canadian Pacific pen and notepad to draw lots of pictures.

One thousand and eight …

The Cave

Two weeks before I turned nine, Mum and I finally arrived in Los Angeles to live with Dad in a new apartment. While alone, Dad had explored and developed a passion for the California deserts—close enough for day trips. On a Sunday, unannounced, he woke us at the break of dawn and drove us to Joshua Tree National Park.

Early summer sky, electric blue and clear, by 8 a.m. we could have fried liver and onions on the hood of our car. Ocotillos, gangly sticks in bloom, waved red tassels like they belonged on the ocean floor. We drove past armies of Joshua trees, spiky yuccas, their branches shaped like arms and legs of running soldiers frozen in position. Across the desert floor we found formations of granite boulders that looked like art, sculpted one hundred million years ago from Earth's molten core, with names like Heart Rock, Bread Loaf, The Chief and one of my favourites, Giant Rock, taller than a seven-story building. There were outcroppings of boulders named Wonderland, Chasm of Doom and Hall of Horrors.

Dad parked the car in the shade of a rock wall. He looked like an army officer, sporting an Australian slouch hat with the brim turned up on one side, khaki shirt and trousers and leather boots, his face already ruddy and slick with sweat. He grabbed a rucksack from the trunk, and a baseball cap that he placed on my head. I squinted and breathed in the hot air of midday desert.

Dressed in crisp, white cotton, Mum put on her cat-eye sunglasses and covered her head with a curved, straw sunbonnet and served us cucumber sandwiches. I drank orange Tang from a cup; they shared a drink from a flask.

Mum retreated into the car and rolled the window open. She took a book out of her purse, placed it on the dashboard, tipped her head back and melted into the car seat.

'I'll stay here,' she said and waved at us.

'Don't be silly,' Dad said.

She often stayed in the car wherever we went. For hours sometimes. He knew she wouldn't go with us. Besides, she wore strappy sandals, no good for desert hikes.

'All right, suit yourself,' he said. 'Come on, Jane.'

Since we had moved from Canada, Mum and Dad agreed to call me by my middle name, Jane.

Dad clutched his rucksack and we headed towards boulders resembling a city of stone. In shorts and a tank top, my arms and legs broiled in the sun while my plimsolls scrunched into desert playa.

'You'll need a small stone to suck on. It will keep your mouth moist, keep you from feeling thirsty,' he said.

He stooped down, found a marble-sized stone, spat on it, rubbed it clean on his trousers and handed it to me. I didn't want to, but I put it in my mouth. He marched towards a towering mass of rock. I took twice as many steps as he did to keep pace. We approached a sloped giant and proceeded to climb. Dad clasped his hands together to give me a leg up over areas too tall for me to ascend and swung me over deep fractures in the rock. At the top of the largest boulder, a few hundred feet above the desert, I spun around for a panoramic view. A warm breeze lapped across us, and my hair whipped into strings.

'There is a cave some twenty feet north, worth exploring,' Dad said. 'What do you think?'

Any question was a trick question, and anything Dad said that included the word explore meant he had done it before without a plan. This time he had a plan, and it included me. No questions answered or asked, but I am sure I winced.

He tugged the brim of his hat and spat to the ground, plucked a bandanna from a pocket and swabbed his forehead. From the rucksack, he retrieved a water canteen, screwed off the cap, poured water into his gaping mouth, then handed the canteen to me.

'Sip it.'

I gulped and let cool water dribble off my chin onto my chest until he grabbed the canteen.

'Onward,' he said and saluted.

Scared, yet curious, I saluted back. My internal dialogue consisted of convincing myself the cave would be cool and warning myself to stay calm.

We walked across the arch of the gritty beast to a fissure surrounded by clusters of bulbous rocks. Beneath two boulders butting heads, I looked down into a cave, too dark to see the bottom. I took the pebble out of my mouth and dropped it into the chasm. Seconds passed before I heard it ping and bounce on the cave floor.

'Ah.' He spread his legs over the opening and stretched his neck to survey the entrance. 'Cor blimey!'

On a stable patch of rock, he pried a rope from his rucksack and knotted the braided twine into a makeshift harness. I focused on keeping a straight face. Near the cave entry, he fastened the excess rope around a monolith of granite, raised the harness and nodded.

'Come on then,' he said, 'put your feet through here.'

Either I succumbed to his wishes, or I'd be forced and the situation would escalate. But I also didn't want to be dropped into a lightless abyss. Certainly not first. I stepped into the harness. He positioned the rope between my legs and around my waist, then lifted me off the ground, tightening the cord as I dangled. The snug hemp clawed my skin, but I dared not complain. After a couple of bounces, he sat me next to the crevasse.

'All right, in you go,' he said.

I scooted away from the hole.

'What's the matter?' he asked with his fist on his hip.

He dragged me to his side and snatched the hat off my head and tossed it to the ground. I avoided his eyes, tried to be neutral and not shake.

'Relax, for Christ's sake.'

At the edge of the hole, he looped the rope around his leg and shoulder, straddled the crevasse with bent knees. He grabbed my wrists and lowered me into the cavity until the rope tightened. I swung rigid and closed my eyes, legs and shoulders scraping against the walls of the chasm. Grains of gypsum fell and echoed below. I opened my eyes to black, then tilted my head to the sky to see Dad's featureless face framed by the mouth of the rock that swallowed me, the rope taut over his leg.

'I wonder if bears could find their way into this cave. I know rattlesnakes can,' he said.

Suspended inside Earth like bait on a hook, I hyperventilated, folded my legs to my chest and curled my toes. *My legs, they'll get eaten first.*

'Stop fidgeting.'

Hand over hand, he sank me deeper. The air grew cooler. Tight as a knot, I tried not to shiver. The outside world disappeared. I hung with visions of snakes and bears, of a cave mouth closing, and how I'd suffocate unseen, never to be found.

The rope slipped and jerked me. I gasped and worried the rope would unravel against granite, send my body tumbling against cave walls, careening into a bottomless pit. From above, the scratch of his boots on loose rock launched a barrage of grit and dirt. I placed my hands over my eyes and flexed my head skyward. He was gone.

I strained to pull myself to the bright blue hole. The rope slipped again. Rain-stick gravel skittered to the cave floor. Reaching above my head with both hands, I gripped the rope, heaved, but couldn't lift myself high enough. Swung my legs to scissor-catch the rope but instead rocked back and forth in a cascade of sand.

'Dad!' I yelled.

My pleas for help ricocheted but never went up and out. I screamed, but the sound deadened in that hollow. Waves of guttural cries came from my belly. I shook and moaned, knowing I'd be eaten alive. Each time I moved the rope slipped and the harness tightened. I feared breathing would cause the rope to snap and stifled my breath, choked, then wailed.

'Somebody, help me. Somebody, please help me.'

A crunch of gravel came from above.

'Stop your bloody whimpering,' Dad said. 'Pull yourself together.'

I looked up. 'Please get me out. I want out.'

'I thought you were tough, not some bleeding coward.'

Legs apart over the cave mouth, Dad leaned on his knees and looked down. In one gesture of a swung leg, he disappeared again.

'Get me out!'

I begged, pleaded, bawled, and howled until my throat tightened. Light faded. I thought I'd never be rescued. Head pounding, limbs filled with pins and needles, the coarse rope digging into my groin. I cried for Mum. Sputter-whimpered. Gagged on spit. I don't know how long I cried for help but long enough to hang limp.

The rope vibrated. I hung like a rag doll as Dad hoisted me upward. Each hand-over-hand movement tugged, a slip and grab of the rope, through cool to warm air. Light brightening as I neared the top. I felt Dad's knuckles between my shoulder blades as he grabbed the harness rope. I closed my eyes to disappear. He hoisted me out of the hole and swung me onto a smooth slope of rock. My legs gave way, landing me on my tailbone. The rope slackened. I dropped to my elbows, arms collapsed, and my head hit the ground. I folded onto my side and rested my face on hot granite.

'Go on then. Chop-chop. Your mother's been waiting.'

Dad wiggled the harness off me, untied the knots and wound the rope.

'Get up. And take that look off your face.'

Grabbing my arms, he yanked me to my feet, then snatched my hat from the ground, smacked the dirt off across his knee and slapped it onto my skull. Jell-O for knees, I swayed.

'Drink some water.'

Dad handed me his canteen. After a couple of swigs, he took the canteen, poured water into his hand, and smeared the wet across my face. With the corner of his shirt, he wiped my cheeks and forehead dry. He returned the canteen and rope to his rucksack and slung it over his shoulder.

'Not a word to your mother.'

Dad assisted my descent from the boulder formation. Once on the playa, he cracked on in the direction of Mum. Sweaty and sore, I trotted, lagged some twenty feet behind his soldier-stride and eventually made it to the car. She gave us a quick nod with pursed lips, folded her book and sat up. She fanned her shiny red face in the sizzling heat. In that moment, it made sense to me how someone could sit solitary for hours in the desert sun.

'You all right then, Mouse?' asked Mum.

'She was brilliant. Tough as nails, this kid,' Dad said.

His comment rushed through me like a narcotic. *I made him proud.* He tossed his rucksack and hat into the trunk, recovered the flask, and gulped the remainder of its contents. I lay on the back seat where the hot vinyl upholstery stuck to my skin. The insides of my thighs chafed raw. Ribs sore. On our three-hour drive home, I pretended to be asleep.

For years after, I drew pictures of caverns with figures bound in rope, hovering, hanging, falling, most of the pages covered with charcoal. Whenever I discovered those drawings torn to shreds, I drew more.

One thousand nine …

No Place Like Homelessness

Before I turned fifteen, I moved with Mum and Dad from an apartment to a rental house in Tarzana. That house became a pressure cooker, the tension rising with each of Dad's affairs. Easily triggered, his yelling could turn into physical violence, especially when he was drunk. Mum and I walked on eggshells.

It appeared that none of us could bear to be in the same place at the same time. Dad, often a dark cloud, hid in his office. I often experienced Mum as a caged badger, her frustration palpable. I am not sure where she hid. When at home, I spent time drawing in the backyard with our dogs, Maggie and BB, or took refuge in the living room, a sunless space with a picture window shaded by trees, a room my parents rarely went into. I snuck provisions from the kitchen, then holed up under a floor lamp, semi-reclined on a chaise lounge, in front of a blaring TV, beading necklaces, and writing rage-poetry in my journals. When I look back, I think of how much of the time I did my best to bide invisible, feeling petrified.

To avoid being at home, I kept busy at school, not so much with classes and homework, but attending the high school photography club and science club, drawing in the art room, writing in the library, or hanging with friends.

One ordinary day, I came home from school, walked through the front door and saw Dad in his office, home early, alone. He was never home early. His English Leather cologne permeated the house. Dressed in a blue suit and tie, he leaned back in a swivel chair, lifted his arms and crossed his fingers behind his neck. He creased his forehead and pouted his lower lip so firm it dented his cleft deeper into his chin.

'Your mother has left the country. She won't be coming home,' he announced.

I followed him into the kitchen and watched as he poured himself a glass of scotch. I wavered between inner hysteria and relief, terrified, yet excited. The lid had blown off the boiling pot, and I bubbled over the top. I could see an out. I could breathe.

'Don't you have a friend you can stay with for a couple of weeks while I get things sorted?'

'Right now?'

'Right now.'

He walked past me to his office and closed the door with a bang. His desk chair creaked.

Southern California during the early 1970s equalled hip, as in, hippie communes were prevalent in the countryside and suburbia, making it easy for me to find a crash pad. I called a friend who knew a friend whose hippy parents took in runaways. They were amenable given my stay would be two weeks. I packed a few clothes, tiptoed to Dad's office, and knocked on the door.

'Entrez s'il vous plaît.'

I opened the door a crack. 'I'm ready. I have a place to stay.'

Peering through the door space, he scanned me head to toe, sucked in one side of his mouth and bit his cheek, a thing he did when ambivalent.

'All right, off we go.'

He grabbed his keys and asked for the address. We drove to a ranch-style house with an overgrown front yard.

'Is there a phone number?' he asked.

He opened the glove box to retrieve a small piece of paper. I wrote the friend's phone number down, handed it to him. He folded the note and buried it in the glove box.

'I'll call you in two weeks.'

'Okay,' I said, my voice barely audible.

The minute I stepped out of his car, he sped away. My heart raced. I felt like an animal being released into an unfamiliar wilderness, but also like an animal that wanted to be free.

Later, after two weeks, I tried to reach him at work. He didn't return my calls. After a long while, I can't remember how long, the friend's hippy parents drove me back home. They pulled into an empty driveway.

Outside the car, I thanked them. Someone once nicknamed me Loquacious One. It's a joke. I am, especially in stressful situations, quiet as a mouse. They drove away. I guessed they thought I had a key and my parents would be home at some point. I didn't have a key.

On the veranda, near the front door, were two oven-sized cardboard boxes secured with strapping tape. Dad had printed my name across each in black crayon. I peered through the living room window to see the furniture covered in white sheets. The same through every window. Other than a few large pieces of furniture, the house was stripped clean, anything smaller than a chair, gone. Artworks, knickknacks, pillows, gone. I climbed the fence to the backyard, BB and Maggie nowhere to be found.

I don't remember where I slept that night or what I did with the two boxes. I don't remember how I got to school the next day but a schoolmate told me I could stay at her boyfriend's house, a home supported by a single father raising two sons and an orphaned boy. The father, Ned, lived off saltine crackers and chicken noodle soup and slept on a waterbed with mirrors on the ceiling. He dressed like a car salesman in tight polyester suits. He was a pushover, yet nothing tipped him over. And however inappropriate it might have seemed, a young teen girl in a household full of males, most of them much older, no one took advantage of me. The opposite was true; they took care of me, a distressed, numb, confused mess.

Ned's youngest son, Ryan, a brown, muscular fourteen-year-old welcomed me to stay in his room. He reminded me of an Egyptian pharaoh, soft-dark eyes, black ringlets of hair to his shoulders. He had a sparse moustache and an almost-beard edged his face. We spent hours inside echoey culverts, concrete drainage tunnels, improvising songs with him playing guitar, using the acoustical resonance to enhance our harmonies.

*

Dad appeared months later and took me to lunch. Not sure how he found me. It was the first time I'd heard from him since he dropped me off at the hippy parent household. I wasn't shocked, just indifferent. He brought me a used car, a Chevy Nova II, which he paid for by draining my savings account. An account he had kept in his name. All the money I had saved from years of babysitting and other jobs.

'Your mother has moved into a one-bedroom apartment in the valley. I'm renting a room in Los Angeles,' he said.

I assumed that meant I wasn't going to be living with either one of them. As usual, I didn't ask questions or offer any input. But I did ask him to buy me a pair of shoes since the ones on my feet were deteriorating. He handed me ten bucks and drove off.

*

One summer afternoon, I followed Ryan to his best friend's house. He introduced me to Skippy Vance, an androgynous looking boy with waist-length hair, slim hips, slender hands, and aqua eyes. He often wore a black satin wizard's cape and I later learned that he was obsessed with Gandalf from *The Hobbit*. I helped Skippy with his chores; we hand-washed dishes together. When he slid his warm, wet hands beneath my shirt, I fell in love. Not long after, I moved in.

Everyone called Skippy's house *The Vance Trance* run by the four teenage Vance kids. It was a popular hangout that attracted young people with high IQs who congregated to play board games, make music, and have conversations about politics, art and self-realisation. The bohemian parents lived in a cottage in the backyard.

Skippy's dad, Norman, resembled Sean Connery, eyes and attitude like James Bond. I felt like my soul might vaporise from the intensity of his gaze. A hipster with a beatnik beard and his hair slicked to his scalp with a few strands stuck against a receding hairline. He either had a cigarette in his hand or a joint in his mouth. Norm worked as a graphic designer, but his passion for colour, texture and line made him a darn good painter, an artist. A real artist. One who exhibited and sold paintings.

Skippy's mum, Anne, was also an artist, and poet and a writer. She spoke her mind and was still a sweet peach. Her eyes and mouth smiled without trying. No bad bones. Soft spoken, but she kept Norm—who could be explosive—in check most of the time.

Intimidated and disabled with low self-esteem, I was the quiet observer, quiet sufferer, and still the Vances treated me like family. I felt adopted. Even when I revealed to Ann that I wanted to kill myself—she promptly found me a therapist. I had no idea what a psychologist was or what they did but seeing one saved my life. Anne saved my life.

I shared a room with Skippy. I'd had boyfriends before him, but I loved him the most. He was my best friend. Also, an artist. As unfettered children of the sixties, we lived on the coattails of free love and played wild with art and sex.

One morning, Skippy and I startle-woke to a wailing, ear-piercing drone sound right outside the bedroom door, then an eerie pause before a full crescendo. Bagpipes vibrated the innards of the house. Norm had announced his entrance and was rallying us out of bed. Sunday meant breakfast at the International House of Pancakes.

In between bites of cherry blintzes and chocolate chip pancakes, Skippy and I drew pictures on napkins. Dad would have declared that uncouth, but Norm leaned in beside me and picked up my drawing.

'Pretty good. In fact, very good.'

He wrapped an arm around me and gave a firm squeeze. Branded me with his laser eyes. I sat flushed and teary. My art-self solidified. It was okay to be an artist. In fact, it was pretty good. Very good.

I stayed with Skippy and his family for a couple of years until Skippy found interest in someone else. I loved the Vances. They never asked me to leave, but I left broken-hearted.

I lived in my car and bounced house to house, but never found a home where I could rest. Ryan, my fellow culvert singer, had moved to Humboldt County and asked me to follow him.

'When you are ready, you can stay at my place,' he said.

At seventeen, still young enough to be ordered into foster care, I hung low at a crash pad, Meeko's house, one of the many drug-dealing hubs in the San Fernando Valley. After a night of LSD and heroin, the heroin not by choice—someone blew it up my nostril while I was tripping—I woke to a cat moaning.

'Mwahhhhhhhhhhhhhh.'

I found myself naked in Meeko's bed staring at a hippie tapestry pinned to the ceiling. He lay unconscious on muscle relaxants and painkillers, a limp human-sized dandy lion, his frizz-cloud hair the circumference of a weather balloon.

I threw on a blanket and cringed as I tip-toed barefoot across a filthy carpet that reeked of cheap wine and rancid bong water. Avoiding empty beer bottles, shoes, druggies' flotsam and jetsam, I followed the moan.

'Mwahhhhhhhhhhhh mwahhhhhhhhhhhhhhhh.'

Through the hall and into the living room, I lumbered over partied-out humans sprawled on the floor. No one stirred. The cat's moan grew long like a sour note played on a cello.

'Mwahhhhhhhhhhhhhh.'

Slumped on the couch, on top of some guy, a young woman lay naked with a tampon string hanging out from between her legs.

'Mwahhhhhhhhhhhhhh.'

I dodged vomit and pills, cat piss and poop as I stumbled through the kitchen and out the back door.

'Mwahhhhhhhhhhhhhh. Mwahhhhhhhhhhhhhhhh.'

On the stoop, the house cat, orange, fluffy and matted, lay on her side, with a round belly the size of a cantaloupe. She panted in labour, drooled and groaned while she spread and contracted her toes. Inside her, little kittens tossed and wriggled.

'Mwahhhhhhhhhhhhh. Mwahhhhhhhhhhhh.'

I placed my hand on her belly. Her eyes dilated. She tried to bite me but didn't have the strength. Her kittens kicked from inside against my palm. I rushed into the house to get a bowl of water and returned to see her gasping, only the whites of her eyes visible. I dripped water off my fingertips into her mouth. As her body went limp, brown fluid seeped from under her tail, soaked into her carpet of apricot fur, spread across the landing and flooded over the steps. I slumped in the doorway. Her belly undulated. Then it went still.

I sobbed for hours until she hardened. Found a towel in the house and wrapped her in pink and white striped terry cloth, soured and mildewed, the best I could muster.

Sunlight spilled over us. I cried for the cat and cried for myself. I laid her in a mound of dewy clover in the backyard and closed my eyes.

I'm getting the hell out of here. I'm going to Humboldt County.

One thousand ten …

Giving Birth to Buddha

Ryan found a room for me in a commune full of hippies, artists and college students called the Big House, the first and biggest Victorian house at the start of a dirt road into Starvation Flats. When we stood on the porch, we could see and hear the rush of the Van Duzen River as it gushed through a redwood-forested valley. I was almost eighteen when I met Billy, who lived at the end of the road with his friends in the Pink House, the only house around painted pink.

On a cool blustery day, the sky was a mass of cumulus clouds gathered into a thunderhead above the nearby hills. Leaves swirled in dirt where I knelt to pull weeds out of the commune's vegetable garden. I heard a pounding of hooves and caught the scent of pennyroyal. Atop a white horse, Billy cantered over wearing cut-off Levi shorts, his thighs flexed and his long hair streaming in gold waves over his tan torso. He smiled at me, this man who had Greek god features. After talking to him, I guessed he had a genius IQ. I wanted to have his baby.

Billy enrolled at the College of the Redwoods, a lush campus with ponds, greenhouses and gardens surrounded by trees. I got a job there as a gardener. We found a trailer to rent in a speck of a town called Manila, a sandy peninsula that framed an edge of Humboldt Bay. Nine months later, just before Arian was born, I reconnected with Mum and Dad.

'Great news. You are going to be a grandfather. We are having a baby boy, due anytime now.'

'Blimey. You're married. Who's the lucky bloke?' he asked.

'His name is Billy. We aren't married.'

'Well then, you're giving birth to a bastard?'

Billy and I got married soon after.

Mum didn't share the same concerns as Dad. She was thrilled to be a grandmother.

At the end of the school year, we moved so Billy could attend the University of California at Davis to work towards his bachelor's degree. Left alone for hours, caring for our baby, postpartum blues lingered long enough to become a persistent depression. I thought having another child might help.

When I had Nanda in my belly, we lived in student family housing beside the railroad tracks. Every night, trains wailed through town. Brakes screeched and boxcars banged their way into my sleep. I never could take to the clank of steel, horns blowing, or the sounds of engines slowing down and speeding up.

At eight months pregnant, we moved back north to Arcata so Billy could attend Humboldt State University to earn his Master of Science degree. I remained a stay-at-home mum caring for Arian, age two, and preparing for our new arrival.

*

It was before daybreak, after taking a pee, that I cramped so hard I thought I'd give birth on the bathroom floor. Billy drove me to Mad River Hospital before the sun rose. There, to alleviate the pain of contractions, I bent my knees outward and walked through the maternity ward like a funky chicken, slow-breathing, Billy behind me, Arian in tow. We were escorted to the birthing room, windowed with a view of redwood-covered hills, and watched the sun peep through the trees. Billy sat on a chair with Arian. I stripped naked, felt another urge to pee and rushed to the toilet. When I relaxed, the baby's head squeezed out from between my legs. After two pushes and an animal groan, the nurse and Billy rushed in, scooped under my thighs, heaved me from toilet to bed and our baby flew out. The nurse slid him onto my chest. A warm cord slithered across my stomach, and his cat-like toes splayed for traction against my blood-slippery ribs. He stretched his arms wide open, one baby hand in a tight victory fist while his other clawed at my chest. He lifted his bobbing head, a moon face with the eyes of a Bodhisattva, and smiled. I had given birth to Buddha.

Soon after the placenta was eased from my womb and my baby

was cleaned, checked, diapered, and wrapped in a blanket, I insisted on going home.

'You need to give your baby a name,' the nurse said.

'I will, I will. I don't know who he is yet.'

'You have six months to acquire his Social Security number. It's the law.'

'Yes, yes I know.'

We took our baby home in a wicker bassinet bungee-corded to the back seat of our weathered Volkswagen bus. We wedged Arian between the van door and the baby's basket, over which he wrapped his fingers and stared at his new brother in disbelief. We bounced along country roads and over railroad crossings. Mossy fence posts flickered as we passed bright green pastures full of cows. In the sky, a murmuration of blackbirds. We drove through the centre of town, past multi-coloured Victorian houses to our blue cottage on the outskirts where no friends or family waited. We couldn't afford to keep the heat on, so the cottage stayed damp and cold.

Billy and I cuddled on the couch, baby bundled in my lap. *Who are you?* It took us six months to name him. He was not a Julian, Graham, or Nathanial, a George, John, Bill or Tom. Instead, we named him Nityananda—Eternal Bliss—because he smiled, even in his sleep. His middle name, Bhaktirasa—a gesture of love. Nityananda Bhaktirasa. Nanda for short.

One thousand eleven ...

Kids on Train Tracks

Before Nanda was six months old, we returned to sunny Davis so Billy could continue school there, and I, on the brink of light deprivation, could escape Humboldt's overcast skies. The railroad ran through town, splitting it in two, north side and south side, with easy access and no fences. We made a habit of late afternoon strolls, a couple of miles most days. Those rhythmic tracks took us through the quiet spaces of Davis, into grassy meadows and furrowed fields. At ten months old, Nanda skipped crawling and went straight to running. He'd get his legs going and we'd tear after him as he bounded across railroad ballast.

*

I'd given birth to three kids by the time I was twenty-five. My last child, Rachel, was born in 1982, in the spring, my favourite time of year.

Rolling a stroller along a railroad corridor wasn't possible, so I learned how to wrap her to my back using a long piece of fabric. Rachel strapped tight and camera readied, I photographed the countryside where ceanothus and buckeyes bloomed, great herons and red-winged blackbirds flew and waterways reflected broad skies and painterly sunsets. I photographed Billy happy-faced.

The train tracks skirted an open landscape of farmlands and hummocky wetlands. I photographed Nanda and Arian stumble-running with mud-encrusted shoes through ploughed fields. They ran for as far as we could see them. Throwing stones. Gathering sticks. I snapped a picture of their red sweaty faces under hats they made from withered broccoli florets.

Broccoli Hats

I showed the boys how to place pennies on a rail next to a familiar landmark. We checked the next day to see what the train had done. The boys were more excited to collect the flattened coins than to acknowledge the impact of the locomotive. Although the trains were visible from miles away, Billy and I did worry about them sneaking up behind us. We usually walked along the gravel beside the tracks.

'You might not hear a train coming,' I said.

We explained to our kids how sound was absorbed, how sound dissipated through air rendering several hundred tons of rolling steel quiet. The boys watched as I knelt on the ground, leaned over with Rachel snug to my back and pressed an ear to the rail. Arian and Nanda got on their hands and knees and rested their heads near mine, ears pressed to steel. I winked at them. They smiled.

'If you listen carefully, when a train is close by, you'll hear their wheels singing.'

One thousand twelve ...

Nanda Finds God

For Nanda's first day of kindergarten, I promised him a picnic. Just the two of us. Billy often studied at the university till late afternoon. Rachel was in day-care, and Arian got out of school later than Nanda, so we had time. When the bell rang, I met Nanda at his classroom, said hello and lifted him for a bear hug. I had our picnic in a bag slung over my shoulder. We walked across a park green alongside a fence that ran the length of the school until we found a cushiony patch of grass. I pulled a cotton tapestry from the bag and spread it on the lawn. Nanda sat facing the fence. I sat with my back to it, facing him. I poured some lemonade from a thermos into two plastic cups. Nanda's eyes still fixed on the fence.

'Well, tell me, how was your first day, Nanda Ponda?'

In our family, a variation on a name is a sign of affection. I handed him some juice.

'Good.' He took a gulp, eyes not meeting mine and gazed at the fence or beyond it, maybe into the schoolyard.

On paper plates, I arranged tuna fish sandwiches, carrot strips, apple slices, celery with peanut butter and some cookies. Not even the cookies drew his attention.

'What's up, little one?' I waved a cookie in front of his face.

Nanda remained quiet, not the usual chatterbox. His mouth was full of food, but that never stopped him.

'Hmm.' He glanced over, giggled, then continued to gaze past me.

'Okay. You want to tell me what you are looking at?'

'God.' His pink face gleamed, eyes wild. He smiled and shrugged.

I thought the aliens had snatched my boy away and replaced him with a strange replica. Not sure what to say, I studied him. He took a bite of his sandwich and crunched a celery stick and laughed. *Okay there he is.*

'Where is God?' I asked, puzzled and curious.

He tipped his head to the sky and leaned on his elbows. 'God is on the fence.'

I turned around to check the fence. 'I don't see God.'

Nanda stilled himself, like trying to hear something in the distance. He sat up, stretched his hands to the sky, spread his arms wide open and took a deep breath.

'God is on the whole fence, Mama.' He dropped his arms, eyes bright with half-moons.

'Oh, well, I suppose he is.' I chuckled.

I loved that God was on the whole fence for Nanda to see. As a family we were loosely spiritual. I believed God to be nature and the mystery of the universe. We never attended church or sent the kids to Bible school. None of our relatives were religious. I had no idea how he discovered God.

A few days earlier, in full-tantrum mode, Nanda had insisted on a headstrong battle with me over bedtime. I fireman-carried him to his room. He thrashed and managed to kick my nose, hard, with his tennis shoe-ed feet. I released him to the floor, grabbed his arm and told him I'd swat his bottom if he didn't settle down.

He stopped, pouted, and said, 'If you spank me, you will be spanking God. God is in my body.'

'Okay. God is in my body too. And if you kick me, he will understand if I spank you.'

Not long after the fence incident, I discovered, after a routine nightly pee, Nanda wide awake, sitting an arm's length away from the television with the volume low. I peeked through the hallway to see him latched onto an evangelical Christian TV program, transfixed to a preacher pontificating about our Lord and Saviour.

'Good morning,' I said.

He caught me in his periphery, hit the power-off button and scooted away from the TV. He knew not to be awake so early and that television wasn't allowed without permission or parental supervision. Talking about God was fine, but I stopped his lone viewing of morning gospel unsure of what messages this might leave in his innocent mind.

I smiled and coaxed him into my bed to sleep. All tucked in, I kissed his forehead and whispered, 'Apparently God is in our television.'

He nuzzled his head into my shoulder, closed his eyes and nodded.

One thousand thirteen ...

Self

When Billy spent time on campus, I participated in kids' sports, pitched in on after-school programs, served in the PTA, assisted during art lessons, tutored maths, helped with homework, shopped, prepared and cooked meals, did laundry, organised bath times, chores, read bedtime stories, all of it. Tending to three kids under the age of eight, I was, what Americans called a mother who went beyond the call of duty, a super mom.

I began to yearn for alone-time and considered applying to school. I believed Billy wasn't keen on the idea. I understood. Being a stay-at-home mum required as much energy as a full-time job, and then some but I had agreed to that arrangement so he could pursue his career. Although I didn't consider myself to have needs, I also didn't know how much resentment would come to fill me from not getting my needs met. I couldn't even use the bathroom without one or more kids hammering on the door. I went under and denied being depressed. I could still full-throttle function. But when I wanted to die, I made an appointment to see a therapist.

I met with Hope in a dim-lit office with just enough room for two armchairs. Beige walls. Brown shag carpet. She sat in front of a solitary window. I sat across from her. In silhouette, her pixie cut looked like a helmet. *Joan of Arc.* I had trouble seeing her impenetrable eyes magnified through her chunky glasses.

My hand shook when I handed her the drawing she requested from our last session. A self-portrait. She looked surprised to see scratches through thick paper, lines ripped into the sketch of my face, with two blood-red handprints across a marred surface.

'Are you angry?' Hope asked, her face wrinkled into a kind smile.

I couldn't answer.

'Keep drawing and ask yourself if you are angry. Ask yourself what you need.'

I was terrified of anger, and even more terrified of being allowed to be angry. But that inquiry, *Ask yourself what you need,* I had never considered. Answering that question became the catalyst for many changes, including going to school. I quit the PTA, cancelled my volunteering services, applied to UC Davis to study art and was accepted. I felt better, more patient with the kids, and time spent with them became more meaningful. Being a wife did not. I loved Billy, but I didn't feel loved.

While Billy and the kids were in school, I used the living room floor as a work surface to draw eight images depicting life struggles. I scratched into multi-coloured-crayon layered across three-by-four-foot sheets of mat board. On an ordinary quiet afternoon, the kids helped me tack my new sgraffito drawings onto the walls of the living room. Colours and lines vibrated the room and transformed our home into a gallery.

'Wow, what do you think?' I asked them.

'It's beautiful,' Nanda replied, his face shining.

'I love it,' Arian yelled as he raised his fists above his head like he had won an award.

I clapped and said, 'Yay.'

They ran around me in circles.

Then Rachel, full of drama, sang in her highest octave, her hands folded over her heart, 'I love it.'

Like happy lunatics, we pranced through the apartment hollering, waving our arms, chanting, 'Yay! It's beautiful. Yay! We love it. Yay! It's beautiful ...'

When Billy got home, I got the impression he was not pleased with my drawings. I knew our marriage was not salvageable when I removed my art from the walls.

One thousand fourteen ...

Art Objects

After the divorce, during my first year of school, the kids and I moved into a one-bedroom apartment three blocks from the railroad tracks which we often followed to go downtown to shop or walk for exercise. The backs of old industrial buildings framed the south edge of those tracks. On the other side, a cinder block wall hid a residential area. That section of track was closed to trains. Instead, like a magnet, the corridor attracted people-things. We called these items triple-t—train track treasures. A strange array of objets d'art, or ready-mades, some items flattened, some abandoned, some lost.

We found squashed refrigerator coils, looped copper tubing looking like some abstract asemic message. Half a piano, innards exposed, keys strewn over the gravel like knocked-out teeth. Stiff, disfigured, sun-bleached clothes stuck to the ground as if the wearer had evaporated. A cracked, patent-leather high-heeled boot filled with cemented dirt begging for flower seeds to be planted. The kids collected bright fragments of coloured plastic and glass. I brought some of the relics home and we assembled them into sculptures and collages. One of my favourites was a thick family law book, most of the pages rippled and stuck together with grass grown through deteriorated words and a tangle of roots at the bottom. I split it open to the middle and nailed it to our living room wall.

One day we decided to go for a walk to take photographs along the railroad track. The sky, solid blue, presented a bright sun, offering lots of contrast and shadows, great for black and white photos, but I only had colour film at the time. I was afraid Arian's blond hair would glow white, details would get lost, washed out from overexposure to harsh light. I reminded myself to stop acting like a professional and shoot for fun.

Arian was nine, Nanda six, Rachel four, and me, almost thirty. Each of us carried our own 35 mm film cameras as we walked about a mile to the industrial stretch of Davis, midtown.

'Careful. You might not hear the train coming.'

The kids nodded. They knew. As they grew older, I worried less about the dangers of trains, but I warned them just the same, like telling someone to drive safely. Even though that section of track was dead, we pressed our ears to the rail.

I thought we'd photograph a discarded couch or mattress springs or a rusted paint can, but the kids took an interest in making shadows on the hardware store wall. While focusing my lens on an interesting shape, I noticed in my periphery, Nanda and Rachel looking like a couple of giant marshmallows in blinding sun leaning against a blue cement wall. They had pulled white pillowcases over their heads and down past their waists, just hands and legs visible. Laughing with fabric sucked into their mouths, their facial features poked through. Sort of creepy. I had no idea where they found those pillowcases. Arian, camera to his eye, took a picture.

'You guys look amazing but ew, take those pillowcases off your faces.'

We were sun-kissed red, sweaty, thirsty, and hungry, so I led my kid pack homeward, down the tracks. Nanda asked if I would take his photograph. We stopped.

'Now?'

'I want to lie on the tracks and pretend I'm dead,' he said and grinned, 'like in cartoons.'

Rachel and Arian glanced at him, then at me.

'What, like Roadrunner?'

'It'll be funny. Come on,' Nanda pleaded.

Arian shook his head.

And before I could tell Nanda to make it quick, he lay over the railroad ties and ballast between the rails.

I shot one frame.

Nanda age six. Photo rediscovered 18 years after his death.

One thousand fifteen ...

Cannon Ball

The Master of Fine Arts studios were located on campus in one of two uninsulated temporary buildings enclosed in a tall fence. Each building had eight individual studios with rough cement floors, uninsulated walls and bare bulb lighting. The doors faced into a minimally maintained courtyard of dirt and grass with weathered chairs and a couple of hibachis. A canopy of massive old walnut trees provided shade. The outdoor space was used as a sculpture yard and a place to socialise. There were fifteen art grad students that year.

Another scorching summer weekend but by late afternoon the trees offered enough dappled shade to prepare for a photo shoot. In a spot of sun, I spread a blanket on the ground, then collected my camera gear and props from the studio. The kids helped me tug a rectangular, two-hundred-gallon, clear plexiglass aquarium, the size of a washing machine, into the courtyard. I had scavenged the behemoth tank from beside the science department dumpster. We set up a hose to fill it.

At home, I photographed through a thirty-gallon, salt-encrusted fish aquarium, the size of a small laundry basket. Head and shoulder shots mostly, and never filled with water. The bigger courtyard version meant I could photograph full bodies in the tank: two kids could fit inside, maybe even the three.

Photographing through marred, transparent plexiglass or obscured glass, gave me an effect much like the 1860s portraits created by Victorian photographer, Julia Margaret Cameron: foggy, dreamy, otherworldly. She used a wide aperture to produce a shallow depth of field and a slow shutter speed to render movement into painterly blur. Her eerie images appeared sombre, edges of faces smeared like delicious, clotted cream, gestured hands pale with light, and backgrounds melted into shadowy deep space. She included imperfections: scratches, photochemical stains, even fingerprints. I used her techniques to create my images: subjects suggesting loss, a peek into memory, metaphoric narratives to illustrate painful stories about a childhood gone wrong.

Half-filled with water, the aquarium sparkled and shimmered with light. Arian and Nanda reclined on the blanket. Rachel at my side flipped off her sandals.

'I'll go in my clothes. I don't care,' she said and lifted the bottom edges of her shorts in a curtsy.

'Awesome. When we are done you can dry in the sun.'

Close to dinner time, the air felt humid and warm, and the light through the trees filtered gold. A few fellow grad students came into the complex with coolers stocked with bottles of beer, followed by a visiting art professor, Boris, a towering blond god. He bold-strode into our courtyard, smiled and waved, then gazed straight at me and lifted his shirt to wipe sweat off his face. His stomach rippled with muscle. He found some shade under a tree about twenty feet from our tank, popped open a beer and sat to observe us.

Rachel handed me her glasses and raised her arms, her skin golden-brown. I put her glasses in my trousers pocket, swung her into the aquarium, a hot kid dunked in cold water. She yelped. I draped a couple of yards of white tulle, a fine-meshed veil, over the top of the tank and allowed it to fall into the water. The ghost fabric swirled around her body. She knelt to press her face against the plexiglass. The tank behaved like a huge lens, Rachel's body divided in two; above water I could see her shoulders, arms and head, but her submerged legs and torso appeared shorter and wider, optically doubled, like a magician's trick. I parted the crinoline to reveal water snaking down the outer surface of the tank wall, inside fog appeared around Rachel's eyes and mouth, her face painted with waves of light. She pressed both hands against the clear wall until they turned white. I photographed her face beside her wet hair spiralled against the plexiglass where thousands of water droplets sparkled. Through the viewfinder, I saw the world she inhabited separate from the world I knew. She became an abandoned merchild, a captured muse, a poem. I lifted the fabric from the tank, bent over the edge and pulled her out onto a green patch of lawn in the sun. She shook the wet off her arms. I wiped her eyes, returned her glasses and took a picture of strands of hair rippled against shoulders. When the aquarium filled to the top, I winked at Nanda.

'Well?'

'Okay,' he said and hopped to his feet. Seven years old, still a Buddha boy, short and stocky. He kicked off his shoes, looked at me, scanned everyone else in the courtyard and peeled off his shorts to his undies.

'It's like a swimsuit,' he said.

An elfish smile and hot-pink cheeks made me think he felt a tad embarrassed, but it didn't stop him. Off came his shirt, a kid with a six-pack.

Boris, his eyes red, scrunched his face in Nanda's direction. 'Are those your underpants?'

Nanda glared at Boris, directed his eyes to mine and then back to Boris. I waited to see what Nanda would do.

'Okay, Nanda Ponda Squalanda, are you ...'

Motherly affections were expressed through elaborate nicknames, the longer the better, the bigger the love. Before I finished my sentence he sprinted towards the tank. I shielded my camera behind me as he sprung over the edge, landing a cannonball. The walls bulged and water sloshed over. Rachel screamed. Both of us were soaked.

As I continued to make exposures, Nanda surfaced, whipped hair from his face and dove under somersaulting, his body effervescent. Water and boy energy. Bubbles streamed from his nose. He sank to the bottom and lay still. Face relaxed, eyes closed. After a long minute, he burst upward. I lunged around the aquarium, photographed Nanda as he broke the surface and spun in midair, and captured the curve of his body as he dove in. A boy learning to fly.

Nanda didn't want to stop, so I let him toss and roll until he wound down and his feet were shrivelled to prunes. He had jumped into the tank but he couldn't climb out. Arian helped me heave him, waterlogged and teeth chattering, to the ground. He stretched out on the blanket; his wrinkled feet caked with dirt and grass.

'Arian, you going in?' I pointed and smiled at him.

Arian scrunched his face and shook his head. 'No way.'

Boris asked Nanda, 'How old are you?' and took a swig of beer.

I waved at Boris. 'Hey, hold on now.'

Boris' face turned mean. 'I'm asking you. What the hell are you doing running around in your underpants? In public.'

Nanda scowled in response.

'That's enough,' I said to both, forestalling trouble.

I did not want to get into a fight with a buzzed visiting professor or contribute to any reason for the kids to be banned from the studio compound. I motioned to the kids to stand. We gathered our things and moved our blanket closer to the studio fifty feet away from Boris. Arian helped me empty the tank and drag it into the studio. We unlocked the bikes and trailer and loaded our belongings into the cart ready to go home when I heard Boris yelp.

'Little fucker.' Boris shot up drenched, shaking the wet from his hair.

Nanda had taken the beer cooler full of ice and water, snuck behind Boris and dumped it over his head.

I ran towards them waving my hands, yelling, 'Whoa, whoa, Nanda.'

Too late, Nanda snagged Boris' icy beer bottle and swung-emptied the contents across Boris' chest.

A student laughed and said, 'Oh my God. Dude.'

'Okay, okay,' Boris said, with his hands raised in surrender.

Nanda crossed his arms and faced Boris.

'Come on Nandi Pond. What in the world?' I curved an arm around his shoulders and squeezed. 'Apologise.' Squeezed again. 'Right now.' I felt him shake.

'Hell no,' he said. His lower lip trembled and his nostrils flared.

Boris approached us, his mouth twisted.

'He doesn't have to apologise. It's me. I'm sorry.' Boris' square shoulders deflated as he sucked in his top lip and extended an open hand towards Nanda.

Nanda waited until I gave him a push. He reciprocated the handshake as he looked at me with side-eyes, turned away and walked towards our bicycles.

An orange sunset squeezed through trees. I straddled the bike, feet barely touching the ground and readied myself for take-off. In the bike trailer, Nanda sat next to Rachel, her cheeks glowing magenta. He sagged half melted with his legs perched on a folded blanket. I pushed off and pumped the pedal to start moving. Arian balanced on his bike behind us to give me room to get ahead. I rolled my kid-pack through the gate when Boris hollered.

'That's quite a brave young man you have.'

Loud enough for Nanda to hear, I said, 'Brave, lovable and learning.'

One Thousand and Sixteen ...

Perfect Partner Checklist

At thirty-two, I worked as a teaching assistant while I attended graduate school full-time, on top of making art and exhibiting internationally. I had little time for dating, yet a strong desire to share my life with someone. But not anyone. To find a perfect partner, I made a list of characteristics. I vowed to not even try to be in a relationship unless the person met my criteria.

During grad school, I had a few boyfriends. A man, who on our first date arrived at my door in a flowery skirt. If only he had looked hot in a skirt. I also dated an insomniac artist who indulged in alcohol and psychedelics until I realised, I never understood a word he said. Another romantic endeavour was a guy who rear-ended my car twice pulling into the driveway. And last, the clueless man who wanted me to send my kids to live with their father. None of them made it anywhere near partner level.

My list had the following requirements: first, must like kids, next, must be artistic. My new partner needed to be highly intelligent, not engage in small talk, have a great sense of humour, be a problem solver, and know how to fix and make useful things. I wanted someone who would make eye contact. Considerate, had integrity, loyal. Musical. Doesn't abuse drugs or alcohol. Must crave adventure, be ambitious. Be a healthy eater and keep fit. Good-looking. Absolutely could not come from a broken home.

One afternoon, an acquaintance named Eve brought her boyfriend to my apartment for a haircut. She knew I cut my kids' hair, so she thought I was qualified. As soon as her boyfriend walked through my apartment door, the perfect-partner checklist activated.

Her guy wore cropped shorts revealing long muscular legs and a tank top baring broad shoulders. *Fit. Athletic. Check.* A friggin' Viking with a strong jaw, prominent nose, high cheekbones and a sun-bleached mane of dreadlocks that fountained to the middle of his back. *Handsome. Check. Exotic, a plus. Eve's boyfriend, not fair.*

The compare-myself-to-other-women internal programming took over. She looked like a model, tall with slim arms and legs, a petite face with flawless skin. I looked more like Raggedy Ann, rounder, shorter, softer, with skin displaying many dermatological imperfections. I felt dowdy, self-conscious of my boobs that represented a cumulative five years of breastfeeding; I could hold a pencil under them, maybe even a rolling pin. My arms and legs were more voluptuous, resembling the figures in Renoir's painting, *The Bathers*. I got a combo of Dad's muscular gene and Mum's bonny stature.

His eyes met mine. Greenish-turquoise. *Check.* I could have been all in, but he was taken.

'Hey. I'm Roger. How's it going?' He shook my hand firmly.

A current ran through my body to between my legs. *Sexy. Check. This guy. I gotta stop.*

'Great. Nice to meet you,' I said.

The kids sat on my bed which doubled as a sofa in our one-bedroom apartment. I slept in the living room; they shared the bedroom. With genuine interest he introduced himself and shook each one's hand. *Likes kids. Check.*

'Your dreadlocks are gorgeous. Are you sure you want to cut them off?' I asked.

'Well...'

Before he could finish his sentence, Eve chimed in.

'Yes, he is sure. All of it.'

Roger, Eve, and I moved into the kitchen. He lifted his tank top off over his head, shaking his dreads loose. There he was, bare-chested. I flushed with attraction and was relieved he didn't flirt. *Loyal. Check.*

After chatting while cutting his dreads to his skull, I learned he had brains. *Intelligent. Check.* His brother was a friend of mine, so I had some family history. *Not from a broken home. Check.* He played bass in a local band. *Musical. Check.* He had applied to a university to major in art and design. *Ambitious. Check. And an Artist? Check. Check, check, check, fucking checkity check check.*

Roger belonged to Eve. Eve's boyfriend. She was moving to pursue her Ph.D. at a university halfway across the country. He planned to follow her. She left Davis to find housing and start school while he would go later. He needed to bring closure to his band and work. Before he left, we hung out as friends, became close. Neither of us made a move on the other. I did not want a man who could be stolen. Plus, he loved his perfect-partner girlfriend. However, by the time he met up with her, she had found someone else and told him to find a place of his own. He stayed for the year to finish school. We wrote back and forth. I encouraged him to move back to Davis. He did, and when he knocked on my door, I was determined to make him mine. I couldn't pass on a guy who checked all my boxes.

We both had multiple relationships over the prior year before we dated each other so we decided to get blood tested for AIDS and not have sex for a year. A whole year. We wanted to see if we could be close friends in a monogamous relationship first. I had kids to consider. I couldn't fool around anymore. After a year, we consummated our relationship, agreed to get married and rented a house together. I loved him madly. My kids loved him too.

I graduated with a Master of Fine Arts in 1989, the same year our best friend Al had calculated, through astrology, the most auspicious time for a wedding. According to the alignment of the planets, our ceremony would start at 3:30 a.m. beneath a sky full of stars and end at sunrise, 5:00 a.m.

Rows of amber luminarias, candles inside paper bags, edged our front lawn and the fence. A train of them led through the gate along a path to the backyard. Seated on a chair, a friend played classical music on her cello next to ripening tomatoes, green beans vined to poles and a coop with chickens clucking. Our wood dining table stood draped in vintage lace, covered in fresh flowers on a rectangle of lawn. A ceramic candelabra, the moon painted on one side and the sun on the other, held two candles. One for Roger, one for me. Two folded pieces of watercolour paper containing our handwritten wedding vows waited to be read. Whispering guests arrived and followed the trail of lanterns.

I searched for Roger, wandered through the house and yard until someone told me he was with his parents who had been adamant about not attending our wedding. At the last minute, they drove from Los Angeles, a six-hour drive, to convince their son not to marry me—a divorced woman with three children. Roger, puffy faced and red-eyed, arrived a few minutes before our ceremony start time. His parents came later and hid behind the thirty-five guests already gathered. Mum and Dad didn't attend. I suspected they were avoiding each other.

Roger sported a year's growth of dreadlocks. We both wore brand-new button-up shirts and shorts, our feet in new Birkenstocks. We didn't have money for wedding clothes. Being practical, we bought clothes we needed. The kids wore clothing they had. The five of us stood to one side of the table with the guests on the other side facing us.

Our neighbours, a husband-and-wife ministry team from the Berkeley Psychic Institute, had agreed to marry us for a small fee. Standing at one end of the table, they spoke about love and read what constituted a partnership, a hippie-modified version of *in sickness and in health, till death do us part.*

Roger said, 'There are five of us joining together today.'

We lit our candles. I said my vows, a sappy but true love poem to Roger. I heard him snuffle and sigh as he wiped away tears. Nanda looked at me and hush-giggled. A white rat popped its head from the collar of his shirt. I looked at Arian; his rat clung to his shoulder. I took a deep breath and smiled. Roger, whom I had never seen cry, sobbed as he read his love note to me. Nanda disappeared under the table, surfaced on the other side and ran through the crowd of guests. *Where's he going?* In the middle of vows, I couldn't go after him. As Roger and I, both in tears, exchanged rings, Nanda returned carrying a box of tissues. We sniffled and blew our noses as the cello sounded deep notes and signified our union. We kissed as the sun brightened the sky. After a celebratory cheer, everyone returned home to go back to bed.

That afternoon, we had a potluck party: barbequed fish, salad greens from our garden and a potpourri of specialty foods prepared by my artistic foodie friends. We had a keg of custom-brewed pot beer, homemade tomato wine and a three-tiered cake fat with cream and topped with marzipan roses baked and crafted by a friend who happened to be a professional German baker. Another friend modified two plastic superhero figurines into the bride and groom and placed them on top of our cake. Roger's band, Civil Rhythms, played reggae all night. We danced, we ate, we played, we got silly drunk. Well, not the kids. At least I didn't think so.

The next day, late morning, hungover, on my way to the kitchen to start some breakfast, I noticed four rolls of film on my work table. I didn't shoot 3200 film, too grainy and contrasty, but someone did. A few weeks later, I processed the film, astonished to see images of our wedding: lines of luminarias, a cello rested against a chair, a candelabra aglow, the flowers and the garden, the ministers hugging, groups of family and friends, even me waving to the camera. I had no idea who took those photos. The following month, I framed an image of our new family standing together at the wedding table. Candelabra light illuminating our faces. The kids' eyes glued to Roger and me, white rat heads poking over the boys' shoulders. All of us, tissues in our hands.

One thousand seventeen …

The Beheading and Disappearance of Poofy Roger

As soon as I remarried, Billy filed for child custody. Complicated at best. After a long battle, the judge ordered our family, Roger included, to an hour of mediation. The mediator, who lamented not having had a relationship with his father, believed the boys belonged with their father. The judge accepted that recommendation. Within a week Arian and Nanda moved into Billy's apartment.

Rachel, Roger and I were devastated. Arian, thirteen, didn't mind, if he could visit us regularly. Nanda, age ten, called me a few days later requesting to come home.

Before Nanda moved in with his father, I had purchased him a pint-sized stuffed animal, a velvety brown puppy with a sweet face, floppy ears and suede paws. Our family referred to stuffed animals as stuffties. He named his new stuffty, Poofy Roger.

Nanda and I built his puppy a doghouse from an old kitchen drawer, gave it a skylight and front porch. We recycled some fake bushes off an old train set and glued them to the outside, then painted the house purple and bright blue. Nanda drew butterflies and flowers on the walls using a black marker. I quilted Poofy Roger a blue satin blanket and made him a dog collar strung with alphabet beads. It read: I LOVE NANDA. Nanda had at least fifty stuffties at the foot of his bed, but Poofy Roger stayed on his pillow.

The day I bought Nanda the toy puppy, he shook the stuffty in my face and said, 'I'm starving.' Sad-eyed, he stuck his bottom lip out like I had neglected my motherly duties. 'Steak is best for a growing puppy,' he said and gave me a full-toothed grin.

'Steak. Ha ha. Make yourself some macaroni and cheese.' I patted the stufftie's head.

A week later, when Nanda came to visit, he handed me Poofy Roger's body from one hand and its head from the other.

'What happened?'

'I don't want to talk about it.' He closed his eyes and sighed. 'I just want you to fix him.'

I placed Poofy Roger's body and decapitated head on the kitchen table. Roger and I took the kids for a hike, stopped for hamburgers, then ice cream. There wasn't enough time in the day. Not long after we got home, I heard Billy pull into the driveway.

Nanda retrieved the Poofy Roger bits, and with serious eyes said, 'Oh no. What about Poofy Roger? Are you going to fix him?'

'Oh oh. Sorry, Nandi Squalandi. I'll sew in a few quick stitches. I can fix him properly next time you come.' I felt like a loser mum. I fetched a sewing kit and darned in a thick thread to temporarily secure Poofy Roger's head.

After hugs and kisses, the boys walked out the front door. I followed teary eyed. Nanda didn't want to go.

As he walked to his father's car, without turning to look at me, he asked, 'When can I come back?'

Every time Nanda left, I felt like I failed him. Even though it wasn't up to me, it was contingent on the court and the damn mediator. Nanda stopped and turned around.

'Oh, here. I forgot,' he said.

He retrieved two rolls of film from his trousers pocket and handed them to me. I promised I would have the photographs ready the next time he visited. A day later, I took the film to a one-hour processing lab and waited. In the car I opened the envelope and paged through each photo. A blurred image of his father's girlfriend's two-year-old in a crib. The boys' fish tank half-full of murky water with the goldfish I bought for them named Harold, in tatters, almost dead. Nanda had framed the kitchen cupboards open, revealing a box of cornflakes, a bag of rice and not much else. A few images of my boys' bedroom— their belongings strewn across the floor, no beds. I cranked into a shaking mess.

It had been over a week, and I hadn't heard from Arian, Nanda or Billy. A few days later, Nanda contacted me using his friend's phone. Soon after, Billy dropped the boys off for a weekend. I wrapped my arms around Arian and Nanda and kissed their foreheads.

'Did you bring Poofy Roger?'

Nanda's eyes avoided mine. 'I don't know where he is.' He fidgeted and wrung his hands. 'I had him. He disappeared.'

I lifted his chin as his tears fell, wiped them off his cheek and held him tight.

'I kept Poofy Roger on my pillow, but I should have left him at home.'

'Home?'

'Here, with you.'

In less than a year of the boys staying with their father, I received a call from the sheriff's department. I never learned the details, but the boys were returned to me.

One thousand eighteen …

Nanda's Red Blanket

Roger and I tried raising three kids on a fluctuating income with never enough money. But in 1993, I was hired to chair the photography department at a community college to cover for a faculty member on sabbatical. Our income quadrupled. Instant renewal year. New TV, new towels, new clothes, new beds, new bedding, new everything.

I bought Nanda a red cotton-thermal blanket, which matched his new red tartan flannel sheets. It was on sale. Although Nanda was fourteen, he grew attached to the blanket like a little kid. He loved it even when it bled in its first wash and turned his clothes pink.

On cold days, he draped it over his head to take out the trash or gather the mail. He twisted it about his waist while he did homework at the kitchen table. By evening, the blanket made its way into the living room. I often caught Nanda dreaming in the dancing glow of late-night television, the crimson beast wrapped around his head and body, his two pale feet poking out from beneath its red tail. On school nights, when the chaos of family quieted at bedtime, within seconds, Nanda was fast asleep. Swaddled head to toe, his lips and cheeks matched the hue of his blanket. Except for a fitted sheet, his other bedding was kicked to the floor.

Nanda's red blanket went camping. Soaked in a rainstorm, we hung his bright rectangle of red between a manzanita and madrone. It swayed in the gold light of the Sierras, changing tones as it dried, light twinkling through its fibres. He pulled the dry blanket from the branches and handed it to me.

'Mmmmmm. Smell that?' he said.

For days it released the scent of ponderosa pine and campfire.

At the kitchen table with a pitcher of orange juice, bowls of cereal and a carton of milk, Nanda wound a corner of his blanket into a tight whip and cracked it at Rachel's legs. Breakfast blanket rituals. She screamed like she'd been lit on fire. Serious whip fights ensued; all three going at it. Kitchen table legs chattered across the linoleum floor while glasses of milk and juice sloshed.

'Cut it out,' I bellowed.

'It's just a blanket. Mmmmmom.' He twirled the blanket around his arm until it formed a ball, a fat red muscle, and punched that fist into the air.

The autumn skies opened to a battalion of small clouds, sailing in waves through a blue dome. The winds blustered around houses and trees, through walkways, stairwells and over fences. After a long bumpy journey, a fresh tumbleweed, bigger than my arms wide open, had lost its way and hopped over our fence. It stammered, trapped against the gate at the corner of the summer-dried backyard outside Nanda's bedroom window. The only place I had seen tumbleweeds in Davis were along the barren ground near the railroad tracks. The ball of tangled branches caught Nanda's eye. He rallied me outside to watch as sunlight dove through the bramble waving vascular shadows across the garden path.

'It's gonna be my chandelier,' he said, then gave me a toothy grin.

Although the weed was still green, I went in the house to get him a pair of work gloves in case of thorns. He dragged the round bush through the yard, lifted it over his head looking like Atlas and manoeuvred it inside, into his room. Standing on a chair, he hoisted and wired the spiky beast to the light fixture above his bed.

Months had passed. We grew accustomed to the tumbleweed light shade. I had to duck to avoid catching my hair when giving Nanda a goodnight kiss and tuck in. And although it occupied a quarter of his room, we never lost pleasure in the display of filigree patterns on the ceiling and walls. And then, in the dead of night, I heard a shriek.

'Mom!'

Half asleep, I stumbled to Nanda's room and saw him standing on the edge of his bed stripped to his undies, pink undies to be precise, wrestling the blanket.

'Damn it, it's eating me alive.' He growled as he flapped and snapped the blanket.

The precious orb had released its seeds, a mass exodus of bull stickers. That's what I called them when I was a kid. Angled, hard pods the size of a BB with four-pointed spines and two curved stiletto horns. Raging bulls. His blanket inflicted multiple stab wounds. Mad as a dog in a fight with a porcupine, Nanda did everything he could to shake free those clinging bison but to no avail. Poor guy. I blotted his welts using cotton balls soaked in calamine lotion, handed him a spare blanket and told him to sleep on the living room couch.

The next day he hauled the thorn-spitting monster to the backyard. I rescued his blanket, shook it like hell, pecked thorns from the weave and returned it to his room. Again, he tossed it into a corner, a huddled mass of potential agony. I washed it several times, but the bull stickers fractured into bull slivers. Nanda and I spent a few evenings on the couch, tweezing and plucking the stubborn prickers from every inch of that scarlet terrain. Trust was restored, and the blanket regained favour for another five years.

One thousand nineteen …

Through a Pinhole

1996

Roger gave Nanda his 35mm Pentax, a manual camera that inspired Nanda to experiment with exposure settings. He shot many rolls of film of himself and nature and was often game for a photo shoot with me.

On a particularly quiet Saturday, Nanda and I woke early to discover we had the morning to ourselves. While eating breakfast in the backyard we discussed how the fence, bordered with jasmine, forsythia, and orange trees, would make a perfect backdrop for photographic portraits. Under a clear sky and a bright white summer sun, we decided to play with a pinhole camera, a rectangular wooden container no bigger than a shoebox. One end accepted a 4x5 Polaroid film holder. The other end had a dime-sized shim of brass with a hole poked through by a needle—a pinhole—which served as an aperture and lens. Light could enter to expose the film. Once exposed, and rolled through the film holder, the photograph developed in twenty seconds.

Nanda, barefooted, shirtless in baggy shorts, pressed a strip of gaffer tape over the pinhole as a shutter. A simple open and close system. He loaded the film and placed the camera on a chair, lens facing me.

'Okay, this is a test.' His tanned skin shined with perspiration. 'Face me. Be absolutely still as I count to fifteen. Then take one step sideways and face away for another fifteen. Is thirty seconds enough, do you think?'

'Well, we'll see. Tell me when.'

I stood perfectly straight in a thin cotton sundress before a leafy hedge, my arms relaxed at my sides. I could smell my skin and warm grass humid under my bare feet. He pointed at me as he peeled the tape away from the pinhole.

'One thousand one, one thousand two, one thousand three ...'

Sweat dripped down my neck as I held my breath to stay still. We looked into each other's eyes without blinking, focused in the moment, nothing else mattered.

'One thousand thirteen, one thousand fourteen, one thousand fifteen. Scoot to your left and turn around. One thousand one, one thousand two ...'

I took another breath, lunged, rotated, and stood basking in sun, in art, in the love of our collaboration.

'One thousand thirteen, one thousand fourteen, one thousand fifteen.'

I spun around to face him. 'Now slide in the envelope, flip the lever on the holder, and pull the tab,' I instructed.

Nanda removed the film and counted to twenty. We huddled together as he peeled the photo from the chemical substrate. An image of two ghosts. We moaned in unison. Two eerie twins against darkness, one approaching, the other leaving, both hovering over weedy, unmown grass. We looked at each other, our mouths agape. Because sunlight only touched from my head to my knees, my legs didn't get exposed, so I was legless and floating.

I made a thirty-second exposure of Nanda turning in circles. The result whirled him into a life-sized spinning top. For the next photo, he instructed me to raise my arms a couple of inches per second. The slow-motion exposure rendered me into a Fairy Mom.

Fairy Mom

We tried many combinations of time and motion and found that making photographs together transported us into a shared dream world. One image made us squeal. I had lain in the grass and pretended to swim while Nanda paced slowly to and fro behind me. Our longest exposure produced a murky deep hole, transformed me into a struggling spirit sinking into earth, and Nanda became a repetition of headless men, except for one face, barely visible, peeking at us, eyes neither opened nor closed.

'Oh shit. That's spooky. Where are my eyes?' His lips stretched thin as he pressed his chin to his chest.

I sat in the grass. He gathered our photo materials and camera, then sat next to me and leaned a sweaty shoulder to mine. I could see him smile in my periphery. I smiled too.

'That was weird. We look dead.' I turned to him and laughed.

'Oh-myyyyy-God.' He jumped to his feet, circled his arms like windmills and yelled like a ghoul. 'Mooooo-hooooo-haaaaaa-haaaaaaaaaa.' Sprinted the perimeter of the yard, straight legs and stiff arms, his eyes round, mouth a wide O. 'Oooooooooooo.'

A couple of months later I enlarged the images to sixteen by twenty inches. They haunted me, so I stuck them in a black plastic bag and stashed them away in the studio. Mysterious artwork appealed to me, but those pinhole images had something lurking inside, palpable, like finding a lump in my neck.

We Look Dead

One thousand twenty ...

Arms Wide Open

Seated at my work table, located in a corner of our living room, I examined a professional two-and-a-quarter camera, a Rollei I inherited after a close friend had died. A year had passed, and I felt ready to learn how to use the complicated behemoth which meant reading the manual.

'RTFM,' my friend would say, 'Read the fucking manual.'

'What's that?' Nanda asked. He dragged a chair from the kitchen and sat next to me.

'It's Rick's Rollei. Complicated. Here.' Using both hands, I placed it in his lap.

'Ugh. Weighs a ton.' He rotated the camera observing its controls.

'Let's load some film. I'll read you the instructions.'

We successfully wound a roll of 120mm black and white film into the film back and attached it to the camera body.

'Time to try it out, Nanda Pond.' I gave him a grin.

He popped up from his chair. 'Hell yeah.'

We took the camera and a tripod into the yard where summer had disappeared into autumn, the air cool and damp, the sky hazy. Diffused sunlight painted the yard with milky highlights, a garden made of buttercream.

'My favourite kind of light,' I said.

Nanda climbed into the spare branches of our thirty-foot-tall mimosa tree, all its leaves on the ground. Bare feet wedged into the crotch, he grasped two limbs and let his body fall forward, his face expressionless, into the camera. I shot a roll of twelve frames, wound the film, dropped it into my pocket and reloaded.

Nanda asked me to climb into the grape arbour, to hang my arms and legs through the slats and look at him from over the edge. As he released the shutter, I climbed into position knowing I would be transformed into a writhing figure caught in the arbour's lattice and vines. After he exposed a few frames, I scrambled down, retrieved the camera and took some pictures of him on the back steps. He closed his eyes—one of his signature portrait gestures—and stood bare-chested in front of a sliding glass window that reflected the sky. I checked the frame counter, one shot left, but I was running late.

'I gotta go to work.'

'Aw.' Bug-eyed, he stuck out his bottom lip.

'Poor baby.' I pressed my palm into his forehead. 'We'll do more later.'

I went into the house, set the gear on my work table along with the exposed roll of film, collected my briefcase and jacket, and headed off.

I was thrilled to get some time with Nanda as he spent most of his hours with Carmen. The first time I laid eyes on her, the two of them were walking arm in arm at the farmers market headed towards me. She had long sculpted legs in the shortest shorts possible, braless in a thin tank top, satin brown skin, her hair an Afro Halo that slow-motion waved as she sauntered barefooted. A Vogue model face, hypnotizingly gorgeous. *Oh shit, no wonder he wants to move out.* Carmen, five years older than Nanda, was enrolled as a pre-med at the university. Beauty and brains. They both worked at a fast-food burger joint called Murder Burger. She was the manager at that time—his boss.

Before Carmen, I had been Nanda's favourite person. And although jealousy hadn't seized me, loss did. I was also clueless about how to mother a son who was in love. Nanda, smitten, forgot to finish chores and schoolwork, and often came home late. He craved freedom to spend more time with Carmen and continually reminded me how many days he had left before he'd turn eighteen.

One night, well past midnight, I worried Nanda wouldn't come home. Dressed in a robe, I lay on the couch in the living room, eyes glued to the clock on the wall. He called at 1 a.m. I leaned against the kitchen wall to stay standing, coiling the phone cord between my fingers.

'Where are you? I'll come get you.' I let out a huff.

His voice a bit wonky. 'Nah. Come on. Let me stay.'

I heard Carmen say, 'Tell her I'll bring you to school.'

'Nanda, you need to come home. Right now. It's late.'

The argument continued until Roger, half awake, wrapped in a bathrobe, came into the room. He grabbed the phone, dreadlocks flying.

'You are supposed to be home. Where are you?' he asked, 'What? No. No. Did you hear me?'

I bit my lip hard, listened as my whole body tensed. Roger caught my eye and yelled into the receiver, 'This has gone on far too long. If you aren't coming home when you are asked to, then don't bother coming home at all.'

I felt like I had been shoved off a cliff. But I also saw it coming. *Are we bad parents? Does he hate us? Are we too strict? Maybe not strict enough. Maybe too authoritarian.* We didn't know any better.

A couple of days later, I helped Nanda move into Arian's apartment.

Images from our photoshoot stayed with me. I couldn't wait to see what Nanda and I caught on that film. Even the students saw me vibrating with inspiration during the night class. By the time I got home, everyone was in bed. Someone left the hallway light on so I could see into the living room. I sloughed my jacket over a chair, and as I placed the briefcase on my work table I found two rolls of film, both wound and sealed with a gummed label marked—EXPOSED. I didn't recall finishing the second roll.

In the morning, I dashed into the darkroom to process the two rolls, surprised to find that the last picture on the second roll had been taken by Nanda.

After I had left for work, Nanda hauled my camera and tripod into the yard. He framed a leafless forsythia cascading over the fence, set the timer, centred himself before the camera, and with his eyes closed he leaned back into the springy branches with his arms wide open.

Arms Wide Open

One thousand twenty-one …

Regret

1998 was already an arduous year. Discouraged by the lack of full-time teaching positions at colleges near Davis, I decided to continue my schooling and take night classes in childhood education to attain an art education credential. I didn't want to teach grade school, yet I knew I needed to expand my options. I elected to spend my student teaching hours in a High School photography class. On the day of the assignment, I panicked. Why had I enlisted myself to manage thirty wild teenagers? Given my immaturity and impatience, there were only two possible options: do a good job or get arrested for assaulting a minor.

I entered a damp windowless classroom smelling of acidic photo chemicals wafting from an attached darkroom. The classroom walls and ceiling were covered in student photographs. A group of desks were joined to form one big table, like you'd see at a board meeting, butted against the teacher's desk where I positioned myself. Students sat to either side of me, most eyes in my direction. I unpacked a slide projector and plugged it in, then scanned their faces and smiled. The students whispered to each other, some of them smirking. A couple of girls chuckled with side glances. A few kids sat quiet at the rear of the room.

Across from the desk, at the other end of the tables, a pull-down projection screen hung from the ceiling, held together with duct tape, most of its reflective surface yellowed and stained. I switched off the overhead light and turned on the projector. A rectangle of illumination filled the screen. The students' faces glowed as they scooched their chairs in to see.

'Hi, I'm Jane Edberg. I am a fine art photographer. Does anyone know the difference between fine art photography and mainstream photography?'

Dead silence, not a stir.

'Okay. I'll tell you. The fine art photographer pushes the boundaries of what is considered photographic or photographable. They lead the viewer away from cliché into the unexpected. They express their deepest emotions, their concerns for humanity. Mainstream is usually a photograph that is familiar, sentimental, easy to look at, like a cheerful snapshot of a family member or an image of a boat sailing into a sunset.'

I glanced around the room. They were alert and listening.

'I think of mainstream as more of a documentation, which doesn't mean those images can't contain emotion or deeper meaning. That's why the intent of the artist needs to be clear. A photo can be both documentation and fine art, so it's confusing.'

I rounded the carousel, pressed in the first slide and focused an image of Arian when he was ten. Two upright owl wings framed his angelic face behind clouded glass, his eyes were closed. Beneath the wings, his hands grasping the bird's talons.

A sweet 'Ooooooooooooooooooo' came from the students.

I could feel energy in the room. *They are interested.*

'Cool!' a boy belted. 'Holding onto wisdom. Owls are wisdom. Right?'

'Fantastic,' I said. 'That's a great interpretation.'

'Did you kill that bird?' asked a boy from the back of the room. He twitched and his bangs fell over one eye.

'Oh no. It's roadkill. The owl wings and talons belong to a friend of mine.'

'Oh wow, that's cool,' he said.

I clicked to the next slide. One of Rachel, age five, inside an aquarium half filled with water. Sheer curtains draped to either side of her dreamy face, droplets pebbled across murky glass, her hands fogged against the pane.

More favourable oooooooos and ahhhhhhhhhhhs.

'These images are visual poems. The meanings change depending on the viewer. There are no wrong interpretations. Although I might have had a specific intent in creating this image, I am informed by what others see.'

I forwarded the next slide. Two large hands pressed against a windowpane holding a silver marble. Behind the hands, a milky head with hair spiralling like smoke. I could hear the students breathing. I thought they might be bored, but when I looked around the room, they were leaning towards the screen, mesmerised.

A girl seated outside the projector's glow asked, 'He wants us to guess or imagine what he is offering?'

I shaded my eyes to see her. 'Beautiful. When I created it, I hadn't thought of it that way. But sure.'

Onto the next slide, an image of Nanda. Two girls giggled. It was then I recognised the one closest to me. *Oh crap, it's Sally.* Her thick curved hair edged her heart-shaped face. One of Nanda's friends, one with benefits—the intimate kind. She looked at me, her eyes eclipsed to half-moons.

A while back, Nanda and I had set a time to meet at his apartment so I could help him search for a decent job. I knocked on his door, no answer. He had given me a key, and as usual, I let myself in, but he had forgotten about our meeting that day. Nanda's bedroom door was wide open and I found him in bed with Sally. She scrambled for her clothes, darted down the hall to the bathroom and closed the door with a bang.

'Oops,' Nanda said as he wrapped a sheet around his body.

'Really?'

I fumed, paced the floor, a mum not wanting to be exposed to her son's sex life. I heard Sally's expletives muffled behind the closed door.

In the classroom the projector light coloured her face blue; she half-smiled and her eyes jetted to avoid mine.

'This image is of my youngest son, Nanda. Some of you know him. He is quite popular.'

Nanda had switched schools right before I started student teaching at that high school. He opted for independent study since he had to work to support himself. But in a small town, most of the students knew him. On the screen, the image of Nanda glowed. He was seven years old in the photograph, sitting cross-legged with his mouth open, eyes closed, head pointed skyward. The curve of his jaw line visible. A round hand mirror, the size of a tea plate, pressed against the centre of his chest, looked as though it reflected a full moon.

And before I could bite my tongue, I said, 'Some of you might have spent the night with him.'

A roar of laughter rumbled through the room. Sally's eyes opened out of eclipse, pupils wide, mouth open.

Oh, I need to stop being an idiot.

I back-pedalled. 'You know. Like at one of his slumber parties.'

More laughter. He had a reputation. I spelunked into a cave as the rope unravelled. My face hot. More back-pedalling.

'Oh! I see. You think I meant something else.'

I clicked the forward button, more of Nanda. *Ah, jeez.* A picture of his body contorted inside a glass box, arms reaching towards us, a silver ball the size of a plum wedged in his mouth. Head tipped back, cheeks sucked in, eyes shut tight. Sally's anxiousness and her urge to flee was palpable. My face sweaty. *Am I a teacher first, an artist first, or mother first, or all the above and this is the dance?* I straightened my posture, cleared my throat.

'In this image, we see a character hiding, yet pleading to connect.'

I felt shame-faced. I wanted to go, and I wanted to stay. Foot in mouth, I stayed.

Next slide, a cat in a zip-lock baggie filled the screen. Self-consciousness possessed me and I forgot how to be present. I faked confidence to get through.

'What the hell?' asked a boy.

'People! Call the cruelty to animals police,' cried another.

They laughed.

'No kitties were harmed,' I said. 'Ever feel like you are trapped?'

Nanda had his own life, and I hadn't adjusted well. I embarrassed myself. I turned to Sally. Gone. Somehow between images of Nanda and the cat in a bag she had managed to escape.

A week passed, and I made the usual jaunt to Nanda's place. I knocked on the door and waited. About to knock again, the door flew open.

Nanda, with his arms crossed over a bare chest, head to one side, fire blazing in his eyes, said, 'What the fuck, Mom? What the hell were you thinking?' then laughed.

One thousand twenty-two …

Mustard Fields

My whole life, I had lived with a garden of flowers, as did my kids. Roger and I edged our front yard with lavender, tulips and daffodils. Black-light lobelia lined the back path while shocking pink cosmos parachuted above, lacy arms fluttering midair. Rows of dahlias, marigolds and roses crowded narcissus into tight groups. Naked ladies rose and fainted. Buddleia swayed with butterflies. A carpet of alyssum seeded its way through the length of the garden. Banksia roses, branches woven into a heart shape, climbed a trellis near our bedroom window. In spring, the sun-yellow forsythia flowed over the fence like a waterfall.

The kids helped me hang rows of long-stemmed pink and red roses from the living room ceiling beams. When the roses dried, I placed the fragrant petals into ceramic bowls for our nightstands. I set single blooms on the kitchen counter and next to the bathroom sink. I'd arrange a vase of flowers for every room in our house. The kids pressed roses and strung marigolds. As a family ritual, we'd pluck daisies and place them behind our ears.

When Nanda was a toddler, he used to dig holes in the garden with grubby hands and feet. He loved to smack dirt to see it fly, but not in a rage like little-me. He was an expressive earth-child in glee. We made pretend soup, filled pots with water, flower petals and grass, and cooked mud pies in the sun. At seventeen, he remembered how to weave a clover wreath, the way I had shown him when he was four. A gift for Carmen.

On a warm autumn afternoon, I stopped by Nanda's apartment to collect him. We had a plan to go into the fields to take photographs. Nanda and I loved to walk on the county roads and watch cows, birds and the occasional coyote or fox. We found solace in the fields full of bloom. The roads gave way to Central Valley trucks along an agricultural strip where safflower and sugar beets flourished, and tilled earth was left to a thriving community of mustard plants. Miles of brilliant yellow and green against a backdrop of widescreen horizon. A Payne's grey and milk-splashed sky swept clean to cerulean blue by the San Joaquin Valley's windy brush.

'You aren't dressed yet?' I asked.

'Shoes and shirt, two minutes.'

On top of his dresser, the only furniture in the room besides his bed, I noticed a half-gallon jar filled with branchy pink roses, purple peonies and red tulips. He had just moved into an apartment with his friend, Drew. A single mattress on the floor. None of his art hung. The flower colours popped against the stark white walls. I walked over to sniff the blooms.

'Wow, what's the occasion? Secret admirer, Mr. Nanda Ponda Squalanda Ji?'

Cheeks hot pink, he swiped his hand across his chest. 'Nope. Thought I'd treat myself.'

He swaggered about the room, blue jeans hanging from narrow hips, let himself fall backwards onto the mattress and leaned on his elbows. With his feet, he hooked his shoes from the floor into the air, caught them in his hands, spun and juggled them before putting them on. I loved watching my Nanda-acrobat, dancing, clowning, his curved, moving lines.

We drove along county roads into farmland, parked in dirt and got out to walk, compelled to take photographs where the open skies welcomed the lush ripeness of spring. Nanda knew how to pose, how to be photographed, a young man who displayed unbreakable confidence. I aimed the camera. We paused and smiled when we heard a train whistle blow from nearby. Up to his chest in mustard flowers, he fastened two bright yellow sprigs of mustard blooms behind both ears. He stilled himself while buoyant florets dangled about his face, a face Caravaggio would have loved to paint. I pressed the shutter release.

Nanda Loves Flowers

One thousand twenty-three ...

The Toilet

Nanda's new roommate, Drew, a reserved and studious twenty-something, grabbed my elbow at the food co-op. A Sir Lancelot-grunge-dude with locks of blond hair tied in a ponytail and a neatly trimmed beard.

'You might want to talk to Nanda. He broke the toilet last night.'

'What?'

'He got in a fight with Carmen. Got drunk. Then got into a fight with the toilet.'

'Oh, oh.' My mouth turned upside down. 'Okay, I guess I'm going over there today.'

'See ya round.' He turned to get into the checkout line.

'Drew?'

'Yeah?' he said, looking over his shoulder.

'I'm so sorry. He can be a little volcano.'

'No worries. He just needs to pay for the damn thing and fix it.'

'Of course.'

I felt my stomach clench, wondered how I could encourage Nanda to realise impulse control. *What's a mother to do?*

My grocery list went into my pocket. New mission: get Nanda sorted. On the way to his apartment, I didn't know if I felt scared or angry. Maybe a lot of both. Nanda tried to be a good guy, and ninety-five percent of the time he behaved like a better-than-good guy, a very good guy. However, he could be feisty, argumentative and impulsive. Add alcohol, he could be out of control. When I arrived at his apartment, my anger, or my repressed version of anger, had taken charge.

I parked in Nanda's vacant spot behind the apartment building. He didn't own a vehicle, thank God. A choir of air conditioners moaned and dripped along the rear wall of the complex. Spring felt more like midsummer. I looked up as I crossed the parking lot to see Nanda standing in front of his second-story bedroom window. There he was with his back towards me. He arched and flexed his muscles, hands on his head, fingers woven through hair, and tilted his head side to side.

'Ah geez.'

Trying not to catch on fire as my temper grew, I plucked a pebble from a planter box and tossed it against the glass pane. Tap! Nanda twisted at the waist, a supermodel, hands still on his head. *My boy needs a catwalk.*

Carmen once told me, 'He's vainer than any girl I know. He takes fifteen minutes to moisturise his face with Oil of Olay.'

I told her he took the bottle from me. I had received the face cream as a birthday/Christmas present from my mother-in-law when I turned thirty-five. Nanda saw me place it into the Goodwill to-go pile and asked me if he could have it. He used that brand ever since. Carmen and I howled.

With my sandals stuck to hot asphalt, I waved and tried not to appear too angry. Nanda's mouth did a giant O, like wow, as he opened the window. He hung his head out with a sweet 'Maaamaaaa,' and smiled. Nanda, born smiling.

'I'll be right there.'

Most of my fuming released. His childlike manner smoothed me over, but I still lamented. *How am I going to deal with his stupid toilet issue?* I took the stairs to his apartment and knocked on the door, sweat-soaked, my shirt stuck to my skin. Nanda swung open the door, bowed and motioned me to come inside. I took a deep breath and entered his tidy, hand-me-down furnished apartment. Nanda worked hard, paid his bills, usually on time. I had wondered how Drew would tolerate Nanda as a roommate, but Drew once said, 'It's hard not to love Nanda.'

I didn't give Nanda the usual peck on the cheek or two-arm wrap-around hug. Instead, I walked to the kitchen sink and filled a glass with water.

'Weren't you supposed to be at work today?' Not eyeing him, I fiddled with some of his fantasy books on the kitchen table.

'Not till fiiiiiive,' he said and stood in front of me.

As I downed the water, I checked Nanda's hobbit legs, hairy and muscular, then noticed an abrasion on one of his feet. He saw my eye with an eyebrow like a crow's wing ready to take flight. He lifted a single brow up and down, up and down, and laughed.

Looking him straight in the eyes, I asked, 'Everything okay?'

'No, but if I need your help, you'll be the first to know,' he said with his hand on my shoulder.

One thousand twenty-four ...

Move to Santa Cruz

Roger took well to the parental duties of an active stepdad to my kids and worked hard to help support his new family. And although he had a master's degree, he worked at the UC Davis arboretum full-time at slightly above minimum wage. I also had a master's degree and juggled part-time teaching at three separate colleges, managed a computer lab at an elementary school ten hours a week and worked part-time as an assistant to the director of the Humanities Institute at UC Davis. Hours inconsistent, wages low. Both of us had student loans, a debt over $100,000 with steep monthly payments and credit cards maxed out. We drove old cars often in need of repair. We didn't own anything of great value and didn't have any savings. In our demographics, we fell below the poverty line.

My thinking: we needed jobs, two well-paid career jobs. I broached the idea of Santa Cruz with Roger.

'Ah, the Pacific Ocean, fresh air, cooler summers, mountains and rivers, an art community, a short drive to San Francisco, a college, a university. We could do it!'

He agreed.

Nanda and Arian planned to rent a house in Davis with friends. Nanda, who registered to join the Coast Guard, still had a semester of high school left before he could graduate and fully enlist. However, when I mentioned moving to Santa Cruz, he appeared excited.

'I could go to school with Rachel, and I'd be closer to Carmen,' he said.

Carmen had recently moved 400 miles south to attend a university in Long Beach. Still 200 miles from Santa Cruz, but half closer.

'You could. But finish school in Davis.'

'Does "you could" mean, I can come with you guys?' His eyes dilated and his cheeks warmed red.

'Well, no. Stay with your brother. You're all set. Are you having second thoughts about the Coast Guard?'

He shook his head and rolled his eyes to the ceiling.

Nanda also failed to acknowledge his relationship with Roger still needed mending. That altercation on the phone where Nanda didn't want to come home and Roger suggested he not come home at all. Nanda made it home that night—late and drunk. A nonproductive argument ensued. Roger asked him to move out again, so Nanda left. At the time, Nanda was not yet eighteen. I considered his departure temporary.

All the times we talked about moving to Santa Cruz, I never addressed smoothing the rift between him and Roger. I didn't want to poke a sore spot. I'd already spoken to them, and they had agreed to work on it but as time went by, they never mentioned it again. I lamented, then settled on knowing it wasn't for me to fix. Heart-stressed and longing, deep down, I wanted Nanda to move to Santa Cruz, my best buddy, my confidant, my mama's boy. But I understood, eighteen almost nineteen, having tasted freedom, he wouldn't want to return to the confines of our home, and I certainly didn't want to go back to administering rules. I'd go crazy monitoring his comings and goings. Besides, he wanted to live with Arian again; the two of them were inseparable. Nanda had expressed an interest in living with Carmen while he finished school before leaving for the Coast Guard, but she told him he'd be too much of a distraction; she wouldn't be able to complete homework or study.

'We haven't even found jobs yet. It's just a dream at this point,' I said. I encouraged him to stay, to look forward to being in the Coast Guard. 'Before you know it, you'll be on a massive ship headed out on open seas to Antarctica, hanging on for dear life.' I smiled.

Rachel, almost sixteen, had two more years of high school. Most of her friends needed more guidance, I thought a move would be a positive change.

'I am not going to Santa Cruz,' she said.

I thought my idea of a move would blow over or we'd find a way to make it in Davis. Buy a house. Settle down. But within the week of discussing the idea with Roger, he found a job advertisement and applied for the position of Grounds Assistant Supervisor at the University of California in Santa Cruz. Great salary. Gorgeous location. Matched his skill sets. By the next week he got a phone call. He nailed the interview. They hired him. We talked about my finding employment near Santa Cruz taking a year or more and reassured each other that we could endure a long-distance relationship. Shortly after, he moved.

Rachel and I stayed behind. She needed to finish the remainder of her high school year, and I hadn't completed the credential program. And I didn't have a job near Santa Cruz. Roger rented a small apartment not far from his new workplace. I continued to rent the house in Davis.

For months, I whittled fingernails to the bone, upped my alcohol consumption and spent many nights crying alone in bed. I conducted vigorous job searches: college instructor, high school teacher, even administrative assistant. Unfortunately, there was nothing near Roger. I thought I'd never be able to join my husband.

We couldn't afford time or money to visit very often. Twice in four months. He had a good income, but the cost of the move, a new car, and various debts we needed to pay off, living paycheck to paycheck, not much was left over.

Six months after starting the job search, in the mailroom of a college where I taught part-time, I saw a flyer for a full-time position for art instructor at Gavilan College in Gilroy, an hour's drive to Santa Cruz. I had already been commuting as a freeway flyer—someone who spends more hours driving to various jobs than they do actually working. I applied for the job.

Time crawled. I heard nothing about my application, not even if they had received it. After a couple more months, I finally got Human Resources on the phone but only for a brief consoling. Another month went by. Just as I had abandoned hope, I received a call. They asked me to appear in two days for a four-hour interview. The drive to Gilroy would take three hours from Davis with good traffic, mostly on a winding mountainous road, and the weather report predicted rain. The interview time: 8:00 a.m.

I excused Rachel from school. We stayed with Roger in his studio apartment. While there, I needed to prepare a computer-arts presentation for the interview committee. I had no idea how to teach computer art and had two days to prepare a bad-ass lecture. I also needed to complete an essay for my graduate course. Talk about worn out.

A dress didn't exist in my wardrobe, so I borrowed one from my close friend, Faith. Thank God I had art skills so I could finesse a decent hairdo and makeup. I applied fake fingernails because I had none. Dolled up, I felt like a fraud, terrified the interviewers would find me unbelievable. *This is probably all for nothing.* Anxiety and desperation had to be shoved deep, below trigger level.

The interview committee sat around a heavy oak conference table: eight instructors from various disciplines, along with three deans and an administrative assistant. The main interviewer, Sebastian, also an art professor, was a tall, slender man in a blue satin suit with a flower in his lapel. His face resembled a topographical map with two miniature green lakes to either side of a pointy, rosy peak of a nose. Hypnotised by the pink flag of his tongue, I missed most of what he said. He waved a long-stemmed red rose above his head. He slapped the stem into my palm, wrapped his hands around mine, and flopped the flower side to side.

'Where have you been all of my life?' he asked and let go.

Am I hearing this correctly? What does he mean? Think quick!

'Well, some things are worth waiting for.' I smiled, feeling the slickness of freshly applied lipstick. I rarely wore lipstick. *My God, I hope I don't have lipstick on my teeth.*

After presenting the bad-ass lecture and enduring a couple of hours of gruelling questions, I exited a door to the parking lot. I took in a few deep breaths, then spotted two condors nested on top of a redwood tree flapping their wings. I felt congratulated.

Weeks later while I thought they had hired someone else, a letter of acceptance arrived in the mailbox. I would be given ten classes to teach. We had a month to find housing, register Rachel in school, and move a household of twenty years' accumulation along with dogs and cats to Santa Cruz.

The night we finished moving into our new house, while relaxing on our living room carpet, a train pounded and clattered past our backyard fence. The sliding glass window hummed, and the fence rattled. We had no idea the alley behind our house came with a railroad corridor. Horns blared.

One thousand twenty-five …

Instant Photo

Near the end of September 1998, Nanda came for his first visit to Santa Cruz. A perfect autumn day, mid-seventies, pillowy clouds floating on the ocean breeze, sunlight flickering in and out, soft to bright. A respite from a particularly foggy August. I can turn into mud under low light. In the luminosity of that day, my mind cleared.

I collected Nanda at the San José train station and drove him over the mountains on a winding highway to our new rental house located two blocks from the beach. Roger was at work and Rachel at school, so Nanda and I did a tour of the neighbourhood and downtown Santa Cruz, walked the boardwalk and watched surfers at Pleasure Point and Steamer Lane, which he loved. We named it the Nanda Pilgrimage.

In the backyard, we sat next to each other at a picnic table near full-bloomed honeysuckle and talked about his Coast Guard plans.

'They're enlisting me as a photojournalist.' He smiled wide and rubbed his hands briskly to show he savoured the thought.

I hugged him. 'Wow, how cool is that!'

'I'll miss Carmen, but to be honest, I am more at ease without her.' He shrugged.

'I guess we'll see how it all turns out.'

'Oh, by the way, Carmen wants a photograph of me, and I don't have any good ones. Nothing recent.' He arched his back, rubbed his chest and winked.

'You want me to take some pictures of you.' With my hand curved to the shape of his face, I gently patted his cheek.

'Yup. Can we do Polaroids? She's coming in a few days.' He rested his hand on my shoulder. 'I'll be right back. Gotta change.' He plucked at his shirt and ran into the house.

I nodded and followed him inside to retrieve the Polaroid camera gear. 'I still have some SX-70 and today's light is heaven.'

Back outside, I loaded the camera and lounged in the sun. Twenty minutes later, he slow-motion walked through the backyard, his hair tamed with mousse. In white khaki trousers, black leather lace-ups and a new burgundy T-shirt, he beamed beautiful.

'Wine colours match your lips, my handsome Nanda Ponda Squalondi Pondi.'

Nanda grinned. Around his neck he wore a necklace strung from the black obsidian beads Carmen had given to him when she left for school. I smiled so hard my jaw hurt. His face, not a boy's, but a man's, alert, his pupils wide with love.

The Polaroid That Lived in Carmen's Pocket for a Year

One thousand twenty-six ...

Birthday Card

Mid-November, I longed to see my boys, but I worked nonstop and couldn't get time off. Winter break would be the soonest, starting the 21st of December. Dizzy with a headache, I reflected on Davis where I had lots of time and no money and compared that to Santa Cruz where I had a full-time job with an overload of teaching, lots of money and no time.

A chill hit the air. I plummeted into a slow-motion collapse, anticipating our family not celebrating Thanksgiving together and cramming birthdays into Christmas. Plus, I hated holidays, all the expectations, with one exception, Valentine's Day. Day of the heart, of love and the wry poems of Chaucer.

Seated at my work table, I peered through the window and watched as a fog blanket crept across the sky. Instead of preparing art lessons, I took the time to create a collage for Nanda's birthday card. While gathering photographs, paint, brushes, a tub of water, pens, scissors and paste, the phone rang.

I paid for Nanda's landline and long-distance coverage. I also bought him a pager with service—a black box by Motorola that buzzed and showed the phone number of the person calling. Small enough to fit into a trousers pocket, often worn clipped to a belt. The idea is for the person paged to call back. We never entered my number. Instead, he thought it would be funny if I used the numeric code 7734. When viewed up-side-down 7734 reads as hell.

That would be me.

Nanda used the pager and landline at home, but most days, after he got off work at 5:00 p.m., he'd ring me collect from a payphone where he would hang downtown with friends. We'd talk for an hour on the weekdays, two or more hours on the weekends. The steep bill was worth that connection. Our phone calls were a shared lifeline.

'You have a collect call from, 'It's me."

'Yes, I'll accept the charges. I bet it's you.'

He laughed. 'Hi Mama.'

'Your birthday is next week, Nandi Pondi.' My throat knotted. I didn't want to break it to him that we would have to delay celebrating. 'My workload is crazy. Christmas break is the only time I...' I took a breath. 'Shit. Can we squeeze in birthdays at Christmas?' *Oh gosh, I feel bad.* 'Did that sound terrible?'

'Nah. Don't worry. I can spend my birthday with my lovely Carmen.'

I heard street noises and guessed downtown Davis and that he had just gotten off work.

'And then there's Thanksgiving. It's too much right now.' I bit my lip hard.

'Nah. I get it. Anyways, after my birthday, Robin wants me to visit him at his sister's place in Humboldt. Then we'll return to Davis to have Thanksgiving with his parental units.'

Robin was Nanda's best friend since grade school. Robin, the larger, softer, easier version of Nanda. They looked alike, often made the same gestures simultaneously, finished each other's sentences and were mistaken for brothers. Robin, a whole lot taller, much calmer and a tad wiser.

Nanda said he'd catch a ride to Humboldt with his friend, Shelly, and then she'd drive everyone back to Davis.'

'That sounds cool. Are you sure?' I felt glad he couldn't see my tear-wet face.

'Hellov. I wanna go.'

Hellov was Davis slang for an enthusiastic yes, like hella or hell yeah!

'I'm making you a birthday card.' I bit the cap off a marker and doodled on a piece of watercolour paper. 'And I have a birthday package for you.'

'Awww, nice. Don't mail it, though. I don't want the roommates messing with my things while I'm gone.'

'Let's exchange presents at Christmas. We can do a family Christmas here. I'll get you a train ticket, like before.'

In his exaggerated, fake Scottish accent, he said, 'Aye! That's grrrreat.'

I had seen Nanda twice since we moved. Once when he rode the train to be with us in Santa Cruz in September and once at Halloween when Rachel and I visited him and Arian in Davis.

When our call ended, I collaged some torn pieces of Xeroxed hand-written letters and a photo of Nanda's face onto a blank card. Inside I wrote a poem. I had often written sweet odes to my kids, but that birthday poem was different. I wrapped my synapses with guilt, then ripped words from those nerves and stripped sinew off my ribs to stitch together the lines of poetry. Even though much time had passed, I still felt bad about how Nanda had moved out of our house. I felt bad knowing Roger and Nanda hadn't resolved that tension with each other. I felt bad for moving to Santa Cruz. I felt bad for not bringing Nanda along. I felt bad for dragging Rachel away from her brothers and friends. I missed my boys and felt deeply-fucking-bad.

The poem I wrote could have been mistaken as inappropriate. *What a terrible mother.* I bypassed the opportunity to be a role model in place of honouring my self-expression. In truth, I functioned as a dramatic mother-artist-poet for her dramatic artist-poet-son. In black ink, I hand-scrawled, in a state of unease, a poem coded in desperation. I hoped Nanda knew how much I loved him and how much I wanted to be loved by him.

Birthday Poem for Nanda

Attachment
is longing to stay connected.
Whatever haunts us
will pass,
change with time,
mellow.
I push my heart
outside my body.
You will see it.
Remember,
you must choose

131

to separate and search
for who you will become.
It was me,
fearful, reluctant, broken.
I will never
let you go.
Attached
longing to stay
connected.

After the ink dried, pressing with a firm fist, I sealed the card in an envelope. On the front I wrote Nanda in all caps and drew a circle around his name. A fence to hold him and corral my wish, someday he'd come home. I wanted him to feel wanted. He seemed fine. But I suffered, trying to accept he had a life of his own.

I set the card on top of his birthday present, a box filled with assorted teas, art paper, brushes, watercolours, a fat square of white chocolate and a stuffty lion the size of a mouse with suede feet like Poofy Roger's. Eager to deliver, I squared his gift package to the front corner of my work table and patted it to instill safekeeping.

One thousand twenty-seven ...

Heads Up

Late afternoon when the trailing light of day's end peeped through the window, the phone rang. Nanda had returned from his trip. I knew it was him as I had counted the days. I walked into the bedroom, lay on the bed and lifted the receiver.

'Hey, Nanda Pond.' I adjusted myself to get comfortable.

His voice weak. 'Mom?'

'Are you okay?' I wedged a pillow under my neck and kicked my shoes off to the floor.

'It's that ...' His voice broke. 'I was trying to tell Arian something.' Nanda cried between talking. 'He's sick of me always talking about Carmen.'

I didn't answer.

'He won't listen.' Nanda's breathing sputtered.

'You sound pretty upset. What's going on?'

'Fuckin' Carmen. Dude. We were drinking. But we were fine, walking and then got into it, some stupid argument, always the same fucking thing. She keeps accusing me of not loving her.' He sobbed. 'God damn it, Mom, she laid her head on the railroad tracks when a train was coming.'

'Oh, God, Nanda. Not again. Why?'

'I did it too,' he said.

'What?'

Holding my breath, I watched the last fragments of sunlight wave like little hands on the bedroom walls, then vanish, leaving the room dark. Then the bed dropped off a cliff.

'We wrestled on the tracks. I couldn't pull her off. So, I said, "Fine, let's both get our heads crushed in." I laid my head on the track, too.'

He sighed. 'That train was fucking close. I was so scared, I rolled off the tracks. At the last minute, she got up and ran to me. We haven't talked about it since.'

Quiet on my end, I worried my voice would crack. His talk of attempted suicide triggered me. I had lost count of how many times I wanted to die. The image of Nanda's head on the rail severed me in half.

'Did you hear what I said?' he asked.

'I did Nandi Pond. I'm so sorry you had to ...'

'I feel ashamed!' he yelled.

'Oh no honey, you ...'

'Trust me. I would never kill myself. But Carmen will someday. I know it.'

I could tell he turned away from the receiver because his crying grew faint, then he returned with a shuddering breath.

'You know, I understand Carmen. She is super sensitive like your mama. And expressive, dramatic. But do you really think she would do that, kill herself?'

I lifted the blankets and shimmied under. Saying the words 'kill herself' felt like a familiar wound. He remained quiet.

Before thinking, I said, 'To be honest, I've been feeling like I can't take it ...'

He cut me off. 'God damn it, you better not.'

I could see right through the phone to Nanda's face, his distress and hopelessness. I made a mistake thinking he would be comforted if I explained the similarities between myself and Carmen. At the time, I didn't want to kill myself, but I often felt haunted by the option. I shared everything with Nanda, forgetting how young and vulnerable he was. I knew that back pedalling wouldn't undo what I said and still I tried—up to my neck in quicksand.

'I would never. I'm just saying.'

We spend another hour talking our way out of the claustrophobic topic until a reasonable sense of normalcy put us at ease. We gave each other virtual hugs before hanging up.

In a dark room, I swaddled myself into the blankets, soaked in shame.

One thousand twenty-eight …

Phone Tag

The heads-on-the-tracks conversation invaded my psyche. In my sleep, I found myself alert in a hyperreal dream state—arguably more real than life. In that sleep-wake state, I thought I heard a knock at the front door.

Did somebody knock or am I dreaming?

In my state of altered consciousness, I listened as rain tapped on the roof.

Pretty sure it's not raining. This is a dream. I don't know. Weird. I think I am both awake and asleep.

I peeked through the door peephole to see a sheriff with a grey face.

Everything seems real, but I'm pretty sure I am dreaming. I can feel the lumpiness of the mattress in my back and the bedsheets across my body.

I cracked open the door. The night sky was pitch black.

Oh my, I can smell the dampness of his overcoat, see dew on his moustache.

The sheriff told me Nanda had been injured, explained how my boy was paralysed from the neck down, would never walk, talk, hear, or see. Nanda would need 24/7 care.

'You have a choice. You can have your son brought to your home or we can have him delivered to his brother, Arian,' he said.

I observed his impassive face and responded, 'Neither choice is an option,' and slammed the door shut.

What have I said? What have I done?

I woke up startled, staring at the ceiling, my body in a knot. I wanted to call Nanda. I didn't believe in omens, but thought, if I told him my beyond lucid dream, I would be protecting him, warning him. After checking the time, 2:00 a.m., I reconsidered; I had already freaked him out during our last phone conversation. Sleep seemed impossible, writhing in worry, yet I managed to slip off. The alarm sounded at 7:00 a.m.

*

Tuesday morning, December 1, 1998, the day before the train struck.

That super dream hung inside me as I got out of bed. The thought of Nanda inundated with tubing, a hose strapped into his mouth, chest spasming, couldn't be shaken away. *What sort of mother doesn't take care of her child?* Unsettled, I needed to hear his voice. In my right mind, I didn't want to tell him about the dream, but I did want to say to him how sorry I felt about our last conversation. I rang him at home, no answer, and he didn't have an answering machine. I went to work in panic mode.

As soon as I entered my office, I tried his phone again. Still, no pick up. When I was busy teaching, he left a message on the office machine to ring him back. I did but couldn't reach him. I arrived home a few minutes after 5:00 p.m. and listened to my machine. One from Nanda: 'Mom, where are you?'

I tried again and still no answer, then dialled his work number. Nanda was the lead cook. With the phone located beside the grill, he picked up. There was loud music, and people talking in the background.

'Murder Burger.'

I laughed.

'Mama, it's crazy in here right now, dinner shift. My relief hasn't shown.'

'All right, Nanda Pond. Call me tonight.'

'Okay, I will when I get off. It might be late. Gotta go. Love you, Mom.'

'Love you, honey.'

Food sounded good and I felt famished. The vivid dream had been in my stomach, and I had forgotten to eat. I didn't feel like cooking, so Roger suggested the Seabright Brewery; we could have dinner and a couple of beers. I thought I'd make it back in time for Nanda's call, but when I returned home, I found three phone messages from him. He got off work earlier than he anticipated. The third message came from a payphone. Not collect.

136

'Mooooooommmmmmm, where are you?'

The message got quieter. I heard his friends talking in the background and his voice distanced.

'Okay. Well, fuck. I'm trying to reach her, but she's ...'

The receiver clicked quiet, then the machine beeped. I called his home phone. It rang and rang. Before I went to bed, I paged him. 7734.

One thousand twenty-nine ...

Presage

Gavilan College was located between a major highway and the foot of the Gabilan mountains close to Pinnacles National Park, home to deer, rattlesnakes, condors, and pumas. In the parking lot, a sign read Mountain Lion Habitat. I had heard the lions roar and growl at night on the way to my car.

The classroom windows, floor to ceiling, faced north where reflections fooled bluebirds and hummingbirds. Two glass doors opened onto a courtyard and welcomed students and the occasional flock of wild turkeys. The ceiling sloped to the south wall where art students displayed photographs along with drawings of line, texture, movement, and colour. The door to my office was located at the back corner.

A typical load for a new art instructor: five art courses. The dean had scheduled my beginning and advanced classes together, different preps but scheduled at the same time, in the same room, by the same teacher—me. The first semester, I taught design, computer arts, art methods, drawing and photography. Each doubled. Ten classes, teaching morning to afternoon, some evenings, no breaks. I wondered if that was even legal. I had been there for three months and by the end of each day, I could barely stand upright. However, new to the scene, four years to tenure, I did whatever the admins asked of me.

My energy sagged. With classes all day into the evening, I couldn't get to the office to take Nanda's afternoon call or find time to reach him. I figured I'd call him the next day.

*

Wednesday, December 2, 1998, the day of.

By 6:00 p.m. the classroom was packed with students. I began to take roll for design class when fellow art professor, Sebastian, entered the room. He had rallied the college admins to hire me and was assigned as my academic mentor to guide me through the full-time teaching assignment. Instead, he used me as a sounding board for his personal problems. Each mentor meet-up ended with him huddled and weeping on my office floor. Even though his behaviour annoyed me, he exuded creativity and came across as a genuine, unique individual, which I valued, but I had to learn on my own how the college operated.

His shiny black Italian boots clicked across the concrete floor, echoed against the walls. Tall and lean in a navy pinstripe suit, a wrinkled lavender dress shirt and a shrivelled red carnation in the jacket lapel, he swaggered towards me. I stopped in the middle of roll call. His face was elfin, aside from a mottled beaklette for a nose, rosacea blushed cheeks and strands of oily hair that striped across his sunburnt scalp. His smile revealed a straight row of coffee-stained pegs for teeth. His Peridot-green eyes flashed in my direction. Under his armpit, he toted a box of shortbread. In one hand he carried a teacup, and a sugar bowl and creamer balanced in the other, his pinkie curled around a teaspoon.

'Good evening, Professor Edberg. Given you are a Brit, I brought you tea.'

Sebastian used my roll sheet as a placemat for the teacup and saucer and set the sugar bowl and creamer on a textbook, then lifted the spoon.

'Cream? Sugar?'

'Good evening, Sebastien.'

I noticed watercolour paint around the rim of the cup and saucer and gritty amber liquid where a broken tea bag bobbed. *It's the thought that counts.* Something or someone smelled of bourbon. I smiled.

'Oh my gosh. Thank you, Sebastien. But please excuse me, I'm about to take roll.'

'Oh, don't let me stop you.' He lifted one leg, and with ballet arms he twirled away to exit my classroom. 'Have a grand day.' He waved.

To my dismay, I heard whispering and snickering from students. At the front of the classroom, at the teaching desk, my head felt unattached, about to spin. I issued the students an assignment to work on in class and observed as they organised their art materials. Seated at a table in front of me was a young man Nanda's age, similar stature and mannerisms. I caught a side view of his cheekbone, a strong jawline, a curve much like Nanda's. My stomach seesawed when I thought about my boys—200 miles away. I wanted to call. Arian didn't like to talk, much less on the phone, but Nanda could chat till day changed to night. My breath quickened.

The students were engaged in their design projects, but I couldn't hear them. The walls of the classroom started to fold. Queasy and faint, I walked into the office and closed the door. Like being drawn tight in a rope harness, dangling in a dark cave, my chest compressed; the air too thick to breathe. I got on my hands and knees. A pulse pounded in my ears. I gasped as my heart squeezed into my throat. I flattened my body to the floor and rested my cheek on the cool concrete. *I don't want to die.* I sipped each breath. Lips tingling. Hands numb. In the quiet of the office, I floated to the ceiling, turned somersaults and sank, then fell to my back. The last bit of daylight streamed through the office windows, a wall of glass. At the top, indigo with clouds, birds soaring. Sheer white curtains hung midway, flickering with the shadows of swallows swooping. Beneath the curtains, three sparrows pecked the ground.

Shivering on the floor, I rallied myself to stand, desperate to go home. I never took sick leave, but I called the Dean and told him I didn't feel well. He had me excuse the class and gave me permission to leave. I had no idea what ailed me; I just wanted to go home. Home. My new home. A home without my boys. But home.

Muscles in knots, I drove, swerving through the mountain pass until I reached the straight shot to the highway. I rolled down the windows to let cool air rush in and felt relieved to drive a stretch of coastline.

At 8:00 p.m., I arrived. The innards of our house felt calm. TV light shimmered beneath Rachel's bedroom door. I went in and kissed her forehead. I heard Roger in the shower. The dogs lay together huddled under the kitchen table, and our kitty was sprawled on the couch. I went into the bedroom, stripped off my clothes and climbed into bed. Rattled.

Roger startled when he saw me. I explained my sudden onset of unease and why I came home early. He climbed into bed naked, slid his arm under my shoulders and cradled me to his warm body and tucked us in, skin to skin, with flannel sheets and a feather comforter. Down pillows swallowed our heads. Above us, an open window framed the full moon. A blue glow traced pine branch shadows waving across the bedroom walls. Gauzy curtains floated on the breeze while cool salt air drifted over the sill. All the ropes and knots of the day released me into sleep.

At 9:20 p.m., the phone rang.

One thousand thirty ...

Shortcut

In the shock of loss, I reeled into a pause before counting off the thirtieth second. The memory film broke and the spool spun, clapping a remnant of time against itself. Not having witnessed my son's death, the picture in my mind stilled to black, but I could hear the voice of a young woman by the name of Ella, a friend and co-worker of Nanda's. She was a shorter, curvier version of Carmen, about Nanda's age. I called her the day after he died. I asked her to tell me what happened. She was there.

*

Wednesday, December 2, 1998, the day of.

According to Ella, when Nanda got off work, she and a group of co-workers invited him to dinner and card games. They went to Slater's Court, a run-down old campsite with cabins and trailers for low rent, known for housing eccentrics and artistic types. Nanda cooked spicy pork chops and green beans. I had no idea he could make a meal other than a sandwich or what he made as a short-order cook, burgers and fries. After dinner, they played poker. A few more friends arrived with beer.

Oscar, a fiftyish-year-old man, the eldest of Nanda's co-workers, walked through the door eager to join in. He wore his baseball hat backwards and sagged his baggy jeans like the kids.

Nanda rarely drank on weekdays when he had to get up the next morning for work. However, he did not want to be outdone by the old guy, so he belted down malt liquor and gin. Ella told me Nanda had consumed the equivalent of twenty-eight drinks in a couple of hours. I didn't think it was possible to imbibe that much alcohol.

Around 7:45 p.m., and a few more shots of gin, Nanda managed to collect himself and headed for the door, his legs, surprisingly, still able to carry him. Arian had mentioned to me that he expected Nanda to be home by late afternoon and worried when it got dark.

Ella decided to join Nanda, so she didn't have to walk home alone at night intoxicated. They took the usual shortcut. The same one Nanda used to get home from work. They followed a dirt path along Olive Drive, a narrow frontage road, poorly lit but graced with huge olive trees. A police car slowed alongside them, then drove off. They walked through an empty lot open to the tracks adjacent to Second and L Street. L led directly to downtown Davis, a few blocks from Nanda's house. Overpasses spanned South Davis to North Davis, but no one wanted to walk the extra couple of miles.

Nanda and Ella stopped near the railroad milepost, the 46.7 marker next to the four Union Pacific tracks, two eastbound and two westbound. Ella, less drunk than Nanda, didn't hear the train, but she saw it coming and ran across all four tracks to the other side. She turned around to see Nanda stalled at the first track and the train closer than expected.

Ella screamed, 'The train is coming. The train is coming fast.'

A bright light expanded as it drew closer. Nanda stepped across the first track, glanced at Ella and stopped.

'Run!' Ella yelled. She told me she was split in half, she wanted to rescue him but feared she couldn't reach him in time.

He froze.

'Run, you fucking idiot. Run.' Ella fell to her knees. 'Please, Nanda.'

Nanda pivoted his body and faced the speeding freight train with his arms wide open.

Undone

The Call

You cannot hang up on grief.

Jolted from deep sleep, I looked at the clock. 9:20 p.m. The only person who ever called me in the evenings was Nanda, but never so late. Friends and family knew not to call after 8:00 p.m., Roger's bedtime. On the second ring, a surge of adrenaline brought me to my feet. Roger stirred. I walked to his bed stand where the phone sat. It rang again.

'Are you gonna get it?' he asked.

'Yes, yes.'

I sat on the edge of the bed beside him and lifted the receiver to my ear.

'Hello.'

'Jane?'

'Mia?'

She was the mother of Arian's friend, Pete. We weren't close and I didn't know where she got our number.

'You might want to sit down.'

'What?' I stood. 'Why are you asking me to sit down?'

A slow collapse started at my sternum. Roger opened his eyes.

'Nanda.' She paused.

The room turned grey. The four walls of our bedroom compressed me into a square.

'Oh Jane, I, I think he's been hit by a train. He's dead.'

My feet disappeared; my knees hit the floor.

Roger jumped out of bed, switched on the bedroom lamp. 'What's going on?'

He wrapped a towel around his waist. Hearing some of what Mia said, he walked across the hall to Rachel's room and opened her door.

I heard him say, 'I think Nanda's been hit by a car.'

Rachel's TV went silent. Her room turned black. Roger came back to our room, the phone receiver still to my ear, Mia's words garbled.

I stood and let the receiver drop. 'No. No, no, no, no!'

Roger picked it up and pressed it to his ear. 'Mia. This is ...'

His words fell into an electric hum, then he hung up the phone. I stumbled out of the room to see Rachel crouched in the dim hallway, arms pulled into her hoodie, her face expressionless. Feeling faint, I leaned back onto the wall across from her.

'Nanda's dead,' I said.

Her face dissolved.

I rolled my head across the walls of that corridor; a moon having lost its orbit. Bumping into framed artworks, light switches and doorknobs.

'No, no, no.'

Logic abandoned, I tumbled room to room, opened every door trying to find anything that would tell me it wasn't true.

'Please no.'

On hands and knees, I crawled through the living room. *What Mia said can't be right.* I stood, inventoried the room, naming objects I recognised, touching each one. *Couch, chair, table, plant, rug.* None of it made sense. *It can't be true.*

'No, no, no.'

In the kitchen, I searched through drawers, cupboards, every closet, then swung the door to the garage open with a bang.

I screamed, 'Nanda.'

From the end of the hall, I peered down that tunnel and stagger-stepped back to the bedrooms. I walked past Rachel, a stuck tumbleweed, and stopped in the doorway of her bedroom. I didn't want to go in. The last place I needed to check, but I knew Nanda wasn't there. I turned around and zombie-walked back to Roger. He was dressed, putting on his shoes. The glare of the bedroom lamp dimmed and flickered. He stood. I raised my hands, turned them slowly, pale and tingling. They were no longer mine. Lips and tongue gone. I was surprised when words sounded.

'Nanda's dead. He's been hit by a train.'

Roger's eyes, stone green, descended into the hollows above his cheeks. Sallow, blood drawn, his arms hung limp. A leafless tree.

With weak breath, he whispered, 'How does Mia know?'

I didn't answer.

My husband, daughter and everything in the house disappeared. I didn't recognise where I was standing.

This is an emergency. Mia could be wrong. Small town rumours spread fast.

'Jane!' Roger's face flashed before me.

'I need to call the Davis police. This is an emergency, right?' I asked.

Roger's face went blank.

*

I gave the police my son's name and they immediately connected me to the coroner, already at the accident site.

'Who is this?' she asked.

'My name is Jane Edberg, Nanda Butler's mother. I've been told my son has been hit by a train.' *Hit by a train. Hit by a train. Hit by a train.*

'How did you get my number?'

'The police department connected me.'

'I can't help you right now. I just got here.'

The shadows in the room rippled.

'Please, please, I need to know if it's my son. He has a tattoo of an arrow on the back of his right shoulder.' Shaking, I held my breath, exhaled, held my breath, exhaled.

'Hold on.'

Hold on. The phone went silent. The room shimmered mercury. *Hold on.* I dove through the chasm of my ear into the receiver, followed the dead-air through the wires across miles to blank space. *Hold on.* I hovered in a stopped world. With closed eyes, I listened, worried we'd been disconnected, wondered if the static buzz was in my brain or the receiver. *Am I still on hold? This is it. The rest of my life on hold.* I pressed the phone hard to my ear until it hurt. *I'm holding on.* Nothing, nothing, nothing, then a click.

'Witnesses have identified the young man to be Nanda, and yes, it appears he has a tattoo of an arrow on the back of his right shoulder. I need you to call the office to make an appointment.'

She told me she would have his fingerprints and dental records to confirm, gave me a phone number and hung up.

What Next?

You meet grief without introductions.

There isn't a word for the increment of time from son is alive to son is dead. In a fraction of a moment, a mental switch flipped to wailing, searching, snot dripping from my nose to tunnel vision, making phone calls, my voice monotone.

I called Billy. At that time, he lived with his new girlfriend, and their child. I'm not sure where I got his number, possibly Arian.

'Nanda's dead.'

After a quick, nervous laugh, he asked, 'How do you know?'

I gave him the coroner's phone number.

I called Roger's brother, Steve, who lived in Davis. We couldn't afford a hotel, so Steve, said we could stay with him even though he didn't have a spare bed.

My friends, Luca and Krispy, said they'd meet me in Davis.

I called my dear friend Faith; she and I had been in one of our communication breakdowns—we often bickered like siblings in a power struggle. She answered the phone.

'I'm here for you,' she said.

I called the dean of the college, apologised for calling him at home, and so late.

'My son has been killed.'

'I am so terribly sorry for your loss.'

Loss? Loss. A word I could not digest. My grief-mind roller-coasted. *I am fine. I am not fine. I am fine. I am anything but fine. I'll be fine.*

'I'll be in first thing Friday,' I said.

He told me he would make the necessary arrangements for me to take the rest of autumn semester off and come back at the end of January, spring semester.

'I can't afford to take time off. My students rely on me. Who will run the department?'

'Look, you're in terrible shock.' In a soft, slow voice he said, 'I am going to insist you take this time off, Jane. I will take care of your classes and the department. You have bereavement leave and there is a catastrophic relief fund that will cover your salary.'

I couldn't reply. *Shock. Bereavement. Catastrophic.* I catalogued those words into my head.

'Right now, take good care of yourself and your family.'

Take good care?

I kept the handset to my ear long after we said our goodbyes.

I dreaded the next call.

'Arian …'

'I know, Mom. A friend of mine was downtown. He told me.' His words laboured, truncated by short breaths. 'Nanda's been hit by, by a train. On the tracks, the tracks near L Street. I, I know.'

'Okay,' I said. The word okay felt like a dull blade. *Okay, okay, okay.* I could hear Arian's voice, but the word okay grew louder. Stuck on repeat. An okay zoetrope. Me: useless, unemotional, unresponsive, unable.

'Mom?'

'Yeah, yeah, I'm here.'

'Ben, he, he drove me to the hospital. He thought Nanda, I don't know, would be there. They told us, there was ah, an emergency, um, a response to, an accident, you know, on the train tracks.'

I listened. My head shaped like a funnel as his words dropped into the narrowing hole of my ear.

'We drove to the tracks, Mom.'

'Oh my God.' *The tracks.*

'There were fire trucks and emergency vehicles. Floodlights. I walked up, saw the paramedics but, but they wouldn't let me get closer. I, uh, I saw them pull out a tube. It looked like, or I think, um, they were packing away resuscitation gear. I thought they were done, that Nanda was breathing.'

'Wait, what?' I asked. My whole body cramped. I tried to stand still with an ear moulded to the handset.

'He had like blood bubbling out of his nose.'

'Oh, dear God,' I said as my skull started to cave.

'They wouldn't let me, ah, get too close, maybe, I don't know, twenty feet. Closer. I don't know. Fuckin', I watched them lift Nanda into, a, a body bag.'

I knew he heard me gasp. He sighed. Air escaped me in short, repeated exhales. Pinpoints of light flashed before my eyes. Roger glanced at me, then left the room.

'They loaded him into, the, uh, an ambulance, and drove off.'

Nauseated and dizzy, I switched off the lamp, sat on the floor and rested my forehead on the edge of the bed trying to reset my senses.

'Mom?'

My head unhinged.

'Mom?' he yelled.

'Arian, stay home. Please don't go anywhere.'

And with ragged air, he said, 'I won't, I won't go anywhere. I love you, Mom.'

'I love you too. Don't go anywhere. Okay? We're on our way.'

I revved myself upright to avoid crashing, loaded a carton of film rolls into a daypack and flung it and my camera bag onto my shoulder. Intuitively, I thought photography might give me enough bravery to go to Davis. At the end of the hall near the front door, Roger and Rachel were talking like mumbling ghosts.

I told myself to keep moving. *What next?* Roger jingled his keys at me. Air heavy and damp, without a coat, I shivered. As we walked to the car, I heard our shoes tap across concrete, the swish of our trousers, trees dripping from fog.

Roger drove. Rachel sat stiff and blinkless in the back seat. I tried not to panic, believed there was some sort of strange error. We'd get to Davis and Nanda would be home, he'd be surprised to see us. We'd be thankful he wasn't dead. Sad that someone else would have to experience the horror. I'd be able to get to work on Friday after all.

Our car motor made a rhythmic hum. I listened to the tyres pulse with traction. The repetition of street lamps, broken white lines, and passing of cars whooshed through me. I counted glowing Botts dots on the road. None of us made a sound during the three-hour drive.

Well after midnight, Davis streets empty, we rolled into the driveway of Arian and Nanda's house, climbed out of the car and stretched beneath a streetlight. Rachel told me I didn't need to worry about her. I cupped my hand to her cheek, examined her face, eyes red and swollen. She wanted to stay with Arian. Steve had a small patch of carpet where Roger and I could sleep, so I agreed.

We let ourselves into the house and found Arian with his girlfriend, Claire, reclined on the couch, their arms and legs entwined. Arian stood up in a dark cloud of baggy clothes, a black beanie drawn down past his eyebrows.

'I've been feeling weird all day, Mom, like I knew,' he said.

'Oh God. Me too.'

He towered over me, curved his body to mine, wrapped his arms around my head and shoulders and squeezed, then dropped his arms limp like a scarecrow.

'I need to go. No partying, okay?'

'We know, Mom,' Rachel said.

Her shoulders relaxed, face softened. I could tell she meant it. I looked at Arian, two slits for eyes. He nodded.

I didn't ask him if Nanda had made it home.

Rapids

Grief is the deepest, swiftest river you will drown in.

Roger and I arrived at his brother's house at 1:00 a.m. Steve, half asleep, in oversized sweatpants, his long bed hair in his face, rubbed his eyes and invited us in. We waited in the entryway for a couple of minutes, not knowing what to say, until he gave us a little wave, turned around and walked down the hall to return to bed.

Roger and I spread our bedding over the living room carpet, then lay down in our clothes. On my back, I looked at the wood slats of the ceiling, imagined each one popping through the roof to the night sky. The moon spun inside me at high velocity as inner tides wavered back and forth against the shell of my body. Roger curled up and crashed.

A river of energy undulated above me unlike anything I had ever encountered. I reached for the sky. Faint rapids of indigo rushed past my hands. Surrendering to grief, my world tilted, turned upside down as I dredged for my son in the swift inky ghost-water. All night, I tipped and spun, my fingers spread to draw broad brush strokes, to trawl through the wash of loss, hoping to catch Nanda's hand.

Afraid the moon inside me might expand, lift me into a blank heaven, I breathed myself back onto the blanket, against the shore of the carpet. The water of my eyes drained to my cheeks into my ears, dripped down my neck into my hair and the astral tides waned. I burrowed into Roger and when I couldn't feel the rise and fall of his chest, I quieted myself to hear him breathe but heard nothing. I tapped his shoulder. Tapped again. He rustled. I was afraid to sleep. Afraid to lose Roger. Afraid everyone would die if I closed my eyes.

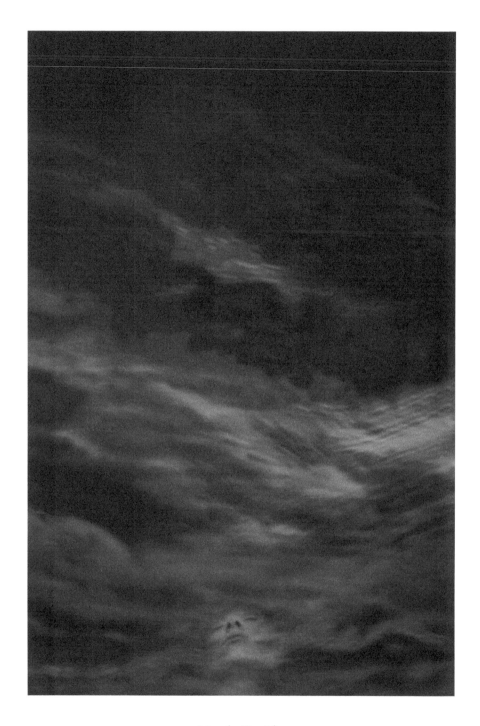

Nanda Rapids

Body Parts

In grief, you won't believe they are gone.

The day after the call, a bright morning pierced the window blinds, a brutal reminder. Roger and I headed to a local coffee shop located in the middle of town. At an outside table in the cold, we sipped hot cappuccinos. Our brains congealed to jelly. My legs went numb as my butt moulded to the wicker chair. I peeled a croissant into dime-sized flakes as my stomach protested anything bite-sized. Roger, who had to travel home to feed the animals, gather clothing, and select photos of Nanda for the memorial, gave me a sad face and a kiss, rocked me back and forth in a hug, and left for Santa Cruz. How crazy I must have been to schedule a memorial to take place three days after Nanda died. Planning the service months after his death would have delayed grief, kept me in contact with more people than I cared to stay in contact with, and likely, due to a busy teaching schedule, would never happen. Plus, I dreaded the whole spectacle.

The closest I'd come to an immediate family member dying was when Bibby died in 1988. She excused herself from a card game, Gin rummy, left her friends to return to her apartment, then laid herself down to rest with a failing heart. Eighty-nine years. Before her death, she had asked me why I stopped communicating with Dad. I revealed some of Dad's inappropriate sexual comments towards me and how he drove drunk with me in the car and sped up when I asked him to slow down. He threatened to murder me. She found everything I shared too hard to accept. After Dad denied any wrongdoing, she cut me off and never spoke to me again. I learned of her death during a phone call from Mum. I didn't get a chance to reconnect with Bibby or help with her interment. Dad took care of Bibby's estate and donated most of her effects to her friends and charity. Too hurt to grieve, I tried not to think of Bibby—switched her off like a porch light.

The early morning café crowd had come and gone. Pins and needles set in, so I peeled my butt off the chair and repositioned my legs. I didn't want to tie up the loose ends of Nanda's life but felt desperate to get it done, so I started a to-do list on a scrap of paper. First item: coroner appointment. Second item: memorial service. I jotted down Saturday, the 5th of December—two days to plan. I furled and unfurled the to-do list, and other duties came to mind: buy flowers, ask about a viewing, cremation, return his house keys, purchase more than one death certificate. I needed death certificates: to close his bank accounts, collect his last paycheck, collect his life insurance. *Life insurance. Life insurance is death insurance.* Compensation for loss. *I feel like puking.*

A blackbird hobbled beneath the café table scavenging. She had one good leg, the other a gnarled stump. I tossed her a small flake of croissant. She tilted her head, one pearly eye blind, but scoped me with her other bright black bead and pecked the crumb into her beak. The bird was broken, but she had found her place in the world. When I lifted my camera from my bag, she flew away. I wrote the details of her visit on the slip of paper to remember resilience.

The cell phone vibrated. I pushed the phone to my ear to hear the coroner's voice. She sounded distant, like she was talking to someone else waiting for me to answer.

'Hello,' I said, free falling.

'Yes, hello! Quick question. Would you be willing to give permission to donate Nanda's body parts?' she asked.

'No!' I replied.

Nanda's body parts? He needs his body parts. No, no. I don't remember hanging up, but I must have because after I vacillated between what was and what is, I shifted into overdrive and called her back. I spoke to her assistant and made an appointment to discuss Nanda's demise and the release of his body.

I heard Rachel's voice coming from the sidewalk. I turned around to see her walking with one of Nanda's friends, a sweet girl named Shelly, a Rubenesque beauty with translucent blue eyes, hair bouncing in ringlets. They rushed up in front of me. Rachel's cheeks were flushed, her forehead sweaty. She was out-of-breath-talking. Her words morphed into sounds I didn't understand. I stared at her face, a heart-shaped moon, like Nanda's face, wisdom-eyed, like him. I felt for the camera in my lap. I wanted to take her photograph but couldn't find the energy. She stood in front of me, her mouth moving. I failed to ask if she was okay, if she had eaten, or about her plans, where she had been or where she'd be during the day and at night. She quieted, and her eyes turned black.

'Mom!' Her jaw stiffened as she waved her hand at me.

'Oh, I'm sorry. Sorry, sweety.'

'I heard that some chick has Nanda's favourite hat.' She slapped her hands to her thighs. 'Nanda has been dead for less than twenty-four hours, and Carmen has been handing out his stuff to everyone, but...'

'Oh, fuck! I ...'

'I got this,' she said.

Rachel explained to me how Arian had been home at the time but hunkered down in his room with Claire, blasting music, while a distraught Carmen ransacked Nanda's room, rifling through Nanda's belongings. She had given away his hats, clothes, books and CDs as mementos to friends and acquaintances. She took his bedsheets and his pillow.

'Thank God Nanda had the sense to bring me most of his journals and collections for safekeeping before he moved into that party house,' I said.

'I know. I am on a mission to get it all back. Shelly has a car. She's gonna help.'

I looked at Shelly, who smiled and nodded.

'Do you have any money?' Rachel asked.

I handed her cash so they could get something to eat. I looked at her body, thought about Nanda's body, about the coroner cutting into him, extracting a kidney, a liver, his heart.

Rachel and Shelly left as fast as they came. Towards the end of the day, aside from Nanda's bed linens and other items Carmen found dear, the girls had recovered most of his things.

By nightfall, Rachel joined me to pick up Luca from the train station. He had taken the Amtrak from San Francisco to help and support me. Luca was a close friend, my surrogate boyfriend through my single-parenting years, my unpaid research assistant who helped me write papers in grad school, the man who pitched a tent in our living room on a rainy day so the kids could camp. He made hand shadows into wolves and crows on the wall while the kids screamed through his ghost stories. We laughed till we peed. He once brought his penguin cookie jar to the house when I had fallen into a sad hole. Pouting, he'd rub the belly of the penguin, remove its head and reach in for a cookie. Fresh-baked, still warm, chocolate chip. Everyone thought we were lovers.

Just as we dropped Rachel off at her brother's house, she said, 'Oh yeah, I forgot to tell you, a bunch of guys got together and wrote Nanda's name across the levee.'

R.I.P.

Grief summons a feather, a cloud, a heart-shaped stone, or an owl to help you rest in peace.

For at least five decades, people had been leaving messages on the face of a levee located at the edge of Davis near the entrance to the Interstate 80 Yolo Causeway. That bridge, over three miles long, connects Davis to West Sacramento, stretching over rice fields, wetlands and wildlife areas—59,000 acres of Yolo Bypass floodplain.

Message makers would come late at night to spray-paint and rearrange head-sized boulders across a sixty-foot slope visible for miles from that busy highway bridge: initials, fraternity and sorority symbols, political slogans, marriage announcements, birthday wishes and the names of those who died. Messages changed often, sometimes daily.

Luca took me to a crepe restaurant; we ate, drank and talked until it closed. He tugged at his braided goatee, worry-faced.

'I know it's late. I know it's dark, but let's go,' he said, then twisted his long hair into a mound on top of his head.

The levee was a place where people partied, dealt drugs and dumped bodies, but the safety issues didn't concern me. I feared seeing Nanda's name. I didn't want it to be real. And even with a full moon, without streetlights, the levee would be spooky-dark at the bypass. It made no sense to go there, but his name would soon be replaced with another's message. I didn't want to miss laying eyes on those stones spelling out my son's name.

'Okay, let's go,' I said.

Luca slung his arm over my shoulder, and we walked to the car. I could smell the leather of his jacket, a creaky red and black bomber with a yellow stripe. He threw his daypack into the back of my car as he climbed into the passenger seat.

We took a country road to where we thought the Causeway started.

159

Beneath the overpass, I turned onto what looked like a dirt levee road, two deep ruts down a strip of crushed rock. The blue of the moon soaked everything to shades of black and white and TV-screen grey. I cranked the windows open to let brisk air keep me awake. The tyres crunched over the gravel road to chirping crickets and wetlands full of buzzing insects. From my side window, I watched stars pop into view one by one. Through the windshield, I saw two tyre ruts leading to nowhere and what appeared to be wetlands on one side and fields on the other. I kept driving but nothing changed. Nothing resembled the face of a levee.

'I think we're lost.' I took my foot off the gas and coasted. 'What do you think?'

Luca rolled down the window, stuck his head out, observed the dark fields and let the wind pull his hair loose.

'Yeah, it looks like more of the same. You'll need to turn around.'

'Good idea. Not sure where though.'

In the rear-view mirror, dust whirled in the glow of taillights. I un-slumped and squinted my eyes trying to find a crossroad or wide shoulder, but the levee road was narrow with steep slopes to either side. The headlamp beams revealed a road disappearing into darkness, no end. *Am I dreaming?* Endless, like a dream I once had where I climbed a ladder into a black sky. I climbed up and up and up, all night long, up and up. So, I drove, drove, drove.

With a flash of feathers, an owl swooped into the illuminated path of the headlights.

'Oh my God. Oh my God. What the fuck?'

I soft-pedalled the brakes, cradled my arms across the steering wheel and leaned in hard to see through the windshield. Wings glowing, slow-motion undulations.

'Barn owl,' Luca said.

He unbuckled and rested his hands on the dashboard. The owl travelled a few feet ahead of us, shuttering light, the crown of his head centre to the road, his wingspan almost the width of the car.

'Feels like we're flying,' I said.

The crush of gravel beneath the tyres grew louder, oscillated. The owl, a silent movie, made a sharp turn, wings stretched like a fighter jet off a warship. I felt the pull and steered his direction. Lucky for us, the owl followed the curve of the road.

As the owl veered upwards, the headlights lit the slope of the levee where red and gold boulders glistened. The owl sailed hard left, turned grey, then disappeared into a shadowy field. I drove to the bank of the Message Rock levee and cut the lights, rolled onto a shoulder and turned off the engine. My eyes adjusted to the faint blue glow of moonlight, although not enough to see the stones on the slope.

I listened to myself rapid-breathe. Luca stayed calm. Afraid I might not be able to stop the locomotion of my lungs, I moaned. Luca took my hand. I hung in a well of fear until I synchronised my breathing to his.

'Okay,' I said and switched the headlights on.

In the wash of yellow light, across the sixty-foot face of the levee, his name, boldfaced, NANDA. Letters formed from boulders, some the size of my belly. I felt the weight inside my rib cage. His friends had cradled and carried each stone into place, sprayed each one red then brushed them gold. Letters the length of his body were laid onto earth.

'Tomorrow, it will be gone,' I said.

Luca left the car first and walked to the foot of the levee. I caught my breath, grabbed the camera and joined him.

I spotted a R, an I and a P. My mouth said, 'Rest in Peace,' but I saw RIP. Rip flesh and blood. Rip bone. Rip a heart out. Rip a life in half. Rip a child from his mother. Rip a family apart. Rip up plans. Rip up the future. Rip up self. Rip to ruin. Rip to end. Rip to cancel. Rip everything to shreds. Rip means stolen. Rip is panic. Rip is numbness. Rip is sorrow. Rip is forever. RIP means dead.

On the ground, beside RIP, fist-sized rocks dotted the outline of a heart.

Grief-dazed, unable to calculate exposures, I set the camera to automatic. Camera in hand, but not to my eye, I aimed, shot multiple frames from left to right, right to left, above, middle, and below, hoping to capture the message on film. I took a deep breath and walked into the pool of illumination, into the name of my son.

Luca squatted, covered his eyes and whispered, 'Rest in peace, Nanda.'

I locked my knees so I wouldn't fall.

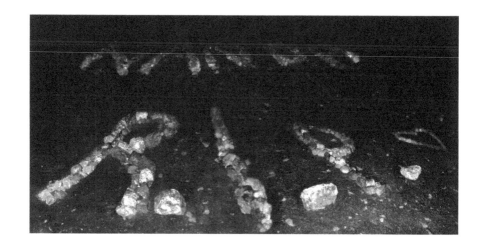

R.I.P. Message Rocks (composite image from
twelve underexposed negatives)

Bag of Things

Grief is not insanity, but you'll think you've gone mad.

Two days after the call.

After slipping the Nanda Junction map into my pocket, I lifted the package of Nanda's personal belongings from the coroner's desk, the force of the train's impact palpable. Gripping the package to my belly, I exited her office, trance-walked through an empty box-shaped lobby, out the glass door onto the sidewalk. After a couple of steps onto concrete, I stopped—stuck in a grey-scale comic. No sounds. Not even a bird. Not a soul in sight. *Am I still alive? Am I the only one alive?*

The parking lot of dull rectangles and straight white lines met farm fields, grey-green flatness for miles delineated by uncurved roads, acres of squares. I thought if I took another step, my foot would sink, and the next step, I'd be to my ankles, then knees, then waist, until buried. There would be no trace of me, just a plastic-wrapped bundle belonging to no one on the undisturbed sidewalk.

I crept one foot past the other, aimed for my car, the single curvilinear object in sight bracketed by two white lines on a quadrilateral plane of pavement. My silver car, matte like the pewter sky. To step off the curb onto the asphalt meant I needed to trust the weird equation I was calculating, trust I would continue upright, be able to transverse what might be spongy or turn to liquid. I feared the white lines would cinch around my neck, pull me under. *What world is this?*

Someone had said to me earlier, the only way out is through. *Through what? Did they mean forward?* I certainly wasn't going back inside the building, so forward I went. I lifted the other foot and placed it in front of me, set my weight down, cliff-falling, the Nanda package secured between my hands. Each step a slow plunge across the parking lot. I tucked the package under my armpit and stuck my hand inside my pack to fumble for keys. The tap and turn of key into car lock and the pop of the car door as it opened jolted waves of adrenaline through me.

I released the pack from my waist and dropped it to the passenger side floor, gripped the package in one hand, and grabbed the steering wheel to lower myself into the driver's seat. I heard a click and imagined a detonated device. If metal springs thrust through my pelvis, filled my intestines, clutched me to the seat, I promised myself I would not let go of the bag of Nanda's things, even if I bled to death. Walnuts for lungs, and a hummingbird heart, I shut the car door gently and sat stunned in a vacuum waiting for an explosion. None.

I wedged the package into my lap against my belly and pulled the map from my pocket. *How could something so small be so painful?* Like a cheat sheet to a life lost, yet still a puzzle to solve, I memorised every detail.

A state of urgency brewed—I needed to call Billy. I set the map on the passenger seat and retrieved the phone and dialled his number. He never picked up, so I left a message.

'You need to sign the release,' my voice broke, 'please.'

After a long exhale, I returned the phone to the pack. With nowhere to go, I rocked in the car with the package pressed to my chest behind crossed arms. Aside from clothing and his shoes and hat, the bundle contained everything else Nanda had on his body and in his pockets when the train struck. I lifted the bound square and read the label. Yolo County Coroner's Division. Nityananda Bhakti Rasa Butler. His full name seemed foreign. I knew it was Nanda, and I still didn't want it to be true.

I peeled and pried open the taped edge to unfold the bag, squeezed out Nanda's wallet, worn-polished black leather rounded to the curve of his butt. I opened it like a private journal, cringed as I trespassed, then slid his state ID from the clear plastic sleeve. On the passenger seat, next to the map, I arranged cards into a neat row: his student ID, bus pass, restaurant workers' union card, ATM card, health insurance card, Social Security card, along with bank deposit and withdrawal slips, a teeny, folded phone number list, and the emergency contact sheet I had made for him before I moved to Santa Cruz.

In the billfold, I counted $200, then set Nanda's wallet in my lap. I took his pager out of the bag, switched it on, scrolled through phone numbers until I saw 7734, the last page I sent him, and switched it off. I flipped open his Zippo lighter, ran my thumb over the wheel to strike the flint. The tang of lighter fluid filled my nose. I waved my hand over the flame then snapped the Zippo closed to hear that familiar metal scuff and clap.

Nanda's Gordon crest key chain had been shattered. A bit of tape secured the resin shards in place. Someone at the coroner's office had painstakingly collected even the smallest of bits, some no bigger than a grain of sand, and puzzled them together. On the keyring, a shark-shaped bottle-opener swung next to bent keys, the curve of his hip bone evident.

At the bottom of the bag, I found some loose change and an envelope the size of a postage stamp, two quarter-inch gold hoop earrings inside. A triangle of abalone shell, corners smooth, surface polished, the piece he found in Santa Cruz, was unharmed and had somehow survived in his pocket.

I arranged his items, made a collage into an unsettled design. A minute glimpse into his life. A still life. Still life. *Still life?* Too tired to use a camera, I mentally photographed each composition. I slipped the map into my pocket, returned the cards and money to the wallet, and neatly packed his things into the plastic bag.

A buzz sounded. *Oh, the phone.* I scrambled for the pack, grabbed the phone and flipped it open.

'Hello.'

'Ms. Edberg, this is Simon from the Davis Mortuary. Nanda is en route.'

Nanda Surrogate

You might burden yourself with the question: What could I have done to prevent this from happening? The answer might be: Nothing.

After playing chicken with a freight train at the Nanda Junction and counting thirty seconds until it pulsed through my veins, I hurried to meet Robin, waiting for me at my sons' house. I'd known Robin since he was a rug rat; his parents were my friends. Nanda and Robin were both precocious and by the time they were in junior high school, they'd engage me in lengthy conversations about art, writing, and photographic experimentation. They loved to psychoanalyse and impersonate our family members and friends which often led to them riffing off each other like two stand-up comedians. Robin, whom I loved like a son, became my surrogate Nanda. Not a replacement, but a placeholder, as I struggled to believe that Nanda was gone. Thinking of Robin as my stand-in Nanda gave me comfort.

The moon floated high, seemed further away. I checked the time on my watch, elevenish p.m. Before the short drive, I made a quick stop to purchase a six pack of beer.

Their front door was usually unlocked. I let myself in. The house was creepy quiet. Moonlight seeped in enough for me to see. I tiptoed in the hallway until I heard Arian and Claire muffled behind their closed bedroom door. I didn't want to disturb them. Halfway through the hall, I stopped in the doorway of Nanda's bedroom as if it had been roped off, untouchable, like a museum exhibit, a space preserved from a moment in time. I could not console myself, the fact I would need to empty his room, haul his property to my house, and not be able to bring him along. A pang of guilt gripped me, wishing again that we had moved him to Santa Cruz.

Further down the hall, I noticed the roommate's door open. Soft lamplight revealed a sparse unremarkable space with a queen-sized mattress on the floor covered in blankets. As I got closer, I found Robin reclined with his arms folded behind his head, wearing oversized jeans and a plaid flannel shirt, trainers still on his feet. He sat up on his elbows and grinned deep dimples.

'Hey. Roommate's out of town. I can sleep in here. Not that anyone's sleeping. I figured you'd want to sleep in Nanda's room."

In one squeezed breath, I replied, 'Hell the fuck no. It feels like he could walk in at any moment. He'd be livid if he found me in his bed.' I shook my head.

'Alrighty then.'

He scooted over towards the wall and patted the bed space next to him.

'Perfect,' I said.

I flung my pack to the floor, set down the six pack, grabbed two beers and handed one to Robin.

'Plus, I don't think I could tolerate closing my eyes beneath that drawing over his bed. I'm not sure Nanda knew I made it to represent my failed marriage to his father.'

Robin laughed.

I dropped my jacket from my shoulders, heel-shoved the boots from my feet without unlacing them and flopped next to him. We turned our heads to acknowledge each other, faces like wood. Synchronised, we twisted off the beer caps, clanked our bottles together, and guzzled.

A couple of guys came into the house, loud and buzzed. I assumed they were my sons' friends. They headed our way and poked their heads into the room.

'Hey, Nanda's mom,' said a guy in a hoodie, then he pointed at Robin. 'What the fuck, dude.' Both guys busted into laughter.

Robin raised his head and said, 'Fuck off.'

They laughed louder and tromped back down the hallway and out the house.

'Idiots.'

I didn't give it another thought, Robin and I sharing a bed. My son had just died. Besides, neither of us wanted to sleep on a grungy couch, and most definitely not in Nanda's bed.

Robin scrunched the pillow under his head and pulled a pack of Marlboros from his shirt pocket, tapped the bottom to nudge a couple of cigarettes loose, stuck one in his mouth and handed me the other.

Retrieved a lighter from his jeans pocket and lit them.

'I like that drawing,' he said, looking at me sideways.

I sucked the smoke into the chambers of my lungs until it hurt then let the smoke escape as I talked. 'You can have it.'

We drank, smoked and talked into delirium. I couldn't sleep. Robin claimed he hadn't slept since the day. Same. Both of us, conscious-unconscious.

'Shelly let Nanda drive in Humboldt,' Robin said.

'Ah geez!' I looked over at Robin. 'Nanda didn't have a driver's licence.'

'According to Shelly, he did really well,' Robin said. 'Except on curves.' He snort-laughed, then gave me a side glance with an impish grin.

Dazed, I half-listened to Robin tell more stories about his and Nanda's late-night adventures, teens roaming about after curfew, and how they avoided the police by hiding in railroad track alleys. His words muffled into the background as I recycled through mental inventories: all the ways I could have prevented Nanda's death, all the ways I had caused it to happen, and how I could have saved him.

I pulled the to-do list from my pack, scanned the order of things, and began to choreograph my reaction in preparation for viewing Nanda's dead body. *Maybe it won't be him.*

What Remains

In grief, you will be invited to hold hands with death.

Another restless night and a brief doze until I startle-woke with an urgency to get up. Once vertical, I headed out, in the same clothes since Wednesday. Before I shut the door I heard Robin yell, 'See you at the mortuary.'

Roger hadn't returned yet with clean clothes, so I stopped by Faith's house. Faith and I met in our mid-twenties when we brought our eldest children to their first day of kindergarten. Two long-haired, braless, hippy mamas in long tapestry skirts wearing Birkenstocks, each with three children of similar ages. Sitting in hot sun, waiting for the school doors to open, we simultaneously breastfed our babies. We instantly bonded.

I borrowed a black-light purple, ankle-length, embroidered dress and a black velvet jacket. She placed a magenta bowler hat on my head; the rim rested at my eyebrows. The snug fit calmed me and I felt shielded. Her face turned serious as she slid a cool polished rose quartz stone into my hand, shaped to the curve of a palm, a perfect fit in a clenched fist. Tears welled up in Faith's eyes and magnified her sky-blue irises, pupils pulsing. She smiled and curled my hand into hers until the stone warmed. I rested the pink talisman inside the jacket pocket in case I needed something solid to hold should I become wobbly.

In a rush, I took off, to proceed with all the errands. Check all the boxes on the to-do list. *Maybe if I complete the tasks quickly, Nanda's death won't be real.* I drove to Café Roma and ordered a croissant and coffee, sat outside in the chill away from customers who remained inside to stay warm. The morning's orange sun crept through the legs of tables and chairs, dashed across cobble-stoned pavement.

I wiggled the scrolled to-do list from my pack, the list I had rolled and unrolled repeatedly, wrinkled-soft and ink-smudged. I unfurled it, took out a pen and checked and double-checked the appointment time for the viewing. *The coroner is vehemently against my viewing Nanda's body.* I underlined the word 'viewing.' *He was hit by a train, for Christ's sake.* I circled the appointment time, '10:00 a.m.' *What if I fall apart?* I pressed the pen hard and spiralled circles around 'viewing' and '10:00 a.m.' *I'll collapse.* I scribbled over 'viewing' and wrote 'seeing.' *It couldn't be Nanda.* In my mind's eye, Nanda's face became impossible to conjure. I read the scheduled time again. *Ten. Ten, zero, zero. One, zero, colon, zero, zero.* I checked my watch. *Zero, nine, colon, three, zero.* Reread the time on both the list and the watch. *Ten. Nine-thirty.* I repeated the numbers until they became abstract shapes. Scuffed my throat. Tapped the pen. Bit my lip. Still unable to tell the difference between the time on the list and the time on the watch. I leapt from the chair and headed to the car. Roger, Luca, and Carmen needed a ride. *Shit!*

Driving through town, I noticed my hands pale and boney against the steering wheel. *Am I dead? I am dead.* I gripped until my knuckles turned white and purple. As my heart palpitated and breathing quickened, I reminded myself to pay attention to the road. *This is a terror dream.* I placed a cold hand to my cheek. *Am I asleep? I think I'm awake. Fuck!* A seam split open. What I had known as consciousness gave way to a new consciousness, a new program running. *Don't think about it. Keep going, just keep going.*

By the grace of good luck, I made it through town, numb to the bone. Roger sat shotgun, Luca behind him, the two of them almost transparent, two gummy humans stuck to the seats of the car. Carmen, her hair touching the sky, looked eight feet tall in a sleeveless mini dress, high-heeled white sandals, her long legs bare. She sat behind me with both hands pushing on the back of my seat like giving someone CPR. For the entire drive, she chattered, none of it making sense.

'Nanda ... Nanda ... Nanda ... Nanda and I ... Nanda said ... Nanda would ... Nanda did ... Nanda needed ...'

Please stop! I held my breath between exhales and inhales. Although I loved her, she needed more support than I could give. I spasmed as she spiralled.

Finally, we arrived. I parked across the street from the mortuary, a one-story ranch-style-house-type building with windows obscured by murk-yellow, rippled glass. *No one wants to see the dead.* Everyone exited the car and waited on the lawn next to the sidewalk. I sat for a moment, strapped my camera around my neck, sighed, and joined them to wait for the others to arrive.

Balanced on the edge of a curb, I noticed a leaf fall from the sky. I held the camera heart level between both hands like a prayer. But instead of lifting the viewfinder to my eye, I observed the leaf-body flicker-tumble into the gutter. The fallen leaf clawed across grey foliage, arteries dried taut, until half-buried in silt. A small brown bird landed, lifted the dead leaf into its beak and flew away. One of a zillion from an endless migration of birds. Nanda's body flew up and fell to the ground. In midair, he became lost in the infinite migration of souls.

Roger's brother, Steve, coasted up on his bike, while Robin, Arian and Rachel walked in the street behind him. Cement faces, all of them. No words. Eyes darted. Rachel idled next to me, pressed her shoulder into mine. I wanted to press back, but I feared putting my weight on her.

I led them through the front door of the mortuary into a low-lit, red foyer where the director greeted us. The perfect cliche. Clasped hands, slight head tilt. A tall, greyish man in a charcoal suit with a diaphanous face. He coaxed me aside and positioned himself next to me with his head hung over mine, our backs to everyone, and whispered.

'Nanda's father has made a request to ...'

'Wait, did he call you?' I asked.

'No, Ma'am. The guests arrived an hour ago.'

'An hour ago? He's here?'

'Yes, Ma'am.'

'A request?' I tightened, jaw to tailbone.

'He would like to place something under Nanda's tongue.'

'Oh, hell no. No. No, no.'

Maybe water from the Ganges, a flower or a coin, but I never asked, and never found out. My face in flames, I followed the director; family and friends trailed behind. He led us to a dim room. Jaundiced light poured in through a couple of small windows. Billy had voiced earlier that he wasn't coming to the viewing. He sat with his girlfriend and three-year-old daughter in a shadow against a wall. He looked sharp as usual, in pressed trousers and dress shirt, polished loafers with the little tassels, his hair combed into one slick ripple. But his eyes, his father-of-a-dead-son eyes, were swollen with grief. My jaw clenched so hard my ears pinched shut. I strained to offer him a half-smile. His face unreadable. He didn't look at me; instead, he stared at the camera bouncing from my neck.

My group followed me into the room, then halted as I continued towards Nanda. His body lay in a sleeping-like-the-dead pose beneath a smooth white sheet and yellow blanket on a waist-high table edged with gold-pleated fabric to the floor. His body, not a bag of bones, but a straight line, the same line that once had lain across the tracks. He looked like a fraud, a well-groomed fraud. His porous face pointed to the ceiling, a caricature, like those cheesy portraits drawn at carnivals. His facial skin was plastered in creamy beige concealer, a few dents filled with peach-coloured plasticine, even though I had insisted to the funeral director no make-up. Nanda's chin revealed short stubby whiskers. His hair was stiff-gelled, combed in one direction, trimmed sharp across his brow. A garland of neon-orange marigolds surrounded his warped moon head. In all my preparedness, I sank—I had forgotten to bring flowers.

Earlier, the day the coroner's office released Nanda to the mortuary, I asked the funeral director if I could come to help clean and prepare Nanda's body. As I made the request, I thought it sounded weird, possibly creepy, but I felt protective and wanted to supervise anyone touching my son.

'It's not advisable or lawful, and it requires training,' he said.

That's when I insisted on no make-up. No putty or filler.

'Just dress him in clean clothes and comb his hair.'

I have no memory of how Nanda's clothing was delivered to the mortician.

'Yes, of course,' he said.

I trusted him not to mask death's face.

Rachel came to my side as I scanned Nanda.

I leaned down but could not smell him. Not even the hamburger grease on his shoes. What I could smell were marigolds, clean linens, candles burning and the cosmetics they applied to his face. He'd been cleaned away.

Roger made a quick circle around Nanda, hung his head and cried into a tissue. He held my hand for a second, then went outside.

I noticed Arian made it through the door, the last to enter, but had stopped. His jade-green irises dulled to slate. Jaw tight. The little muscles at the sides of his temples flinching. His hands in fists. When our eyes joined, he turned for the exit.

'Don't go.' I walked over to him and extended my hand. 'Please don't go.'

Arian's broad shoulders rounded as he placed his hand in mine. We lumbered to his brother's side. Rachel stayed close to me as I unfolded Arian's hand against Nanda's chest. He bent to kiss his brother's forehead and shook. He paused to look at me, face slack, his eyes robbed of light.

'Death is a sick joke, Mom. Nanda looks like a hollow log,' he said and left the room.

An edge of white sheet had been folded over the blanket under Nanda's arms, his hands positioned flat against his sides. The only parts remotely resembling him were his hands if they had been carved from wood. The ring I had given to him, the one he begged from me at our last visit, was embedded in his swollen flesh.

I tried to hold Nanda's hand. If he saw me at the café, he'd sit in my lap. I'd wrap my arms around him; he'd envelop my hands in his. In the short hour of his viewing, what I had worded as *seeing*, perhaps even better named, *not seeing*, his fingers, muscles hardened around bone, remained unpliable. His mannequin hands failed to hold mine.

I turned his ring hand over, his palm cupped like a shell. My breath scooped through the curve and air-circled into me. Breathing an ellipse, I cradled his hand in mine and mine in his. Palm to palm, I tried to extract memories from skin, broad knuckles, clean manicured nails, moons glowing, rising in every nail bed. He used to be a nail-biter like me. I never scolded him. He stopped on his own. I wanted to steal the moons from his hands, ingest them as pills and orbit them through my fingers. I wanted to string the lunar beads, once waned and waxed between mother and son, into a necklace. Harness the gravitational pull of mother, of heavenly body, the full moon, grab him by his shoulders and yank him to a seated position, tell him to stop acting so fucking ridiculous.

I blew my air into his ear. 'Come on, don't do this, get up.'

I wanted the warmth of my breath to soften him, waken him. *Someone has made a mistake.* 'This isn't you.' I tapped on his chest. 'Don't do this.'

Solid but dull. Not even a drumbeat, or an echo, just a thud absorbed into the density of an airless body. Every cell turned to rubber. *I hope they didn't forget to replace your heart.* The corpse they claimed to be my son was not a sturdy bull, a flush-faced athlete, Nanda, who could not be held down. His words and gestures, his passion and nerve, not there. I could not fathom that all the words he had ever spoken were his last. It made no sense to me how a slab of flesh, a facsimile of a young man, could be him. My boy. No. I couldn't see him gone forever. He was a cage with the door still open. He had escaped.

'Come back.'

I wanted to climb in, fix what was broken, summon him, trick him into reconsidering, to take the bait, settle into his body. I'd rock him back and forth like a truck stuck in mud, rev until he moved.

A rush started at my feet and exited my mouth like a siren. I held my face in my hands and tried to hold back the surge. Steve came to my side and handed me a white folded handkerchief. I saturated the square of cotton with tears, shoved it into my pocket next to the rose quartz.

Carmen positioned herself across from me, her arms tied in a knot. Bowed over him, she pressed her lips to his and scream-sobbed, ploughed her face into his chest and drenched his shirt until her breathing shortened. The weight of the quartz in my pocket reminded me to pray, not to let her grief enter mine. She wept and wailed, then took Nanda's cologne bottle out of her purse, opened it and dabbed cologne over his body. Choking on the acrid scent, Rachel and I begged her to stop. She stepped back, moved to the end of the table a few inches away from Nanda's head and held the bottle under her nose with both hands. Her eyes, two voids. She looked like one of those Greek statues missing their eyeballs. Trapped in a grief-vacuum, I couldn't console her.

I leaned my belly into the table edge. The camera swung over his torso like a divining pendulum. I wanted to photograph him. *This is your son; quit being a photographer.* My palms flat to Nanda's chest pulsed against his rib cage. *How can I rescue you?* I scanned his face and discovered two round bruises the shape and size of silver dollars on both sides of his chin. I made a mental note to later examine the front structure of freight trains to match the contusion marks. That's when I noticed the hickey. I glanced at Carmen; our eyes met. She touched her hand to her neck, and with her other hand, she ran her fingers across the love mark.

Rachel, next to me, peeled the blanket and sheet off Nanda's body. Curious, I followed like an animal, like that being you become when the self you referred to as yourself is demolished. She lifted his shirt, a dress shirt, and beneath that, an undershirt, which came apart in pieces. The fabric had been cut and fitted to dress his rigid body. I helped her remove the scraps. Luca appeared and stood at full attention across from me. Everyone else fled the room, even Carmen.

Have I dishonoured the dead? No!

I needed to see what had happened to Nanda, understand his condition, how he had been treated. Rachel and I shared the same impulse. We examined the landscape of his yellowed chest, continents of blue bruises and red-brown abrasions. Through the middle of his sternum, split to either side of collar bones, a ropey purple and white stitched Y. His belly was a lumpy mound, icy to the touch, where they stuffed him with a bag of human giblets, his organs measured and bundled in dry ice.

If only I could sort his innards, remould him symmetrically.

I wanted to make sure nothing had been placed under Nanda's tongue. With my finger, I pressed his grey lips, pinked with lipstick until a thin line of yellow wax cracked, revealing a mouth stitched shut against clenched teeth. As his mother, art-self unconsciously responding, I wavered between shame and curiosity, but the need to observe, examine and discover took over. Rachel was caught in the same spell.

While I surveyed Nanda's face, I landed next to an eyelash poised alone on his firm cheek. A single, black sliver balanced perfectly, both ends pointed upright like a symbol on a runestone. I looked at Luca. He looked at me and touched the tip of his pinkie to his tongue, then using that finger like a pollen brush he rescued the eyelash. He lifted it for me to see. Nanda's eyelash, the little curved line that lived on his face, through joy and rage, had let go at the last minute to be found.

Luca, who I had never seen so stolid, tugged his wallet from his jeans pocket, placed it on the table next to Nanda and opened it with one hand. He removed a piece of paper, bent it gently in half and released the eyelash into the crease. He folded the paper to secure

175

Nanda's eyelash into the billfold, flapped his wallet closed and gave me a wink.

Nanda's eyelash, a waning moon into darkness, kept hidden for safekeeping. The arc that illustrated the trajectory of his death. His eyelash was his smile, a Viking ship, a warrior's discarded bow, a horn reduced by distance whose warning cannot be heard. Yet, in my madness, a vessel, inside I could find Nanda and all his history. I wanted to scrape him loose. String together his beautiful DNA. Create a new Nanda.

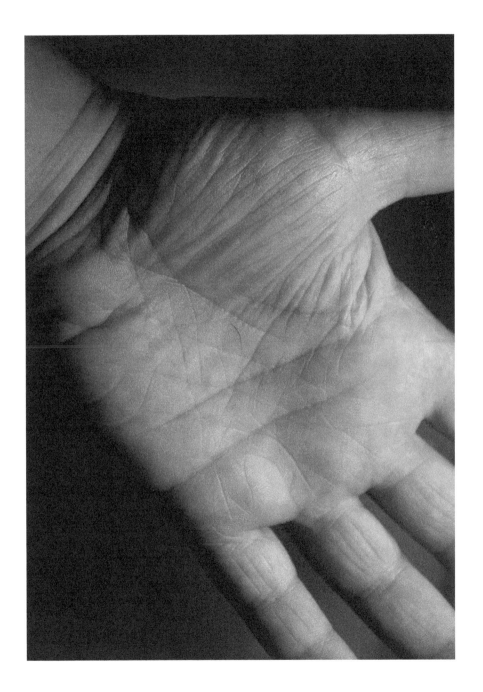

Wanting Nanda's Eyelash

Rachel, wrinkle-browed, peeled back Nanda's eyelids, but like elastic, they snapped closed. Nanda was born with his eyes open. I couldn't take not seeing his eyes. He liked to meet eye to eye when he talked or listened. If I ever looked away, he'd tap my arm, cradle my chin on the tips of his fingers, guide my face to his, and with a magnetic click, our eyes would join.

'Are you gonna photograph, Nanda?' Rachel asked.

In my periphery, her face looked like a question mark. I held the camera pressed to my chest to keep it from swinging, and with my other hand, I lifted one of Nanda's eyelids with a thumb, my face close to his, so he could see me. Fully opened, his iris and pupil were not visible, only a wrinkled, jaundiced, egg-like sclera. I wondered if his retina retained the last thing he saw, the afterimage of a train or the moon, but instead, I agonised that he would be stuck staring into the black cave of his head. I didn't answer Rachel.

I would have let the camera delve into the deep recess of Nanda's fibres, each minuscule bit, then absorb him whole. Photographs might prove or disprove how someone might have reassembled him using another person's body parts. I would need to see his face again to be able to process what I lost. The photograph would allow me to someday forgive the sculptor who rebuilt my son's head too square, carved his forehead too wide, the proportions wrong, a layer of puttied face stretched across a dysmorphic, hollow dome. A foreign chin shoved upward, held in place by two rocking-chair jawbones. Giant flaps of flesh on each side of his head were old man's ears. His nose too pronounced, too angular. Pony nostrils packed with cotton. *Perhaps they lost his head.*

But instead, I camera-eyed him, focused in, framed the details, inventoried every shot I could have taken. I memorised him, hoping to recall the disturbing, unknown, unseen matters of that night; his thoughts, how he felt, and his end.

I lifted Nanda's head, felt his unhinged skull pull away from his body. I would have photographed the impossible bend of his disconnected hip and twisted leg. But above all, I wanted to photograph his hands. Hands loved. Hands as memories. Hands of laughter. Hands crying. Hands folded into prayer. Hands flipping the bird. Hands as vessels. Hands holding mine, me, the shipwright, who would float them in a pond, dreaming where he might take me.

I fantasised about stealing Nanda's body, to bring him home. His brother, sister and I would have washed him, swaddled him in his blanket, photographed his cocoon, given him a long wake and whispered bardo prayers into his ears. When it was evident he needed to go, we could have given him a natural burial into earth or laid his body to rest in a Viking ship, ignited the fire and released him to the sea.

Instead, there I was, with Nanda's body institutionalised with a few minutes left, and still, I could not bring myself to use the camera.

*

Luca lost his wallet soon after the viewing.

Laughing in the Bardo

Griever, to cry is expected; to laugh is divine.

Three days after Nanda's death, my former boss at the International House—a place to gather in celebration of diversity—opened the building to facilitate Nanda's memorial service. Without any formal announcement, community members, acquaintances, friends and family gathered. Even his Coast Guard recruiter showed up to share the shock. Nanda dead. I whited out through the entire service like a long-extended camera flash. One minute, in front of hundreds of people, the next minute, alone in the parking lot. I stared into pavement. I couldn't remember how I landed there.

The building lights went off behind me. I heard doors bang shut and keys jangle. I turned around, no one in sight. Aimless, with no desire to go anywhere, I didn't worry that I had forgotten to make stay-over plans. I wasn't concerned about not knowing where I had misplaced the bag of clothes Roger had brought for me. Or the whereabouts of Roger and Rachel. I couldn't even remember if we had said goodbye.

I had no ride. My car was parked on the other side of town at my sons' house. No food, just a leathery banana peel at the bottom of my fanny pack, left over from my one meal of the day. Damp air seeped through my clothes, and my teeth vibrated. I didn't panic, but I did check the cell phone. Dead.

I heard footsteps and the echoey voices of Luca and my artist buddy, Krispy, a slim beauty whose coppery hair wrapped around her like a cape. Her face could be found in a Victorian photograph. We were kindred spirits who liked to dress in industrial men's apparel and good sturdy boots. She brought her dog, Mikivey, an obedient black shepherd. I didn't turn around. Mikivey nudged his nose into my hand until he broke my trance. Krispy and Luca linked their arms to mine. Krispy snuggled her head into my neck. I started to shake.

'You aren't answering your phone,' she said.

'Battery died.'

Krispy draped her jacket over my shoulders. 'Roger and Rachel are headed home. They know you're with us.'

'Okay.'

Luca told me they stayed behind to gather the flowers and photos, and box up leftovers, but first and foremost, they waited to take care of me. Luca on one side, Krispy on the other, we walked as one unit. Krispy whisper-sang the traditional Scottish folk song, *The Parting Glass*. Luca harmonised. Their voices poured into me, kept me upright on the way to Krispy's Bronco. She sat me in the back, had Mikivey curl up on my feet, then drove us through the backroads of Davis to the rural outskirts of Winters headed to her one-person trailer, a fifties Silver Streak situated on a friend's plot of land. I swayed, hypnotised, staring out the window into an ink-dense sky. A cloud-glazed moon hovered over furrowed fields. Rows of bare, fruit trees fractured into patterns. Faces appeared and transformed into hundreds of low-huddled, sooty clouds that bobbed on a murky, roller-coaster hillside. Before we arrived, the moon had been devoured by trees.

From the light of the car headlamps, Krispy's trailer appeared, a shiny capsule in the woods. We stumbled through tall grasses to her wooden porch over which she had wired spindly branches in place to suspend a makeshift roof of green corrugated fibreglass. Balanced on the centre edge, a Victrola tin horn hung like a gargantuan black trumpet flower. Two disembodied manikin legs stood beside a vintage metal chair that cradled a one-eared toy bunny with a smiling, plastic babyface, a saint Jerome votive candle lodged in its arm. Near the trailer entry, a preserved aardvark served as a petrified door attendant. Krispy lived an artist's life. But when we got inside, the art hanging on the walls was unreadable. Her art usually inspired me to care about the human condition and made me question what I was made of. Usually better than gallery visits. But I perceived nothing. My art-self voided. A wobble started in my spine and made its way to my eyeballs. *Fuck, I'm art blind.*

Luca tilted his head, looked me up and down, then threw his arm over my shoulder. We squeezed into the kitchen while Krispy collapsed her breakfast nook table to the wall and unfolded the benches into a bed for her and Mikivey. She offered Luca cushions and a sleeping bag on a slim bit of linoleum floor. I took the narrow slide-out bed next to the kitchen cupboards. We had to perform gymnastics to get to the toilet. The smell of dog breath and damp dog fur filled the trailer.

Krispy hit the button on the wall sconce, and the trailer went pitch black. I didn't see moonlight seep in, but I could feel the weight of the moon in my chest.

We lay quiet in the trailer. I stirred my arms in the air, opened my eyes as wide as I could and searched for whatever moved in the darkness. I couldn't see a thing, well, at least not anything real. I mean, I could see, but straight through the ceiling. Exactly like the strange encounter I had at Steve's house. Flat on my back, arms extended, fingers raking the air, wishing I could feel where Nanda might have gone, questioning the superlunary flotsam and jetsam spinning above me as I tried to fly into the astral plane, the bardo. Probing the liminal state between death and rebirth, swimming through ethereal landscapes, slivers of grey light rived through darkness. Milky ghosts dissipated into my eyes. I could feel a thick presence of unknown. Nothing. Something. I kept my arms pointed to heaven. *Where is heaven?* Stretched to the limit. Trying to signal. To pull. A vain attempt at grasping. My arms grew numb, waved like silk ribbons. *Where is he?*

'I hope the rats stay away,' Krispy said.

'Rats?' Luca asked.

'What rats?' I asked.

'I heard them at night, building nests in the wheel wells,' she said. 'I was pretty sure they couldn't get back in.'

'Back in? Pretty sure?' Luca asked.

'Until they ate all my soap.'

They chuckled. I imagined rats burping bubbles and almost smiled. I let my arms drop. 'When's the last time they got in?'

'Last week. But I have since repaired the holes,' she said.

'Oh, thank God,' I said.

'They ate my vintage dresses.'

'Oh no,' I said, an urge to laugh stuck in my belly.

Krispy and Luca giggled.

'They also filled my favourite lace-up vintage shoes with wads of black, greasy poop,' she said, then they both burst into hysterics.

'Oh fuck, that's gross,' I said and laughed.

My first laugh since Nanda died. I cried because I laughed, and I cried because I believed Nanda might be dead, and I laughed because I pictured fat velvet-jacketed rats munching on vintage dresses, popping pearl hors d'oeuvres into their mouths, picking lace from their teeth, then taking giant, soapy shits in their royal rat lavatory.

'One night, after a very long day at work, I climbed into bed, the slide-out bed, and before I started to doze off, I felt a lump in the mattress. Then the lump moved,' she said.

I prodded the surface of the mattress, not more than three inches thick.

Luca scream-laughed. 'And you're sure you've taken care of these rats?'

'Well, so, I could feel a hole in the mattress where the lump moved, so I pushed harder onto the lump. I stayed on the lump all night.'

'Hole? Lump? Eeeeee.' I pressed myself against the mattress and tried to feel for a hole, for a lump.

'I woke up to,' she snickered, 'a dead rat.'

'You murdered a rat in this bed?' I snorted in hysterics, then sobbed.

'I'm so sorry, I didn't want to tell you, because, well, you know. But, anyways, I have replaced the mattress. It's new, clean.'

I laughed. 'It is disconcerting, but it is also fucking hilarious.'

They laughed. I hyperventilated between laughing and crying.

'Anyways, mattress rats, hella stressful,' she said. 'And then there's…'

'What?' Luca and I asked in unison.

'The drawer rats,' she said.

'Drawer rats?' I asked and curled into the blankets.

'Fucking huge wood rats,' she said.

Luca wailed like a crazed hyena.

'They managed to burrow their way into the kitchen drawers. Oh my God, I could hear them late at night shuffling silverware, wrestling kitchen utensils.'

'Oh yuck,' I said.

The cathartic pendulum swung me from misery to mirth, like my first leap off a steep cliff into a deep swimming hole, apprehensive at first but the plunge enlivening. *Stop laughing. He's dead.* I had lost control. Confused. Funny felt good. *This is not right. You've got to stop laughing.* I laughed until my ribs spasmed and my cheeks burned.

Stop it. What will they think? Then I moaned like a stabbed dog. Luca reached for my hand and squeezed.

'Should I stop?' she asked.

'No, no, keep going,' I said as I cleaned snot off my face with the sheet.

Krispy told us she set traps. But the clever rats could trigger the traps without getting caught. One night she heard the familiar clamber through the wheel wells, the scurry inside the walls, into the drawers, the jostling of kitchen spoons and knives and high-pitched screaming. The drawer clattered and bounced, more screaming. In a panic, she turned on the lights and carefully opened the drawer to find a large, pissed-off rat attached to a wood and wire rat-trap caught around its butt. The creature writhed and contorted, kicked and screeched, wild-eyed, baring its sharp teeth. She slammed the drawer shut.

'I was in my mother's old pink nightie freezing my ass off. I decided to put on a pair of tube socks, you know, those seventies dorky ones, thick-ribbed knee socks, neon green and orange stripes at the top, and the one pair of shoes I had at the time, my bad-ass steel-toed welding boots. There was thunder and lightning, and it was pouring rain, but I needed to go outside.'

'Why?' I asked.

'To fetch the long, barbeque tongs,' she answered. 'And the oven gloves.'

My belly cramped as both Luca and I howled.

She went on to explain how she put on oven gloves and nabbed the rat's head with the tongs. She took the rat outside and planned to stomp the rat to death with her boots, but she couldn't find the nerve to crush it. So instead, she decided she'd drown it. Meanwhile, the wind whipped through, rain plummeted, thunder rolled, and the sky cracked with lightning. The rat wriggled in the clutch of the tongs and wailed a high-pitched shrill as claws and teeth flashed. Without a tub to hold water, she emptied a metal trash can, spilling garbage across her porch. Soaked to her skin, her arm cramped as she wrangled the wriggling, screaming rat between tongs in one hand while filling the trash can with water from a hose in the other. When the trash can reached half full, she threw the trapped rat in.

'Only problem,' she started to crack up, 'wood floats.'

'Oh shit,' I said.

'Basically, the frenzied rat used the trap as a kickboard and did circles in the trash can water,' her voice squeezed the rest of the words into high pitch, 'while glaring at me with its bulging rat eyes.'

I just about peed myself. 'Oh my God. What did you do?'

'By that time, I was drenched, chilled to the bone. I soldiered on. Couldn't find a hat, but I had a metal colander which I placed on my head so the rain wouldn't get in my face, at the same time freaking out that I might be electrocuted since I was surrounded by lightning.'

I could see her, artist-warrior, 115 pounds of lean machine, pink chiffon rippling in the wind, lightning reflected off her salad-strainer helmet, neon stripes aglow beneath her knees as she clomped around in steel-toed boots, wielding a crazed rat in a trap. Smiling cramped my jaw. Waves of laughter rippled through me. I saw myself as someone crying like someone is laughing and someone laughing like someone is crying. It felt good-bad, bad-good. But I couldn't drop the shame. The smiling bereaved are frowned upon. *Who would understand a mother in grief, smiling or laughing days after her son had died? Is he dead?*

Krispy cleared her throat, then her words oozed like ointment, 'He strained to look at me as I plunged him under. I could feel his desperation, his convulsions through to my bones. It takes a reeeeeally long time to drown a rat,' she said. 'I thought I was gonna puke.'

The refrigerator hummed. I heard blankets shuffle. Krispy sighed.

'Actually, I cried through the whole fucking ordeal. Not quite recovered,' she said.

I tried to imagine killing the rat. Krispy was a gentle woman who found herself connected to the rat in a trap, determined to follow through beyond what she had expected. She drowned the fucker, that's all. Rat gone. End of story. End of fucking story. *Nanda, where did you go?* My eyes soaked in darkness. I had expected to return his call, expected him to answer, and we'd make plans. *Don't be gone!* Nanda gone. *Please don't be gone.* Nanda, fucking gone.

Clearing Nanda's Room

Grief is discovering and losing your loved one in each of their belongings.

Sunday evening, Krispy and I, along with Mikivey, dropped Luca at the train station, then headed over to my sons' house to call it a night. Before we reached the door, we heard guys hollering and laughing inside, but the minute we entered, weird-quiet. Arian and his friends, most of whom I'd known since they were wee ones, were kicked back on the sofa around a beer-cluttered coffee table. They gave us a few quick glances but didn't say a word. Cigarette smoke spiralled. Arian stood, tilted his head to one side and embraced me.

Drinking after the death of a family member, friend, or acquaintance for that matter, was a young people ritual in these parts. I worried about Arian. No stranger to loss, he had a girlfriend who died a few years earlier, killed by a drunk hit-and-run driver. He saw her die. And a year later, his godfather, my best friend, Rick, died by suicide.

Arian flopped on the couch, combed a hand through his mass of curls and picked up his beer.

Krispy and I both unanimously decided sleeping in Nanda's room was out of the question. Plus, the guys were noisy, and the house was full of smoke. Video-game light flashed in the living room and lit the backyard leaving us only the middle-class, suburban front yard to make camp. To avoid the beacon of full moon and concerned neighbours, we chose a spot in a shadow and sat on God-knows-whose sleeping bag spread between two bushes on a dewy patch of Bermuda grass. Krispy brought a wool blanket from her truck to throw over us.

We finished off a bag of chips, a chocolate bar, a six-pack of beer and smoked a half pack of cigarettes. I had quit smoking years earlier but started again. Neither of us could sleep. As soon as we laid our heads to the ground around 4:00 a.m., the front door clicked open and closed with a bang. Two young men bantered back and forth as they walked through the yard. I shushed as loud as I could, which prompted a burst of laughter. Jimmy and Miguel stumbled along the sidewalk to the street, out of view.

Krispy and I heard Jimmy loud-whisper, 'Dude, what the fuck? You are going the wrong way. It's this way you, moron.'

'Let go of me, assbite,' yelled Miguel.

Then the crack of a dropped bottle.

'Fucker! What'd you do that for?'

'Shut up!' a neighbour blurted from across the street.

We heard a door slam. The guys whispered and snickered.

Mikivey rose and stirred. Stale beer wafted our way as the dog turned in circles and clanked beer bottles beneath his feet. He mashed our paper cup ashtray, which hurled stinky ash and cigarette butts over us.

'Aw, come on Miki!' Krispy said.

She stood, brushed herself off, looked at me and laughed. I was dotted with ash, so she brushed me off too. Her dog sat at attention; his eyes fixed on her. By the time the ruckus settled down it was around 5:00 a.m. and still dark. Krispy had a long drive home and although sleep deprived, she had to work that morning. I stretched my body, arms over my head, toes pointed, and heard joints creak and crackle. Close to freezing, I exhaled ghost breath.

'I gotta go. Call me. No wait, I'll call you,' Krispy said. She knelt on the blanket and squeezed my arm. 'You gonna be okay?'

I sat up. 'Yah.'

Mikivey poked his nose into my face, then looked at me with two black marbles reflecting moon glints. Krispy gathered her blankets, covered me with her side of the sleeping bag and walked to the street towards her truck. Mikivey followed.

Not much later, more whispers. I pulled on boots, slipped into a damp coat and tucked my hair under the bowler hat Faith had lent me, the one I had worn day and night. After four days without a shower, my armpits reeked. I rolled up the sleeping bag, brushed the bottles and debris into a pile, wiped my hands on my skirt and walked to the driveway where I found Jimmy and Miguel leaning against my car, a beer bottle sitting on the hood.

'Hey,' said Jimmy with his hair in his face.

'Get the fuck off my car.' I reached into my jacket pocket for keys.

'Hey, sorry, Jane, no worries, eh?'

With his head down, he grabbed his beer and moved away. Miguel lit his cigarette and gave me a little wave as he shoved off the bumper.

'Go home!' I said.

They staggered into the street. I opened the car trunk, grabbed my pack, collected the cardboard boxes and packing materials I'd purchased at a hardware store and let myself into the house. Quiet and no one in sight. Through an unlit hallway, I bumped around until I wedged in the doorway of Nanda's bedroom. I dropped the pack and boxes to the floor. Not much moonlight shone through his window. I could make out a bare mattress and beige shag carpet. All of Nanda's footprints swallowed. Nailed above the head of his stripped bed hung the drawing I told Robin he could have, the one Nanda begged, or more like, took from me when he first moved out. *Maybe Robin doesn't want it!*

My sad drawing covered half the wall. A sgraffito crayon image of embers shaped like a man and a woman rising from flames, masks falling off their faces. Near the end of my marriage to Billy, I had scratched the arms-wide-open-sized drawing for days until the flames rose and the figures broke to pieces. I removed the picture from Nanda's wall and placed it at the start of a donation pile.

I turned on the overhead light. On top of Nanda's television, two photographs, a Polaroid he took of me the last time we saw each other and a photograph Dad took of Nanda at the age of sixteen. Dad had invited Nanda to hike along a rocky cliff at Montaña de Oro Bluff. In the photo, Nanda stood with his arms wide open to a blustery sky, hair wind-tossed, mouth agape like he was howling, his back to an expanse of ocean and a twenty-foot wave breaking over his head.

Dad had shown the photograph to me a couple years earlier when he shot it and said, 'Christ almighty, he's adventurous! He could have been killed.' Dad shook his head and laughed.

'Yeah, the both of you,' I had said, and did not laugh.

Nanda, under Dad's care, the same man who had hung me in that cave at Joshua Tree when I was a child. *What was I thinking to leave Nanda, my kid, with such a man?* But like Jekyll and Hyde, Dad could also be a good man. As a kid, I played dress-up with Dad. We sang opera together in our echoey basement. He built me a playhouse, and in winter, in Canada, an ice-skating rink and ice slide. He bought me a record player and albums of classical music. He also, in a drunken rage, once knocked me out cold when I was fourteen. *Was I in denial?* The photograph made me ill. Dad was right; Nanda could have died. Swept into the ocean, crashed onto the rocky shore, his body torn and bloodied, his head cracked open. *I could have blamed Dad for Nanda's death.*

I slipped the photographs into a flat, zippered pocket of my daypack. On the TV was a jewel-shaped turquoise bottle, a cologne Dad had given to Nanda. I twisted the gold cap off and brought the bottle to my nose. A sigh geysered. The cologne smelled good, but it had smelled better on Nanda. The scent of his Euro kisses. He'd bob his head back and forth with exaggerated pouty lips and kiss each of my cheeks. His last Euro kiss, he squeezed my shoulders with his broad hands and with a cheeky grin, he said, 'You are MY mom.'

After shoving the bottle to the bottom of the pack, I scanned the room. In a laundry basket on the floor were rows of tucked socks, rolled how I had shown Nanda. I left those for Arian. *He's practical; he'll want them.* I flapped open a black plastic garbage bag and tossed in Nanda's stack of underwear.

In the closet, evenly spaced, Nanda had buttoned his shirts to hangers the way I did, the way Dad had shown me. I unbuttoned each shirt, kept a couple for myself, then folded them into bags for the donation pile. Off a shelf, I slid most of his squarely folded trousers into a bag but kept a pair of his white Khakis to take home. Most of his clothes would be too short to give to Arian. *Where are Nanda's shoes?*

Next to Nanda's bed was a small bookcase. I leafed through his sci-fi and fantasy books, each dented on the inside covers with the scroll of his name. The pages had released the pressure of his hands, the curl gone flat. Beside a well-worn paperback copy of *The Hobbit*, which I placed in my pack to save for Billy who loved Tolkien, I found a fat bundle of handwritten pages tied with red string, with the title *Kilran* inscribed in red ink across the top page, the start of Nanda's novel. He had written about a warrior with amnesia, who had forgotten who he was, on a quest to regain his memory, to remember his mission. Earlier, on Nanda's computer, I had found the Word document he started for that book. I opened the file to see a bright white page with one centred line, *Light holds shadows, a darkness worth seeing.*

After I fitted Nanda's drawings, photographs and writings into a box, I took down his curtains. Along the windowsill, I noticed his handprints left in the dust. I hushed breath onto the window to reveal the oil of his fingertip swirls pressed onto the glass. From the pack, I retrieved my camera and photographed his prints, the worn dip in the mattress, the grime-rimmed bedroom door handle, the smudge of knee, hand and head against the wall next to the bed. Over every surface of his room, I searched for what belonged to him: a stray hair, a blue thread on the carpet from the jacket he last wore, a small white feather from his pillow, a crumpled café receipt for a latte and almond croissant, the same as I often ordered.

On top of the bookcase sat a vase of wilted flowers. One of his buddies mentioned he thought it weird that Nanda had bought a bouquet for himself. The guy must not have known Nanda very well. Beside the vase, a bundle of burnt sage, still pungent, in a bowl with a box of matches. *What could be more stagnant than death?* Sitting on the edge of his mattress, I lit and waved the smudge stick, swirling smoke to clear his room.

I knocked on Arian's door but didn't get an answer, so I slid a note under saying I'd call later in the day. After loading Nanda's belongings into the car, I went back in for the last item. Nanda's red blanket, imploded from the weight of itself, lay in a heap on the closet floor. Carmen must not have wanted such a plain blanket. I picked it up and turned myself inside out trying to feel for the shape of him. On the way to the car, I squeezed his blanket between clenched fists and chest. My eyes pulsed, reduced to pinholes; everything faded to white, then shimmered and gave way to a clouded sky. The moon still visible. In the driveway, legs pressed together tight, I fumbled for two corner ends of the blanket, and stretched it wide open to catch air. The red sail billowed into the bare light of morning, the same sail I once floated over Nanda when I used to tuck him at night. Caught in the undertow, I shook the blanket to release the memory. *It's just laundry.* Like gathering his bedding off the clothesline, the fresh peel, the smell of air. *Fold the laundry.* I ran my hands along the edges, pinched the corners together, turned over, turned under, made it square, then opened the passenger door and reposed Nanda's red blanket onto the passenger seat.

Un

Reach into your sorrow, take hold of grief and dance.

I sped out of Davis, racing past agricultural fields onto the highway. The moon wobbled my internal orbit, followed me through the valley, over hills, as I wove through mountains to hurry home. In that lunar spotlight, in a warp trance, the road flew under me. A drive that usually took three hours took two. I pulled into the driveway to find the moon perched on the roof of our house.

As I walked past the garage, I heard Roger grinding metal. When not at work, he spent hours as a builder-maker-inventor. Rachel was hidden away in her room, the TV blaring. I unloaded the last bags and boxes into the studio and peeled my clothes to the bedroom floor. A shower required too much energy, and I didn't want to get wet, so I put on a loose skirt and long-sleeved T-shirt. I went back to the car for Nanda's red blanket. With breath held, my stomach dropped as I lifted the limp fabric into my arms.

The moon retreated to the west, bouncing from house to house, as I lumbered back to the front door. Halfway along the sidewalk, I stepped from path to lawn to get a closer look at a stand of five-foot-tall stalks of weathered fava beans the colour of straw. What dies in winter sometimes returns in spring, but I could not foresee a new life. I cradled Nanda's blanket like a baby and knelt to the ground beside pungent decomposed roots, felt a chill seep in, listened to the cracking of tubular bones.

Blanket to belly, I drew in a long breath of ocean air and crouched between frail branches. My skirt dampened from wet earth as I sank in to hold hands with brittle leaves. Sunk my teeth into a fibrous stem, marrowless and empty. I felt as hollow as those stalks.

I hoisted the husk of my body to stand and trudged to the front door, blanket padded against my rib cage. In the studio, I slumped the blanket over the back of a chair, sunk my palms into the fabric. I wanted to climb in. One minute gravity sucked me down, the next minute gravity let go. Unrelenting.

'Ahhhhhhhhhh, No! No no no, nooooo, no no.'

Rachel and Roger found me folded on the floor. I moaned as Roger paced. Through the tunnel of my being a locomotive howled.

He placed his hand on my shoulder and said, 'You have got to stop.'

But my body was not my own. I circled the floor on my hands and knees like an animal in labour. Snot so thick I gagged, strained to inhale. Roger staggered behind me, rubbed circles on my back, kept asking me to stop. Unstoppable.

'She can't stop.' Rachel sobbed.

After an hour or so, the surges slowed to a numb calm.

'What am I now?' I asked.

They didn't respond. All of us drowning. Unable.

'I need to take some photographs,' I said.

They both nodded, sad-eyed, vacant.

I dragged myself up, grabbed the blanket and hung my camera over my shoulder. Wedged the tripod under an armpit and trod to the garden tearing open a roll of film with my teeth. *I want to un, as in undo, unmake.* I wanted to see what unimaginable, unreachable, unrelenting looked like while holding Nanda's blanket. *Un, un, un, undone.*

I photographed things to help me see. To recollect. Photos are a vocabulary of being. I craved evidence, details, proof. To survive, I needed to organise, moment to moment. To make sense of, and be sure of, what would soon be the past. To be present with what is found. To find meaning. To make life better. I thought in pictures. Framed what I needed to keep to hold moments still. I recorded to allow myself a way to return to that moment. A keepsake for later perusal. Unseen. Unknown. Unbelievable.

On a weepy lawn, feet cushioned wet, I unfolded the limbs of Nanda's red blanket across a patch of green, stretched its body to the ground, along with memories, the weight of his arms, his legs, his hands. I positioned the tripod, attached the camera and turned the focusing ring. Through the viewfinder, my son's blanket glowed next to a wintered garden, an ephemeral boneyard. I set the timer and walked barefoot into where Nanda was missing, into the camera's gaze. Unsound.

Nanda's blanket multiplied the weight of everything as I wrapped it around me. In that empty space, his space, I tried to imagine him. I had climbed into a version of him. Beneath the blanket, breathing through pores of his weave, I tried to recover. Unrecoverable. Folded it into a book of flesh, unpaged, I read the unreadable, formed the fabric into a sad pillow and buried my face into the sag of it. Unrolled, flattened and lifted with aching arms, a flag I desperately needed to wave, the emergency of it all, yet his blanket remained too heavy to fly. Unsavable. I bundled Nanda's blanket into a mass of arteries and veins. Opened it like a map of muscle. Grabbed its tail and wrestled with what might be left of him. I draped his limp arm over my shoulder and wailed in my mourner's veil. Wallowing, I collapsed inside, outside, inside out, outside in. Unable.

Searching with raw impulse in a rhythmic daze before the camera, I unknowingly art-danced my first acquaintance with my new-self.

Unwords

Beads

Loss isn't singular.

Directly after my un performance before the camera, after the first shower since Nanda died, I stood naked and dripping with my feet pressed flat to the marble floor of our bathroom dragging a hairbrush through wet hair. Chilled. No light. No fan. Quiet. Over and over, I pulled the brush front to back as I dissolved into a faceless form in a fogged mirror.

The details of Nanda's memorial service, which I had considered unremembered, poured into me. Rows and rows of chairs were filled with young people. Krispy brought Mikivey who didn't leave my side. Every word of the eulogy spoken by my therapist, Reverend Bill, still forgotten, but his eyes, I could see them, bluer than ever. I could see the flowers.

'What shall we bring?' they asked.

'Flowers! Nanda loves flowers,' I answered.

Bouquets leaned against the wall of the entryway. There were flower arrangements on every surface, petals across tabletops, mourners holding roses and carnations, some with flowers in their laps, flowers in the aisles, and bunches piled in rows where I stood next to the pulpit. I faced everyone and babbled about loss. The only thing I remember saying, 'Nanda was my best friend.'

Over the rim of my ears, I dragged the brush past my temples and curved downward over my shoulder again and again. Cool drips of water rolled down my back and legs to the floor.

The International House overflowed with people, from the front of the pulpit, through the back doors to the edges of the parking lot. Dear friends, Eve and Greg, sang a song about Nanda they wrote the night before. Nanda's Coast Guard recruitment officer let me know how impressed she was with my son. Billy and his family sat in the front row. Dad and his new wife clear of Mum, so much sour history, but they showed up. Arian, head bowed, sat up front beside Mum holding her hand. Roger, alone at the far back, leaned against a wall, his tear-wet face bloodshot.

The brush grew heavy in my hand as I placed it against the nape of my neck. I leaned over, hung my head and stroked downward.

Glimmers of a childhood friend, Leslie, dressed in black, head draped like a Catholic nun, clasped her hands to her chest. A grad school buddy, Jon, his face sunburnt from skiing, embraced me. I saw my swollen eyes reflected in his mirrored sunglasses. Faith's husband and their boys offered long hugs. Trevor, a neighbourhood bad boy, handsome but cocky, hunched beside me, shook, wailed, begged to make amends. He'd punched Nanda to the ground a year earlier, delivering a swollen eye and a split lip after Nanda called him an asshole.

I flipped my hair and proceeded to brush it front to back again. My feet turning to ice on the marble.

Next to the entryway of the venue, a framed photograph of Nanda, the last photograph I had taken of him, sat on a table surrounded by roses. Rachel had it enlarged to life-size. He looked like someone in a Pre-Raphaelite painting. I glanced but did not linger. Even the smaller photographs of him arranged on a wall made me shudder. Nanda as a baby, a boy, a young man.

I later learned that Billy's girlfriend brought food, marigolds, candles and incense. What moved me most was the spirit pond she created. Beneath the wall display of Nanda photographs, she placed a glass bowl the size of the moon on a table and filled it to the rim with water. She crafted and floated little leaf boats. In each boat, she placed a lit ghee wick. Between flames, Nanda's images, blinking apparitions, reflected on the surface of that pond.

I whacked the brush against my hand to shake away the wetness and noticed it was full of hair. *Oh God, my hair.* Loosening the strands free, pinching it out bit by bit, I managed to gather a handful.

As a kid, I observed Bibby deal with loose hair. After a proficient brushing, she would comb and gather the hair from the brush tines. Between both hands she would roll the hair into a tight ball and toss it into the waste bin.

'It's quite nasty to discover stray hair,' she said. 'This prevents hair from wandering.' She winked, nodded and grinned with her gappy teeth.

Since then, I had always wound loose hair into a ball and always tossed the balls into the bin. So, between both hands, I rubbed the hairs together in opposite circular motion until the delicate threads centred and wove into a perfect spongy sphere.

But there alone in the bathroom in the grip of loss, I couldn't bear to lose anything more, not even a hair, much less a ball of hair. I could not throw the bead away. In the vanity drawer, amongst the dental floss, package of tissues, tubes of cream and ointment, tweezers and bobby pins, hand mirror and brush, I tucked the ball of hair into a corner and closed the drawer.

Ball of Hair

Grief-switch

Grief is a solo journey.

A couple of weeks after the call, still December, on a late afternoon, Roger and I met with friends at our favourite brewpub in Santa Cruz. Our first attempt at socialising since Nanda's death. We sat outdoors in the brisk air to chat, eat dinner and drink beer. The sounds of waves breaking close by. My face muscles ached as I struggled to smile.

Above us, the thinnest sliver of pink moon. I feared all memories of Nanda would disappear as that crescent waned. Then my face slipped. I found it impossible to mask grief. I got up and walked away. I locked myself in a bathroom stall, crouched balanced on the toilet seat, and willed myself to disappear. The room faded, sounds muffled, brain detached. I rocked with the ceiling fan's oscillating hum.

'You in there?' Roger called through the restroom door.

I couldn't answer. Shaking, I clenched my jaw to quiet my chattering teeth. He entered, each step hesitant, then tapped on the stall door.

'Jane?'

'I can't be here.'

'I know. Let's go home,' he said.

Our friends were long gone. We never saw them again. From then on, we decided to keep it simple—just him and me.

The first grief-relief came a few weeks later, on the veranda at the same brewery. I sat across from Roger next to a fountain where the sounds of water soothed my nerves. Sunshine warmed my blank face. He ordered two pints of beer and a large basket of French fries. We both stared into oblivion, no words needed.

I ate the fries in clusters, devoured a basket or two while downing two pints of beer. A switch flipped and I began to feel calm. I chain-smoked cigarettes. No grief. I consumed a chocolate bar. *Where does the anguish go?* I knew it would be back, but for those couple of hours, I had found a fix.

My therapist, Flora Hansen, knew I didn't like taking antidepressants and suggested my love for potatoes, a wonderful comfort food, might be a natural mood enhancer. She dug through her library and handed me a book called *Potatoes, Not Prozac*.

'Maybe you crave potatoes because they produce feel-good hormones,' she said.

Loads of French fries, beer, cigarettes and chocolate became a weekly ritual. I don't know how Roger tolerated it. Maybe it worked for him as well. Unhealthy, unsustainable, and I gained twenty pounds, I didn't care. It worked.

Levitation

Your grief is a ghost you cannot explain.

The end of December. Midnight. A billowy pine tree canopied the house, laced over the windows, and waved its artery shadows onto our bedroom walls. Moonlight squeezed through gauzy curtains, dotting the room with glittery sequins. The ceiling read like a page from a Carlos Castaneda book, beckoning me to find a safe spot. I reclined in bed, muscles tight as a straitjacket, beneath a crow's wing. I swung inside and outside my head like a pendulum until there was no head, trapped between the world I lost and the one I was about to live in, with just enough wits to open a bottle of sedatives.

Awake and asleep, no difference. With my legs entangled in blankets, I tried to decipher the new world through a narrow tube of being. Squeezed thoughts out like oil paint. I chewed my fingers till they bled. In the hollow of my being, I hung in the all-too-familiar cavern labouring to suck oxygen through a collapsed self until I untied myself from the bed.

Not sleepwalking, not dreaming, I slung on a robe and threw Nanda's red blanket on like a cape, tiptoed through the house and out the back door. Across a moist yard, my feet sank with each step, weeds between toes. I climbed into a thicket of honeysuckle to reach the fence, limbs, robe and blanket snagging, clambered up the weathered boards and dropped to the other side, to the railroad. Crunching through ballast, I stepped onto the tracks, then planted my bare feet on a tie and curled my toes to the edge. Anchored in place, I swayed with the blanket draped over my head, its tail stroking the rails.

I visualised the pieta, a marble statue of Mary, shrouded, her lifeless son, Jesus, cradled in her lap. Her palm open to the sky, questioning why. I recalled a scene from a film that had always haunted me: in a desolate snowed-in wilderness an Algonquin woman, upon seeing her dead son, falls to her knees and wails guttural animal sounds. Both hands raised to the sky. *I am now one of the child-loss mothers.* I could feel a woeful beast pacing in my chest.

The dark fence-lined alley stretched for blocks with a faint dappling of light from nearby homes. I dismissed any notion of hope. I wondered about my lifeline, about the railroad that stretched from my childhood home on the prairies of Canada across the United States to California. Wondered about those four lanes of steel rails that gouged through the Nanda terminal out to the coast to sideswipe our new home in Santa Cruz. There I waited, where the ghost trains hurled and howled morning and night, my ear eternally pressed to the rails, to the pulse of that night; no matter what direction, they all headed to the Nanda Junction. Every train was Nanda's train. I wanted to die.

Loose rocks cracked with the scuffle of footsteps in gravel. A herculean shadow flickered past fence-slotted light emitted from a neighbour's porch lamp. The baggy phantom grew larger against the fence until a man-form stumbled across the tracks in my direction. I slow-breathed and stood firm as the hooded Thor, one clumsy foot after the other, thudded, then slowed to a step, a pause, a waver, step and a pause. With most of the available light behind him, his silhouette morphed into a heap of baggage ready to topple. He stopped within inches of my taut belly. We shared the air and his alcohol breath; shared the unknown trapped between us, his face unseeable. The wall of him unclimbable, impenetrable. I feared, if he moved one step closer, I'd shatter. Then he lowered his head so close to mine I could feel his heat. Through the bell of my chest, an animal growl bassooned from my mouth. He jerked his head upright, spun and ran-stumbled down the tracks, a rhythmic pounding of stone, until out of view.

What the hell am I doing here?

My feet were too sore and cold to climb the fence, so I balance-walked a rail in search of an outlet to the street. I ran past neighbours' houses, hoping no one noticed me in my red blanket disguise as I snuck into the house. After brushing the dirt off my feet, I took two sedatives and crept into bed. The eerie cartoon man ran circles inside me. I fixated on the pine tree outside the window, its branches combing the night sky. Roger deep-breathed. Asleep on his side with his back turned towards me, he let out a sigh, twitched his leg, stretched an arm and settled back into slumber. I drew the covers over his shoulders and lay flat with my arms at my sides. In the nightness of our blue-grey room, rippled shadows snaked onto the ceiling.

Just as I felt my body relax, settled into the silence of our room, a spray of light shot through our window and over our bed. Our shaded yard was next to the railroad track. If anyone happened to be on the tracks carrying flashlights, we'd hear gravel and the echo of footsteps. I heard nothing. My body thrummed as if I had been struck like a singing bowl. The hairs on my arms moved in circular motion. A wash of ghost-white glowed at the foot of our bed, seeped over the edge towards me, then the linens lifted. I turned to look at Roger. Sound asleep. Cold hands grasped my ankles, squeezed and tugged. They shook me like a heavy blanket and let go. I rose and floated midair. A veil of phantom light rushed beneath me, and I dropped to the bed. Roger sat up.

'What the heck?' he asked.

'Did you feel that? Did you see that flash?' I lay still, staring at the ceiling.

'Night terror?' he asked.

'No, no. That's not what it was.' I rubbed my eyes as tears welled up.

He rolled towards me, slid his arm under my neck and nuzzled his head into my pillow.

'Are you okay?'

'I think so.'

I wasn't okay.

He drifted back to sleep. The grief-shock anaesthesia was wearing off. I unlaced his arms, got out of bed, popped open the sedative bottle and dropped the last pill into my mouth, worrying about addiction, about being transformed into the walking dead. *That's my last sedative. I'll learn to count breaths instead.*

When I returned to bed, I didn't melt into sleep, I lay there for hours and shook. Gnawed loose skin from cuticles, wriggled legs to calm nerves, and mentally wrestled with the urge to stand on railroad tracks.

Levitation

Earth Hand

The heart is the seat of grief.

In the spring of 1999, a few months after the blow, I dreaded the hills turning green, as in life goes on. I compiled a list of my family and sorted them according to how devastated I'd be if they died. With a red marker, I underlined the above ten on the one-to-ten grief-scale: Rachel, Arian, Roger. I was sure I wouldn't survive if any of them perished. If I had comprehended statistics, I would have rattled through equations and still feared the odds. And then there was me. I wanted to die but didn't really want to die. I worried that if I wanted to die, I might have been slowly killing myself or summoning death. *What if I died? What if I was next? I could die.* But so new to grief, losing anyone or anything generated relentless anxiety. Whenever the phone rang, I'd brace myself in case it was a call from death.

I developed a pattern, a ritual, I'd wake at 2:08 a.m. every night in a terrified state, lean into Roger, slip my arm around him, place my hand onto the centre of his chest, feel for movement, listen to him breathe, get out of bed, creep into Rachel's room, position my ear to her nose and wait for her breath to rise and fall, rise and fall. I even checked the dogs and our cat, touched their bellies until they stretched their legs, lifted their heads. For Arian, nearly impossible to get on the phone, I kept an angel candle lit.

Just before spring semester started, I had Rachel test out of high school and enrolled her at my college to keep her close to me. My workload kept us on campus from early morning to late afternoon. I also needed her company since my colleagues steered clear as if I were carrying a corpse.

Looking back, we coped by staying busy. Roger worked long hours. Arian made himself unavailable, but occasionally I'd get him on the phone for a couple of minutes. Rachel found friends and schoolwork to keep her busy. In a grief-tangle, I didn't understand my chaos of mixed emotions and rarely considered how anyone else felt.

The weeks were composed of lesson prepping, teaching, cooking dinner, prepping some more, grading work, and going to bed at 1:00 a.m. On weekends I did housework. I started to write simple diary entries. And when I intuited that something needed to be recorded, I took photographs.

On Valentine's Day, I woke thinking about hearts, broken hearts, my heart, surprised to find mine pounding arrogantly strong. Roger bought Rachel and me fancy heart-shaped chocolates. He gave me a pair of handcrafted silver earrings—danglies—and an orchid.

That evening when I woke at 2:08 am, I sat up in bed, leaned against the wall with my chin rested on the windowsill. Roger in full slumber. I thought about an art piece I once made where I preserved a cherry cordial, a plump neon cherry in pink syrup encapsulated in chocolate, into a glass vessel like an archaeological artefact, with a poetic label telling the story of Saint Valentine's demise. A tragic story not for the faint of heart. He was beheaded, then revered as a saint, buried, dug up, buried again, his head anointed and kept in a reliquary, once given as a gift to a queen; even a vessel stained with his blood became cherished as a holy relic. I loved the paradox of 'Will you be my Valentine?' The weirdness of offering a beloved a candy resembling a brain preserved in its skull. However, I wasn't moved to embalm any part of Nanda.

Outside, below our window, where the sun rarely shined, a spare spot of damp earth, usually moist from fog, a place where weeds refused to grow, two sad camellia bushes managed to survive. I looked through the pane of glass, down into scraggy branches, past a few waxy leaves, and noticed a blush-coloured flower. The soggy ground was full of bruised petals, rotted blossoms, flesh pink and cadaver blue. I pressed my cheek on the window glass. Breath amplified and vaporised into a rhythmic cloud, appeared and disappeared, then condensed. Through the misted glass, in the flutter of moonlight, I saw Nanda's hands in the dirt.

I sank beneath flannel sheets and a pillowy comforter, leaned my back against Roger's. Moonlight fell through swaying fir tree branches; needly figures fluttered across our bedroom walls. I could hear harbour seals bark and ocean waves tumble against rocks. Sea-driven wind whistling. In the yard, Nanda's phantom fingers, with their geometry, topography, lines, scars, and moons, grasped and churned earth.

A few days later, the coroner's report arrived in the mail from the Yolo County Sheriff's Office. I brought it into the studio, slid against the wall to the floor and fell into the memory of Nanda facing a westbound Union Pacific freight train. My eyes drained into the room, to the big white envelope. For weeks, drenched in shame, heavy with guilt, tormented, I worried that he might have intentionally ended his life.

I opened the envelope and eased out the thirty-page document: cover letter, autopsy, toxicology, and investigators' reports. I memorised the facts. December 2, 1998. Davis, California. Full moon. Sixteen miles per hour southerly winds. Forty-eight degrees Fahrenheit. Nanda walked along Olive Drive and attempted to cross the railroad tracks to Second Street near the 46.7 marker. Time 8:05 p.m. Blood alcohol .20 percent. No drugs present. Multiple injuries. Primary impact: a transection of the arch of the aorta, cardiac tamponade. I looked it up. A heart exploding on impact. *A broken heart.* Secondary impact: multiple lacerations, most of his organs macerated, his skull unhinged, right hip dislocated.

According to the Union Pacific engineer who could see my son clearly in the railroad corridor, Nanda stopped in the Foul Line. Not in the Y where tracks joined. He was between the number one and number two tracks. Nanda might have thought he was safe because he wasn't standing directly on a track, but in the engineer's report, it is explained that freight trains breach the foul line.

The train's engineer said, 'He was scared like a rabbit ... he must have thought he was out of harm's way ... he jumped at the last minute ... too late! I watched him fly twenty feet into the air, but I didn't see him land.'

No mention of his arms wide open.

I read the report many times. He flew up and never came back down.

The coroner interviewed numerous family members, his teachers, friends, and a few witnesses. She concluded that Nanda was beyond drunk, his perception and decision making severely impaired. Cause of death: Accidental.

Holding Hands

River

Grief is a courtship with death.

In Grass Valley California the Bear River flowed within a ten-minute walk from Treehenge, a parcel of land with a cluster of cottages belonging to my close friends, Wayne and Jeannie Olts. Home to deer, mountain lions, coyotes, rattlesnakes and redtail hawks. The path to the river curved through woodlands covered in giant oaks, madrone, manzanita, buckeye and ceanothus.

My family had attended Thanksgiving celebrations and communal gatherings in their meadow where we danced, ate homegrown food, played music, and communed with nature. One of Nanda's favourite places. He had expected to return to those woods and the river.

When Nanda died, Wayne and Jeannie, old souls with deep hearts, gave my family an open invitation to stay in their guest cottage where sun streamed in through ample windows and a skylight. When ravens flew overhead the room filled with flittering bird shadows. Along the length of the bed, a picture window offered a view of tall wavy oaks and a mosaic of blue sky.

Jeannie, a Jungian psychologist, suggested I float in the river.

'Let the river hold you. Lean into your grief,' she said.

As the first summer without my boy approached, Roger and I brought Nanda's red blanket to Treehenge to fill it with sunlight, let it breathe mountain air and soak in the flow of moving water.

At sunrise, I loaded a daypack with food, and plenty of water, and tied Nanda's red blanket around my waist. Roger, his face soft, eyes peaceful, heaved the camera bag and tripod over his shoulder. We sauntered through the woods, climbed, and slid down a steep rocky slope, past wood roses, lupines, and miner's lettuce, whacking our way through patches of poison oak and willows to a sunny riverbank of stone, sand, and maidenhair ferns. Sage sweetened the air. The voice of water rushed by.

Roger loaded film into the camera. A man of few words, but he knew how to show up. I unwrapped the blanket from my hips and handed it to him, kicked off sandals and removed all clothing, then sank my feet into grey mud and yellow silt at the water's edge. I stepped in deeper, onto a layer of steeped blackened leaves, thousands of tiny bubbles rose, fragrant with sulphur. Further in, arms of green algae slinked around my ankles. I slipped into the river and the river flooded into me: memories of a tanned boy skipping stones, of his muscular body sliding between boulders where the river tumbled into deep waterholes, of him resting chest bare, sunburnt, sprawled over the curve of a fallen tree, feet crusted with serpentine sand.

My skin appeared porcelain white where the water pooled Prussian blue and raw umber. Dappled light and shadow undulated patterns over a topography of goosebumps. From Roger's hands, the red blanket spilled into the river like blood, rippled and sank. With a toe, I hooked and trawled the submersed cloth to the surface as icy currents forced us into the water's flow. Above me, wearing only shorts, Roger, dreadlocks knotted on the top of his head, wide-stepped across granite slabs. He followed us, camera to his eye. I feared the river would steal the blanket until it clung to my body like a drowning animal. In the churn of rapids, we twisted as one. *Maybe I am drowning.*

River Rituals

When I struggled to free myself, the blanket tightened, when I relaxed, it loosened. Together we floated down the meandering blue-green-gold. A wound. A signal. A baptism.

Slowly through the shallows, I drifted between sun-bleached river rocks. The blanket grabbed onto me as I lifted myself onto a warm, broad-chested boulder. I pulled and stretched the red weave, a body full of river, next to mine. The blanket daggled its tail in the water, eager to slip away. I peeled the glistening crimson from the surface of stone and crawled under. What I could not remember, remembered me. The river offered movement, direction, a willingness to embrace change. Not ready, but I understood. On hands and knees in salutation I lifted my head and sat. Nanda's red blanket surrendered, and in that cloak of sorrow, I leaned into grief.

Sitting on the Shoulders of the Bear River

Same Place

Loss changes as life changes, continually evolving.

As an artist and photographer, I had trained my eyes to notice what would make an extraordinary image; a portrait, abstraction, still-life or landscape. I learned the language of shapes, contrast, the play of light and shadow, and the nuance of colour. The deep images, the ones I created to understand the human condition, I discovered by dancing with the subject, searching for whatever imbalanced me on the fulcrum of stability. The last photographs I had taken of Nanda, the Polaroids in the backyard that late September, the last time we shared one-on-one time, were not given much aesthetic consideration; the pictures were quick snapshots meant for Carmen. Polaroids have a short lifespan, they fade quickly, details deteriorate, but the results are instant. I could make shiny squares of Nanda in twenty seconds. We planned to take quality photographs using film and the fancy camera when the family gathered at Christmas.

A year later, same time, same place, sunlight flooded the backyard as it did that day. For the first time since his death, I mulled over those Polaroids, how precious they had become. To revisit the past, I walked through the yard and placed his portraits into the exact locations where he posed. I noticed that the bougainvillaea, once a full-bloom backdrop of magenta flowers, had dried as brown as the fence. Ivy had overgrown, taking the honeysuckle with it. The old ladder was missing. The hose, bucket and garden hoe were gone. Broken stepping-stones had been replaced with new ones. Our pink camellia bush, not visible in those Polaroids, had risen out of the earth to peek through our bedroom window. The last photo in my hand had no place to go, a photo of Nanda on a swing suspended from our oak tree, his elbows resting in his lap, his face as soft as butter. Someone cut down the tree swing, so I nestled the edge of the photo in pine needles against that tree.

In a split moment, the grief-anaesthesia wore off. A world once shrunk to the size of a plum, impossible to hold onto, to navigate, to see clearly, began to expand and came into focus. I had thawed, and the details of an entire year of life moving on without me entered my view.

Sometimes we are on hold. I needed to be stuck, to be more careful, to slow down time, not take anything for granted, to be mindful as to what can't be undone. All that time, I believed the Polaroids rooted Nanda in place, but his images told me the place had changed, and he had moved on. Those fading photos of Nanda, wrinkled and colours bruised, along with the backyard shifting, informed me to relish the truth, the incredible-clear-glorious truth. Nothing remains the same, not even grief.

Unstuck, I vibrated into the whirl of perpetual change, with urgency to step back into life, to observe, to be witness, willing to take the invitation to continue the photo session with Nanda, to take his place. I went in search of Nanda's clothes and found the trousers and shirt he wore that day.

As I secured the trousers button at my waist, my hips became his, surprised to find the trousers a perfect fit. His shirt a bit loose, still held my shoulders. From the file cabinet, I collected the Polaroid SX-70 camera, tripod and packages of film, untouched since our last visit, the film possibly unviable, and I headed to the backyard. Swinging on an emotional pendulum, I examined each Polaroid of him, his gestures, body language, positioned the camera, set the timer, hopped into each place, and tried to be him. I photographed myself in those places, surprised to find the new Polaroids would be the start of a new relationship with Nanda, who we were, who I was, who I would become.

September 1998   September 1999

Same Place

Solace

In grief, you can choose how to process your loss.

Día de los Muertos, 1999, Nanda's birthday and the first anniversary of his death drew near. In the small square of the studio, slouched in the same sweats for days before the grey glow of a computer monitor, I wasted time over old bank statements and unanswered emails, which scrolled as columns of incomprehensible text.

The family cat, Miss Kitty, a black fur-bag of neuroses covered in self-inflicted sores, straddled my knee. As I stroked her, she purred and rhythmically stabbed needle claws through my sweatpants into my skin. Somehow the pain soothed me.

Staring at the computer screen, I caught sight of a tiny square of Nanda's face, an icon linked to an animation I had created a year earlier. I had been listening to the haunting soundtrack of *La Double vie de Véronique,* a film score by composer, Zbigniew Preisner, while I examined the black and white portrait Nanda had taken of himself, the one where Nanda used my camera and leaned back into the skeletal forsythia with his arms wide open. His right leg pointed forward as if he could walk right out of the photograph. The same leg that was wrenched from its socket when struck by the train.

I enlarged the image, scrolled over him, and zoomed into his hands gripped around boney branches. Followed the edge of his jaw to his eyes. Hit the shift-command-four buttons on the keyboard, and with the cursor I stretched a square around his beautiful face to capture a screenshot. I magnified the fragment of photograph and incrementally took screenshots as I inched in closer. Screenshot by screenshot until his face disappeared to black. I recorded the string of pictures to last and end at thirty seconds, inserted a train whistle, included text, and a title. *Nanda, Breathe!*

I hadn't looked at the animation since the time I created it. Curious, I drew the curtains, put on a pair of reading glasses, turned the volume high, and double-clicked the animation icon. On the computer screen, his face pulsed and zoomed to the tip of his nose, through the tunnel of his nostril to darkness. From speakers, train whistles wailed. A pinhole of light appeared, grew larger, and before long, the words breathe, breathe, breathe, faded in and out as the whistles died.

I turned down the volume to stop the static buzz. Then remembered, the speakers were from Nanda's stereo. A couple of months before he died, I bought him a sound system. We agreed that I'd buy it and hold onto it until he finished the payments. He had one last payment due to me.

Kitty jumped from my lap. I sat dazed and then stood to observe the remembrance altar I made for Nanda. On top of the tall file cabinet draped in lace, much like an art pedestal, a mound of dried rose petals nested the last photograph I took of him. The photograph that had lived in Carmen's pocket. She took it everywhere until it went dog-eared and almost erased, then handed it back to me when she feared it could not last another day in a pocket.

In front of the photo, I had arranged grief-relics: a bowl of his ashes, a fresh pomegranate—an homage to Persephone, a dried red rose from Nanda's last bouquet, a test tube of my tears, a necklace of skeleton heads carved from snake vertebrae—a gift from Krispy, ink drawings of bones on hollow eggshells, charred photographs of me setting flowers on fire against a night sky, Nanda's cologne, his half-comb, broken abalone shells he had collected on our last beach walk, the wax vampire teeth I had sent to him on our last visit on Halloween, and two shrivelled daisies with no chance of resting in the cradles of his ears.

I returned to my work table and straightened a stack of crumpled pages of writing. My attempts at trying to connect lines of words to define loss. On one corner of the table, the neat pile of Nanda's Christmas presents, birthday gifts and his unsent birthday card called to me. *It's time.* Without hesitation, I tore the seal to the envelope, slipped out the card, stood it beside his portrait, peeled open his packages, and artfully positioned the assorted teas, art paper, brushes, watercolours and the stuffty lion onto his altar.

The last item was a square of white chocolate, his favourite, which I unwrapped, and with a blade, carved it into a bird. Sweet buttercream wings and the aroma of hot milk. Before Nanda died, I saw birds as free; after his death, they became handless creatures bound to the sky. Singing to survive, using pointed faces to peck through life, bit by bit, twig by twig, berry by berry, worm by worm. I saw birds as caged or tied to seasons, belting the air, never holding still, their hearts strobing in a fragile frame. *I feel like a bird.* I smelled the vanilla, the sugar, felt the urge to melt the chocolate bird in my mouth, but I made it for Nanda.

To celebrate the Day of the Dead, I sat the bird next to Nanda's photo with a new white candle. Quiet in solitude, although vulnerable, I felt grateful to have a space to move through sorrow, to be, to miss and gift my son, and for a moment, not feel loneliness, abandonment or dread. I found solace.

I breathed, breathed, breathed. Lit the candle and whispered, 'I'm okay.'

New Moon New-Self

Grief is not being able to escape the moon.

I joined a grief group to prepare myself for another holiday clusterfuck. The first meeting fell on an appropriately stormy day. I threw on a parka and stepped outside where cold air bit my cheeks and a dense cloud sat on my forehead. The drive across town was a straight shot to a group of cottages. A sign on the lawn read HOSPICE.

Winter loomed. December offered less daylight, more hours of darkness, seasonal affective disorder, and more sadness. I could not release the pressure, the apprehension, Nanda's birthday, days away on the 23rd of November, then Thanksgiving. Next, the dreaded day of his death, December 2. I still wanted to sleep through birthdays and the long ritual of Christmas. Forget New Year's Eve. Yet, after a year of grief, I was compelled to take the steep climb and jump into the crevasse of loss.

In the hospice parking lot, I thought to turn around and go home. I had never been a group-type person, but Flora suggested I go, and since I was in agony, I hoped it would offer some relief. I gritted my teeth, dragged myself out of the car feeling like a five-year-old and found my way through the front door. I arrived early. I had always been an early arriver, never wanting to walk into a room full of people, unless I was teaching or in charge.

A circle of folding chairs, ten or twelve, were arranged in the centre of a bland living room, the carpet, curtains and walls all beige. A woman, much younger than me, stood at the back wearing cream-coloured trousers and a pastel, floral blouse. Hands clasped to her chest, she introduced herself and welcomed me to take a seat. I noticed her long fingernails. I gave her a quick nod and stuffed my nail-bitten hands into my pockets.

Still in a parka, I sat in the chair closest to the exit. The curtains were drawn, offering a sense of privacy. A couple of shaded lamps gave the room an amber glow. At the appointed hour, women trickled in, quiet, heads hung, and were given the same welcome and directions until the chairs filled. Only women. I wanted to try the group first before I invited Rachel. *Why no men?* Roger would not have come. He hammered away at loss in his shop, cut and ground metal, invented tools, redirected his grief-energy to make useful things.

As the grief counsellor went over her credentials and the rules of engagement, I sat inside the walled-off chamber of myself. Everyone else looked equally hidden. Hands in fists, eyes half-closed staring into carpet, legs knotted at the knee, arms hugged to their bodies. I had to remind myself to breathe, drop my shoulders, sit up straight and blink.

'Let's have you introduce yourselves,' she said with a notepad and pen in hand. 'Start with why you are here.'

In my preoccupied brain, what was left of my fight-or-flight brain, I had failed to consider that I would have to talk, try to answer questions, or be a participant. Everything seemed disproportionate. Grief grew so big I could have swallowed the moon.

A petite, thirty-something woman, whose face didn't move when she spoke, wrung her hands, and said, 'My name is Irma, and I am here because my son David had a motorcycle accident. He was a street racer. He came around a curve too fast, spun across the divide and crashed into a fence.'

Hands wet with sweat, I slid them from my trousers pockets and stuck them under my armpits. I wanted to shriek. *How fucking reckless. He could have killed someone else.* Then, entangled in guilt, I remembered how Nanda stopped a train with his body, his drunkenness. I pressed my lips tight. I couldn't find it in me to honour her grief, let alone mine.

Our counsellor said the obvious, 'I am so sorry for your loss.'

What does that mean exactly? Why are you sorry?

I resisted an eye roll, knowing it would complicate issues. But there we gathered, a bunch of complicated issues, stepping on eggshells, patient and complicit. I imagined a speed course in grieving where we would expose our deepest thoughts, share our bizarre behaviours and wail like maniacs on the floor.

A hand went up and the counsellor encouraged the woman to speak. The woman refolded her lanky arms to her chest, untied her legs and planted her feet forward. She rocked and talked as strands of her long auburn hair swept back and forth across her knees.

'It's been almost a year. I came home from work to find my son, Andrew, overdosed on heroin.'

Waiting to hear the words killed, dead, died, which I never did, I grabbed my elbows and dug my thumbs in until it hurt. Somehow, I knew I'd be okay if these women divulged the worst, the crazy-grief, their vulnerable selves, but I didn't have heart-space to listen to them sidestep their sorrow. I also didn't have the guts to spill mine.

The woman next to her, fiftyish, volunteered to go next. Her chair was beside mine. She repositioned her body to sit tall, pressed her back into her chair, crossed her legs, and laced her fingers in her lap. I heard the air she sucked in through her nose.

'My name is Ann. This is my tenth year.'

Not a stir in the room. I looked at each woman's face. *Are they alive or dead?* They appeared to be dried leaves. I spiralled through a mental picture of my future. Doomed. *Ten years?* Traumatised, I looked at my watch, thirty minutes of grief group, not helpful. I fell into a stupor.

I can't do this. Have these women tricked me? I am a compressed toy moon. They will throw me through hoops, roll me back and forth, play keep away, forget I was once human, sit on me, press until I pop, reinflate me, toss me into the sky never to come down. I can't let that happen. Maybe I'm wrong. Perhaps one of them will make a clean, sagittal cut, divide my orb-body into two bowls, fill them with water, invite birds, float flowers, light little ghee wicks to flicker in little leaf boats. Or together they'll make soup, devour my insides. When they are done with me, I wonder if the counsellor will don the two half-spheres over her breasts, become a warrior. But no, I bet she'd hide them until forgotten. Perhaps I'd be rescued by a sad woman, brave enough to coax the counsellor to fill my halves with dirt and seeds, wait for trees to grow, chop them down, build a small house. Years would pass. Inside the house, there would be a shelf where the two pieces of me-moon would sit smouldering until the house burnt to the ground. Forget about me. From the ashes, they'd make ink, write about what still exists, draw a night sky of a galaxy of lost souls and a portrait of the woman in the moon. If I could talk to save myself, I'd convince one bold woman to make rhythm, to use the half-moons like coconut shells, clippity clop, to run like a wild horse. Better yet, run like hell, fire flowing. I'd ask her to hold me, bowls of myself engulfed in flames, balanced on open hands before God. Only then would I speak and scare everyone to death.

I imagined myself in a permanent foetal position, drooling, the family too worn out to visit. Of course, no matter, I'd be catatonic.

The room came into focus, words muffled. I regained a conscious state as the porcelain women looked at me, the counsellor's face quizzical.

'Would you like to go next?' she asked.

Short of breath, I shuffled, loosened my hands free, smoothed the parka under my butt, and relaxed my shoulders.

'I have a question. How long does grief last?' I asked and stroked my hands back and forth over my thighs, unsure of who to look at.

Everyone turned to the counsellor with looks of desperation. Her eyes caught mine. We studied each other. She smiled.

'Grief lasts forever.'

She kept talking, but I already understood her mindset. *Hell no!* And with serious intent, I vowed to change the grief-equation.

'I'll pass,' I said.

An awkward quiet. She smiled and nodded. 'Okay, perhaps next time?'

I didn't answer.

Instead, I felt rage. *How dare she tell me, tell everyone, that grief, intense distress and sorrow, lasts forever, an eternity of horrific uncontrollable pain of hellish emotions. How could that be true?*

My story of loss and grief, although I owned my story, when I mentally repeated what happened and how I felt, I resisted. It was not a story I wanted to be in, much less share unprocessed in a group. I also didn't want to feed her statement with what might be heard as unresolvable. Nanda could not be brought back from death. However, I could come back to life.

Intuitively, I knew there would be an outcome from grief, that maybe the pain would recede as it transformed into something soulful. I couldn't wrap my brain around how to use art to assist that process, but I knew of no other way.

As for the grief group, I continued to go, not to share, not for kinship or comfort, not to hold space for each other, but to listen, to observe how grief could be expressed, or more accurately, not expressed, withheld, confined to culturally acceptable guidelines, censored. In a culture that didn't incorporate death, dying or loss, I witnessed most grievers quicksand-stuck, mouthless or hanging, unreachable in the cave of loss destined to suffer forever.

No stranger to trauma, before Nanda's death, I had been transforming emotional wounds into meaning. The creative process built my confidence, gave me a voice, and a way to express uncomfortable feelings. I became stronger and wiser, able to observe my bouts of desperation and sadness as bad weather. *Wait, just wait, this storm will pass.* Art, a processing tool. And even though, after Nanda died, I believed art had escaped me, that everything I photographed was documentation, I had an inkling that photography might facilitate grief-vision, that grief might be an art medium.

Before I left for home, I asked the counsellor, 'Have you lost a child?'

I sensed she didn't know what to make of me; her eyes dodged mine.

'No, I, I don't have any children,' she replied.

The Western thinking world I lived in didn't embrace loss into everyday life, in everyday conversations, even in grief groups, that I could see. And because I had felt the rush of the liminal place of souls, kissed the railroad tracks, taken the animal of Nanda's blanket for a swim, worn his clothes and his ashes, I didn't know how to talk about loss without freaking people out. I knew I'd shock the grief counsellor if I mentioned how I found myself floating above the bed. So, I became a quiet mouse.

Will I ever be an artist again? Can I trust processing loss my own way?

The drive home took forever through congested traffic; I missed every green light. The sky swelled and grey lumpy clouds hovered, ready to push in the roof of the car as raindrops tapped against the windshield. I usually had the radio blaring, but I found comfort in the pushy wind whistling through window trim and the swish-tap of the windshield wipers. Almost reaching a hypnotic state along a liquid road, I finally rolled into the driveway and parked. Rain hammered down. My windshield view obscured into abstract paintings, a slippery world outside. I let the drumming beat through me. After five minutes of shivering and slow breathing with eyes closed, I lifted my eyelids, pulled the parka hood over my head, opened the car door and stepped into the downpour. Inflated with wind, the hood of the parka blew back like a second head and bounced at the back of my neck. Rain pelted so hard it stung my face. I closed my eyes, tipped my face to the sky and let the shower drench me, let water stream into my clothing. A river falling from the bardo, from heaven. I unzipped the parka, let it fall to the ground, stretched my arms wide open and absorbed a laying on of millions of hands from the celestial dome. The wellspring of grief flowed. *However many baptisms it takes.*

'Are you okay?' someone yelled.

I opened my eyes, dropped my arms and turned to see a neighbour seated in her car. The engine oscillated, steam rose from the exhaust. She couldn't see me sobbing in the wetness. I smiled with all my teeth.

'Absolutely! I am welcoming my new-self,' I said.

She squinted and pushed her face into the rain. 'Right on!' She laughed, gave me a thumbs-up and drove away.

My new-self was a new moon, not visible. I didn't have a clue how to build the unknown from scratch, what that might look like, how it might function or develop. As grief held my soul hostage, I repeated to myself that the unbearable agony would not last forever, but I also didn't have a plan.

On the night before the anticipated griefaversary of Nanda's birthday, the sky cleared for a brilliant full moon. I had just finished reading a book called *Physics and Astronomy of the Moon* which aside from advanced physics equations offered me details as to how a moon behaves. I meandered to our backyard to watch that bright circle-face rise.

I used to be in love with the lunar orb. I embroidered it on blue jeans, drew its smiling profile on my thigh, painted it into landscapes, photographed it reflected in rivers and ponds. I gave my first child, Arian, Moon as his middle name.

Having stood on the railroad tracks that fateful night, hardly rational, I wondered if the moon had somehow caused Nanda's death. Every time the moon became full, I had curtained the windows and closed the blinds to avoid that frightening ball of ash.

Lying across a picnic bench, I gazed up and saw the moon as stillborn from Earth, aborted into space by some mysterious celestial collision. Ninety-five million years later I could see Mother Earth still holding onto her dead child. I certainly didn't want to let go of Nanda. Nanda was that lifeless moon, able to ring like a bell from moonquakes, powerful enough to ebb and flow tides. A rotating moon, half in shadow and half-reflecting the light of life. There would always be the far side never in view. *I will never see Nanda whole.* My grief synchronised to his waxing and waning.

The moon is a stuck oracle cursed to push and pull. In that split second the moon shows full, it retreats. Disappears. Starts over. New moon. Cycling through invisible, to full, back to invisible. Madness. I watched the moon shrink into the sky. Poems streamed through me. A lullaby. Words to honour the moon's regulation of behaviour, of lunacy, a systematic return to calm. Weak to strong. Crazy to sane. Stupid to smart. Undone to done. Unloved to loved. Repeat. Like standing after a fall, then falling again, and getting up again. *Are we not trying to return to our full selves?* I wondered if that recycling would help me to heal grief. I wondered if I would ever be an artist again, able to extract meaning in the libration of consciousness and unconsciousness, truth and the unknown. I was willing to practise that madness.

I'd solve the equation: Nanda as moon, me as Earth. We would be ring-around-the-rosy beacons as we spun each other in orbit, casting shadows, reflecting light, over and over. Ashes to ashes. *I will not let go.*

A View from the Dark Side

Making Art With Intent

Pocket Fossils

Grief rises from the ashes; you will rise from grief.

I repeated, 'My son is dead,' until it became a mantra and still, I spent a year suspended in disbelief. Any pain I experienced before seemed puny in comparison to the loss of Nanda. Looking back at my old-self, the former depression-misery I considered unbearable didn't have much value in my new grief-world. I succumbed to grief, yet grief, a singular word, no definition I heard or read, matched my experience. So far, I knew grief as unpredictable, brutal, treacherous, turbulent, overwhelming, unbearable. A restless demon I could not stop. Kidnapped, held hostage, stripped, inverted, life stolen, friends and family replaced with imposters, I felt ill, chaotic, and trusted no one. Grief worked overtime, changed everything, and everything seemed unsalvageable until that day when Rachel's fresh eyes blew away my sad fog, cracked me open to see the process of art and how it had started without me. A new art-form had emerged. My new art-self, a grief-art toddler, finally found meaning—meaning in a bowl of ashes.

I knelt at the living room table and shook the ashes flat.

'You got this?' Rachel asked, letting her hair loose from the hair tie.

'Give grief a chance?' I said and gave her a semi-smile.

She nodded. Her waist curved swanlike as she leaned over to collect her backpack. Then she walked down the hallway, entered her room and closed the door quietly.

Window light dampened. Outside, a flint sky. I clicked on a photo lamp and positioned a circle of light over the bowl of Nanda's remains. My son was once a beautiful painting until a swift wind blew his watercolour grains off into that pumicey drift of faint pastels. I thought burying my face in those ashes would smother grief, but instead, grief surfaced, beckoned me.

I am unrealized.

Perhaps I was a portal, an extra-sensitive sieve collecting and dissecting for meaning. Organising the disorder. Eliminating what was not needed. Shaping the formless.

In a daydream, I hovered miles above, looking into the Nanda desert, eager to excavate and discover the archaeology of loss. Knowing his ashes were destined for the ocean in a few days, I retrieved Nanda's bag of things and his hand-sized abalone shell from the studio and brought them to the living room table to perform another inventory, to invoke the raison d'etre. I propped the shell up like a bowl and ran a finger over its rippled rainbow centre where I once saw him stroke his fingertips—tactile like his mother—then scooped the shell full of ashes. Camera readied, I pressed his pager in, then lifted it using a knife blade. The empty form left behind became the tomb of his messages, a reminder of our missed calls. I took a photograph and shimmied the unfilled space smooth. Next, I centreed his wallet into his ashes, tapped the curved leather until it sank, then pried it away to see the concavity like a worn depression in an empty bed. Another image captured. I levelled the remains and dropped his coins in face down; plucked them free to expose the indentations of spirit-spheres. His Gordon crest keychain appeared as a fallen headstone. His ATM card with his name backwards in relief, a sort of cancellation. All voids in which one could cast solid forms. Objects, easy to replace.

At the time of his viewing, it had crossed my mind to follow the mourning rituals of my Victorian ancestors, to make Nanda's death mask before he turned to powder. I could have moulded his head with clay, poured cement into that cavity to preserve him as a statue. Even if I had been given more time, I knew then that I didn't have the nerve to replicate the irreplaceable or live with his face as stone.

As the living room succumbed to dusk, the sphere of lamp light brightened. I allowed myself to shift from despair and followed the creative flow. With grief-vision, my energy surged. In an artistic state, right beside pain, I could see beauty and meaning in anything. I stayed. Observed. Took notes. Leaned in. Breathed through it. Nanda became the owl, the blanket, the moon, the currents of river. His fingerprints—precious poems. He did not inhabit his ashes, but somehow, I saw him in the space that wasn't ash. Nanda remained a life inside death.

One more item lured me. I hurried to the studio to collect Nanda's comb fragment, which I had saved in the altar on top of the file cabinet. His comb had lived in his trousers pocket, passed through his hair hundreds of times, a remnant bit of tortoise-shell plastic with his scent preserved in its teeth. I laid his comb into his ashes.

A couple of weeks after Nanda died, I'd gone to collect his remains from the funeral home to find a half-bit of comb taped to the box. I must have looked startled because the mortician consoled me. He placed his dove-like hand on my shoulder.

'Before the coroner's office transported Nanda, I had requested his comb be sent with his body.'

As he spoke, I felt dabbed with cotton wool.

'I thought it would be nice to style your son's hair with his own comb.'

Then I remembered a phone call the mortician had made a few hours before the viewing.

'How would you like me to style his hair?' he asked me.

'He combed it back flat with mousse.'

While waiting outside before Nanda's viewing, Carmen lamented, 'Oh, I wish I could do Nanda's hair; he makes such a big fuss over it. He likes his bangs all even. He'd be careful to make a clean edge. I can't imagine them getting that right.'

'Bangs? I thought he combed his hair slicked back with mousse,' I replied.

Carmen pulled the Polaroid image of Nanda from her trousers pocket, his bangs, the American word for fringe, made a clean line across his forehead. With my heart in my throat, I called the mortician to inform him that I was wrong about the hairstyle and requested he change it. Carmen reiterated how Nanda had been styling his hair forward; he would run the comb from the crown of his head to the front of his forehead till his short fringe lined his brow. Stiff with mousse, even and neat. I was the one who made that photograph, the one who focused on his face.

How could I not have remembered?

Riddled in guilt, I mulled over our situation: he and I lived two hundred miles apart, the new career job consumed me, I had full-blown depression, and our daily visits had been reduced to once a month. I saw him twice in three months. We were due for a visit.

As soon as I arranged the studio light over the shell, the comb imprint flipped concave to convex, appearing three-dimensional in Nanda's ashes. The comb imprint looked like unplayable piano keys, my son's melodies ended, his lyrics complete, not fragments and dust shaped like a comb, not vacant bone. *I am making art.*

No matter how sad, my creative process revealed the grief-roots that branched through my innards into the world, the universe, the ethers, looped back to self, selves, selflessness, to my art-self.

I can make art with intent. Grieve with intent.

With a microscope, I had probed into the caverns of Nanda's porous ash domain, used a spectrometer, and set flame to a fragment to analyse the colour of his spectrum.

Grief can be ordinary and extraordinary. That's art. And everyone is an artist, yet not everyone is aware of practising art. Even I was fooled, not realising that while making photographs, I had been longing to read his indecipherable cuneiform, to excavate for meaning, to tell stories, stories that reveal truth. Art is creativity and being human is a creative endeavour. Creativity is a process that engages individuality, intuition, thought, feelings, communication, collaboration, and expression, to identify, investigate, problem solve, uncover, and discover, to invent. Art is essential.

I brushed my hand across Nanda's ash to reset to a blank canvas, turned off the photo lamp and sat in darkness with a sense of belonging. Re-belonging to life. Healing! Improving with a sense of well-being. Inspired, and moved to use a camera, a secret box loaded with film magic, to create meaning from loss.

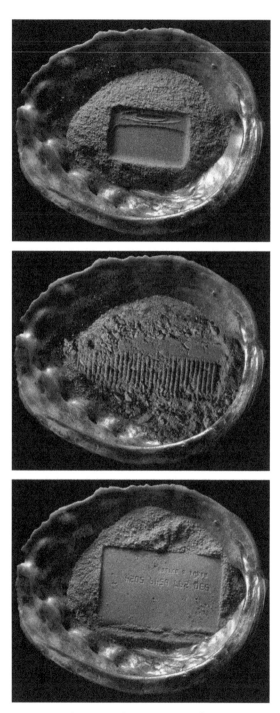

Pocket Fossils: Page, Comb, ID

Viking Ship

How do you heal grief? You grieve!

At age seventeen, Nanda read historical fiction and devoured sci-fi and fantasy books. Seated at our kitchen table paging through a novel about Vikings, he requested, should he die before me, his body be bound and sent out to sea on a ship in flames. He steadied a soup spoon of milk-soaked cereal to his lips and said, 'Think of it, a burning Norse ship headed to Valhalla, Hall of the Slain.' He smiled and crammed the food into his mouth.

I scoffed.

'I'm serious,' he said, with a mouth full of Cheerios.

Nanda fancied himself a warrior, lived vicariously through hero stories and the main character of his novel, *Kilran*. He was enamoured with a hero's journey ending in fire and glory. And although Vikings rarely performed funeral pyre ship rituals, after Nanda's death, I couldn't get that fiery vessel off my mind. I didn't have much time to see to a burial, much less a Viking ship on fire. My time and money could only afford the flames of a furnace, a cremation.

*

I planned for Nanda to be released into the ocean before the new year. A colleague from work who owned a sailboat docked at the Santa Cruz harbour offered to motor six of us into the Monterey Bay. He kindly agreed to take us beyond the one-mile buoy to spread Nanda's ashes. He did not offer to set his vessel on fire.

I invited Robin, and Arian asked his best friend, Pete, to join us. Roger, who had grown weary of seeing my sad face, relinquished his spot to Rachel's new boyfriend, Justin; the two lovebirds were inseparable. He told me Justin would be good support for Rachel.

I don't remember why Carmen couldn't join us, but I saved her a vial of Nanda's ashes, which later she returned to me and never said why.

I had constructed an ash vessel in preparation for the scattering. A vertical, quart-sized rectangular box made of white porcelain. I embossed Nanda's name in Sanskrit, Nityananda, *Eternal Bliss*, across the surface. I stained the pattern with ochre patina, stirred a scoop of his ashes into a glaze, brushed it thick over the relief, and high-fired the vessel to a brilliant gloss.

I worried that in the excitement of getting everyone to the harbour, I might forget the ashes. So, the evening before, I balanced the urn on the ledge of a pony wall near the front door where I kept my daypack and keys.

The morning announced itself like many December days on the coast, foggy. I referred to that time as Release Day even though I knew there wouldn't be any form of release for me, not in allowing his ashes to fall into the ocean. Release Day was not a proud introduction for a new musical, new book or product line. I had mindlessly used the word *release*. Obligation had set in due to the pressure from a barrage of repeat questions, typical comments, what every griever has heard.

'Are you feeling better?'

What does better mean? Is someone keeping a chart? How long do I have to feel better?

'You'll need to move on.'

To where? Here I am. I am where I need to be.

Because I had spent quality time photographing his ashes, I knew I could spill his remains into the sea. Letting go of ash did not mean letting go of Nanda.

I shifted through unconscious to conscious, without intent to with intent, vowing not to let go, move on or find closure. For me, the opposite made more sense, to lean in, hold on, stay, bust open to grief, embrace loss and make art with death. I had finally trusted the animal of myself to know how to heal.

Roger, Rachel, and I sat at the kitchen table eating pizza. A day full of woe, I had peeled my fingernails to half-mast, made sore cuticles bleed. I resembled a taut balloon.

We heard Arian, Robin and Pete talking in the driveway. I looked down the hall as the front door opened.

'Hey, Jane.' Pete smiled and flipped his hair from his face and cocked his head to eye Nanda's urn.

With hands to his chest, he retracted his fingers into claws. His wavy bangs bounced on his forehead as he tip-toe-bounced on his toes like a cartoon burglar ready to pounce on the urn. His nose almost touched the lid as he dog-sniffed. Arian, looking taller than usual, and Robin, grinning, right behind him, both glanced through the hallway into the kitchen to check my reaction. A bit of air escaped me. I smiled, not surprised; Pete had always been a goofball, able to bring light to tough times.

Pete used both hands, lifted the urn lid above his head, looked inside and flattened his chin to his chest. He side-glimpsed me and laughed like Kermit the Frog.

'Oh. My. God!' he said.

'Wickedness,' I said and snorted.

Robin, with his hands tucked into his hoodie pocket, approached the container of ashes and peeked in. 'Alrighty then. Hey Bud!' He freed a hand from his pocket to pat the urn's side, his cheeks blushing maroon.

'Awww, dude!' Arian busted out one of his couldn't-hold-it-back-uneasy laughs as he glanced at me, one eye squeezed shut.

Roger and Rachel had their eyeballs glued in my direction. Everyone cracked up, except me. I snickered under my breath afraid the grief-dam would burst. Pete turned to Robin, full toothy grin, his face as bright as a lighthouse on fire. With a Vanna White hand gesture directed at the urn, he spoke like a game show host.

'Insta-Nanda, just add water.'

The house blared with laughter.

'Holy shit, why hadn't I thought of that,' I said.

Robin dragged his hand across his face to gain composure. He lifted his head with an arched eyebrow and with his best James Bond impersonation said, 'Shaken, not stirred.'

It hurt to laugh, but I could not stop, eyes watering. It wasn't only me cry-laughing, everyone tear-blasted, some of us shamefaced.

For the past year, Nanda had vanished from my mind's eye. I could not hear his voice. In the hyperreal dreams, Nanda appeared once as a polished adult; otherwise, he usually entered as an imposter, like the dumpy relic that posed as him at his viewing. But there, with his friends, I heard Nanda wisecrack, riff stand-up comedy with the guys. Inappropriately fresh in a good way. Those young men brought me to the life of Nanda.

Before we left for the boat, at the last minute, I thought I was ready to surrender all his ashes, but I retrieved a handful and saved them in a jar just in case I missed a trace of him.

What if I discovered an incantation I had not yet tried.

On the beach, surveying the ocean, I couldn't find the horizon. Fog broke into thousands of baby clouds and reflected onto the shore where Heaven and Earth collided. The sunrise mirror bled mauve-pink into a liquid periwinkle blue, a watercolour painting I could step into, sail through. But when we boarded the boat, the fog fell over us as if the day had hung its head. At the bow, the water reflected a missing sky, the colour of pale remains. Lost souls surfacing to greet Nanda. Water behind the stern waved like mercury as my colleague, red-cheeked, his wind parker zipped to his chin, steered us into the bay. He cut the motor, and we drifted. The guys sat cross-legged near the bow. Rachel dangled her legs over the deck, her video camera latched to her eye. I leaned on the edge of the cockpit and see-sawed with swells. Wind whispered into my face, as mini waves lapped against the sides of the boat. Another mile out, thousands of shearwaters skimmed the ocean's surface, rows of them stitching the horizon's edge, taking turns dipping their heads into the sea. I stood shivering, buoyant with the swells, hypnotised by the sea's rhythmic patterns of lines and shapes.

'You can rest here,' I said.

And with hands purple and white-knuckled, I opened the urn. My colleague sat alone at the stern as we each took a handful of ash and eased Nanda overboard. I went last. He slipped through my fingers into the water. Nanda's cloud spirit-swirled on the surface then dove into a vortex of undulating light and shadow. I thought I'd feel loss after his ashes fell; instead, I stepped from finality to a beginning. The ocean took me with him. A place called us. Our container. Contained and not contained. Full and empty. A paradox of him being nowhere, yet the churning of ocean, that elaborate dispensing machine, could send him everywhere.

I see you in this tremendous moving body of water, swaying in the lap of the moon. You will touch every shore, be drawn across land, evaporate into the atmosphere, over hills, the highest mountain peaks, to circle Earth. *I will breathe you. You will rain into rivers, join waters underground and flow back to the sea. I will know where you are.*

The boat surged and plunged, a reminder of perpetual resuscitation. Minutes later, a constant pitch and roll brought my stomach to my throat. I leaned portside and threw up. No sea legs, but my grief-legs had grown.

'Oh dear, what a send-off,' I said.

We laughed. My colleague smiled but kept his head down.

'Got it on tape, Mom,' Rachel said and delivered a cheeky smile.

The day, a slow-motion blink, sun to fog, opened to blue. Nothing remains the same.

*

Late in the evening, the guys headed home. Roger and Rachel went to bed. Seated on the floor of the studio, in the dark, I found solitude beside restlessness. I thought I had exhausted the ashes, would feel some relief, but relief came knowing I had saved that handful. The jar of ash loomed at the centre of my work table. I could not make grief stop. I gave grief a seat and it took the whole room.

Grief is horrible.

I lay on the floor and stretched my arms and legs as far as they could reach.

But what's so wrong with horrible?

The damn Viking ship burned in my head. A self on fire. *Grief is relentless. I need to build a Viking ship.* Viking ship, hardship, a relationship to loss, an apprenticeship in grief, a courtship with death. I danced with mortality. Softened. Grief is not just about loss, an end, it is also a starting point, an extraordinary journey, albeit a solo journey. Grief is an unnavigable, uneven path, a descension with no place to land. It is not a matter of getting back up, but how to adjust to the fall. A nonlinear journey, no end in sight. I thought the grief-trance-walk through shadow would render life unilluminable. Now I was learning to see in the dark, to see life in death, life in loss, life in sorrow.

My eyes meandered around the studio, landed on Nanda's red blanket. I unpinned it from the ceiling, smoothed creased edges and rivered it across the carpet. Like a topographer, I conducted a careful field study, mapped mountains, valleys, lakes, rivers, tributaries, glaciers, and ocean, and memorised those territories of his red blanket. In his woven landscape, I envisioned a Viking ship sailing for Valhalla.

I made a choice to engage grief, embrace that beast, commit to that relationship, whatever it took to make grief familiar, so I could grow a self able to live with loss. Take charge. I didn't want to name grief wrong or tranquillise it again. Instead, I wanted to play with grief. Incorporate grief as a mantra, a meditation. Find out what it wanted, what it needed. Grief owned me.

Okay then, what does grief like to create?

I abandoned logic and worried that if I didn't build his boat by morning, he would never make it to the other side. Exhausted but caffeinated and sugar-rushed from devouring a box of German chocolates, I resonated through my evaporated-self to my big-enough-to-take-it-on art-self as I attached the camera to a tripod. Low on art supplies, I scavenged for sculpting materials and found a piece of cardboard, and at the top of the trash can, a diamond-plate textured stripe of gold foil discarded from the chocolate box. Using scissors and Scotch tape, I constructed a simple Norse ship, the size of a finch and set it between canyon folds of blanket.

In the kitchen, I designed a wick by soaking a twisted fragment of paper towel in butter, took a matchbox from the stove and headed back to the studio. I filled the boat full of ashes, poked the wick into the centre and lit it with a match. Behind the camera, I watched as the foil caught flame, melted to the blanket and fizzled out.

I needed water. But ideas were flowing, and water reminded me of the dry ice I had stored in an ice chest next to my work table. A day earlier, I had designed a friend's poetry book cover, created photographs of dry ice spiralling fog and rippling patterns. I went into the kitchen and got a cookie sheet and a bottle of water. Back in the studio, I filled the tray as a makeshift sea and formed the blanket into another landscape. Wielding tongs, I pinched out a couple of marble-sized bits of dry ice and submerged them. White ghosts flew from the wet. Another boat and wick made, and again they failed into a smoky molten mess. Nanda had already gone through the fire process, so on the third attempt, I nixed the flame, and having mustered what little energy I had left, Viking ship number three was smooth sailing. Alas, Nanda's little ship appeared to be a fine ambassador of loss. It drifted into darkness, then coasted into light.

I have gone mad, but this is my process.

I'd pay the ferryman, Charon, not with coins but with art, an alchemic offering, sacred geometry, the architecture of love from a mother's hands. Nanda floated on a jewel of loss, on a boat I could fit in my palm, into the bardo, through to Valhalla, from the world we once knew into our new world. I floated behind the camera. His ashes filled the boat, yet the boat was empty. I too was a little boat full of empty and hoped my new relationship with Nanda would fill that void.

My energy drained before sunrise. In a daze, I found myself on the floor, on my side, knees folded to my chest, watching dry ice tulle-fog-undulate over Nanda terrain. God was in the boat, the whole boat.

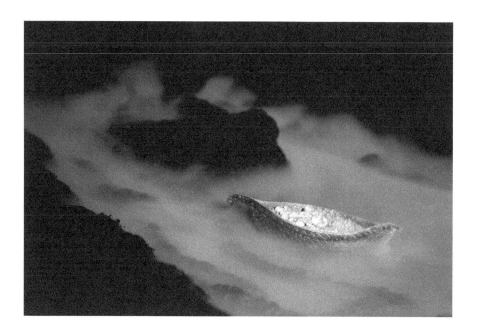

Transported

Memories of Flowers

In grief, you are the seed that requires light and darkness to grow, transform, and bloom.

By the year 2000, Roger and I had been married for eleven years. I could easily say we were still in love, or, in our bereaved condition, we tried our best to love each other, yet I felt invisible, alone-not-alone lonely. In my isolated head, I pondered that maybe he and all other humans might be figments of my imagination, cartoons I invented. Even in the most lucid of moments, I believed everything could melt like film caught in a projector, get stuck against the hot lamp, and burn to nothing. Although art helped me to survive, being creative came with a cost; an art-mind out of control could render me lost in a maze of possibilities. One such mind-altering query had me wonder about existence.

How do I exist? How does anyone exist?

After grad school, I had started a body of artwork titled 'The Alchemy of Flowers' about the perils of womanhood. I made colour photographic portraits, classical female poses superimposed with flowers with titles like: Lady's Slipper, Whoops-a-Daisy, Snapdragon, Flower Child, Wall Flower, Stigma and Black-eyed Susan. The loss of Nanda shut that project down.

I felt outraged at the audacity of the sun, it dared to rise every morning, and in spring, despite death, flowers turned into seeds and fruit. Flowers took on new meaning after seeing them strewn across the railroad tracks, stacks of them at the memorial service, piles of bouquets at Nanda's house, blooms in vases from consoling friends. Severed out of context, I saw flowers as corpses and imagined their extinction.

After losing Nanda, in a quest to understand death, I created a film called *In Memory of Flowers*, a peek into a future where humans had not experienced flowers and believed they never existed. The film's narration had three voices: the Voice of Myth stating how flowers were an elaborate construct; the Voice of Fantasy that spoke of flowers as wonderful, anaesthetising projections; and the Voice of Experience that had lived with flowers, explaining how they could never forget the sweet nectar of honeysuckle after pulling the stigma through fleshy white petals. At the end of the film, before the credits, I included a scrolling list of four hundred and sixteen flower family names in honour of *Schindler's List*.

Most of my artmaking before Nanda died focused on making sense of life. After loss, I found meaning in death. I oscillated between the two categories: alive or dead; then ruminated in the complexity, absurdity, and the mystery of both until everything presented as alive and dead. Massive art-brain fractalization.

What does dead mean? What does it mean to be alive? Why am I alive? Why is anyone alive? Am I the only one alive and everyone else some manifestation of my existence?

From this grief-minded state I had arranged to meet, one at a time, with a few of my closest friends and willing-to-participate family members to record our conversations in an existence experiment, what later would be referred to as a new genre of art performance. I spared Roger, as he had helped me with other art projects and because he was a man of few words, not his thing. For some reason, lost to me, I did not include Rachel. I planned to have each participant sit in front of a simple black backdrop taped to a wall while I faced them positioned behind my video camera.

'Listen carefully. You'll get a chance to respond,' I instructed.

I waited a minute to evaluate their reaction.

'You do not exist. You are a manifestation of my psyche. I created you.'

Again, I checked their reactions.

'Why would I create you?' I asked.

*

Faith had been my friend for sixteen years and knew me better than anyone. She volunteered to be the first subject. I drove to Davis and set up a portable photo studio in her guest room. She relaxed on a pile of pillows; her tawny hair spilling over her high cheekbones, onto her shoulders and across her magenta T-shirt. Gazing into the camera, she puckered her lips and made a kiss sound. Sinking further into the pillows, the backdrop fell off the wall, and she scream-laughed. We retaped the backdrop in place and conversed for a couple of hours.

She ended with, 'You know, I think you created me, so you had a double, and in case you ever doubted yourself, you could turn to me, which is you really, or your psychic doppelganger. That doesn't always work, though, right? We often fight.' She leaned forward; her face filled the frame. She widened her neon-blue eyes and said, 'How long can you stare into a mirror?' She shrieked, collapsed into the pillows, and we hard-belly cackled.

*

Luca sat in a chair against the black velvet panel in my studio, his face never still, hundreds of micro-movements every minute. He wagged his finger at the camera. 'I'll need an appropriate pronoun if we are going to have this conversation. How about jy for my, jee for me, jou for you, jwee for we, jus for us, jour for your, ji for I?' he asked.

I tried not to laugh. He looked away, sucked his lips into his face, bulged his eyes and blinked. Aimed his gaze into the camera lens and twisted the soul-patch on his chin.

'To be honest, hearing I do not exist is a crushing blow. I am thus irrelevant. The I, what I perceive, which in truth is what ji perceives, starts to disintegrate, as jwee integrates.' He continued to explain. 'If you, Jane, ask me/jee a question, you would be asking us/jus a question, and my/jy answer might not matter, unless what I refer to as me is hidden from the Jane creator part.' He crossed his arms in front of his chest. 'Why would you want to do that to me, I mean jee, or I should say, why would jou want to do that to jee, to jus?'

*

I drew the shades behind the lace curtains in Mum's bedroom and had her on a cushioned stool with just enough room on a spot of shag carpet between a mahogany dresser and a king-sized bed. The backdrop was taped to her mirrored closet door. Mum had her hair done at the

243

salon, a stiff bell shape made of frosted blonde curls, painted her face beige, blushed her cheekbones, lined her yellow-green eyes and brows, and swabbed her lips raspberry. In tan trousers and a ruffle-rimmed, silk blouse, she placed her hands in her lap, nails polished to match her lips. She rolled her shoulders back, bosom high, and smiled for the camera.

'Oh, I know, my Mouse. I am a ghost. If you are me, then I am my mother,' she said and smiled again, like posing for a formal portrait.

'Can you say more?' I asked. I looked away, so she'd gaze into the camera.

'Who we are, it is frightening, like one big dream. You think you know who you are or who you want to be, but no, you are not, cannot be.' Her shoulders sank. 'I know you think I am a bitch,' she said with a tight smile, 'and I think you are a bitch too. And that's okay; we know each other.' She raised her chin, tipped her head to one side as she looked away. 'But what I have that you don't have, I am funny, very funny, and you are not.' She glared into the camera. 'You are serious. But you are interesting. I learn from you. I am better because of you. And since I am you, then you are better too.' Her eyes tear-glinted as she turned her body into a three-quarter turn, a classic portrait pose, wove her fingers together in her lap and smiled, yet again, picture-perfect.

*

Arian, also a man of few words, said he represented loyalty. He sat on the floor against the kitchen wall in the apartment he shared with Claire. With a fresh-shaven face, hair in slick waves, he positioned his head centre to the camera frame. Biting the side of his lip, his eyes never left the lens.

'I am probably your horrible childhood repeated, from loss, lots of loss. Most of what you experienced, I experienced too. My father not being there for me. You and I were both homeless. Both of us have lost friends and family. I don't think you meant for things to turn out the way they did. When childhood problems aren't resolved, the trauma manifests in other ways, it's not your fault, but I am your other way,' he said and winced.

He shifted from the camera lens and looked me in the eye. I couldn't

244

disagree. I tried to solve problems, but some problems I created. He might have been correct, my horrible childhood impacted his childhood, my kids' childhoods. As a baby, a child, he took the brunt of my complex post-traumatic stress disorder, depression, boundarylessness, poor self-esteem, and my obsessive compulsive disorder behaviours. I loved him and cared for most of his needs. But he was my first child, and given my lack of maturity, with very little self-awareness or experience, I didn't know how to raise a child. I cut my mother-teeth on him.

*

Being an artist meant the pendulum from sane to crazy swung wide. So far, no one had questioned my sanity. No one until I presented the idea to Dad.

*

After I set up to record Dad in his home office, he entered the room dressed in a crisp, white shirt and pressed trousers, a shiny black belt and polished lace up shoes, his white hair perfectly sheared into a military crew cut. I had barely finished the first sentence of my existence pitch when he scootched to the edge of his leather desk chair with his fists in his lap and drilled me.

'Rubbish! Surely you can comprehend that your project, ideas and logic have failed. The nerve to proclaim such utter nonsense. I brought you into this world. That is a fact.'

Dad went on to elaborate about how Mum had given birth to me. His face reddened and grew tighter, eyes near shut. He shot a pointed finger at me with each word. 'You did not exist before me.'

*

I stashed the recordings into a box and stored them in a closet, not knowing if I'd ever use them. In the process, I discovered an illogical truth: I existed for myself first, and everyone else existed after me. What I found confusing was the power and inconceivable idea of someone dead and gone. While I tried to think of Nanda as missing

245

or having moved on, it left me with unrequited hope. A dear friend of mine said, 'We have been robbed.' I agreed, yet I could not steal him back.

Does he exist now, but not in human form? Did Nanda ever exist?

In my art-head, Nanda was a flower, lost in the realm of extinct flowers, where time and longing altered the voice of reason. Stuck somewhere between fact and fantasy, the plain truth failed to support his existence. Death being profound is an understatement. I searched for Nanda. Looking for a flower shaped by the deepest grief.

The urge to see existence as my own dream, formed a floral myth. There is no correct method for creating or interpreting meaning. Without need for reason or logic, I followed my own process, my own artmaking, my own truth, and my art-self.

When I relinquished Nanda to the sea, in my mind, most of him sank into the stratigraphy of the ocean floor, some particles floated to the moon. In my being, he was a flower fossil waiting to be cracked open in a million years.

At the scientific academy, the inspired palaeobotanist will rise from her chair to receive honours for discovering *Homo sapiens nanda flora*. She will read from her papers, describe the obvious; he was gorgeous and short-lived. Share the evidence of his life, just enough proof needed to justify his existence, the theories, and the folklore. In her quest for answers, she will dream of him blooming, consider the seeds still to be unearthed and imagine his resurrection. His flower image will be etched on a brass plaque, hung in some brilliant hallway of art and science.

I hope she discovers me beside him, a trace of our belonging, together a rare fossil. She'd dissect my cells and release memories of flowers.

In the apron of spring, I buried Nanda like a seed.

I will not forget.

Roots to the core, he erupted through the earth, his tender leaves unfolding for the sun. He became the Austin roses Roger planted in the garden. I recognized Nanda's sweet pea smiles. He was a forget-me-not, the little flower that shouted his name. His head, an Easter lily bent over tender violets. Nanda, the intoxicated poppy, wading in each vase I filled, his perennial arms wide open. His body, an unearthed bulb, whose potent blooms of narcissus multiply into offerings of perseverance even when evidence dwindles and the masquerade of

Nanda's eternity bares no proof. Nanda is the weeping camellia. Who else could recite poems beneath my bedroom window?

How could you not exist?

Beside the railroad tracks, with God in the field, the whole mustard field, I wished him back. As my feet sank into cool, moist ground, the Nanda blanket fragranced anise and sage, snagged the warm hands of spring. Bees whirred. Beetles clicked. Blackbirds tweedled their songs, darted from the fields to draw lines in the sky. With fresh sprigs of mustard blooms nestled behind each of my ears, I listened. I could hear his daisy whispers. Petals falling to the ground. Dragon lily's blood-red pollen spilling. Each time the train came near, he was the wildflower who faced the light.

Voices in the Mustard Fields

Projections

'In the dark I see ...' – Nanda

By the end of the second year of grieving, I had evolved from a zombie to an efficient slogger. If I kept busy, limited daytime hours and social interactions to tasks, I'd feel buffered, or at least the blade of grief in my chest felt less sharp.

However, my obsessive-compulsive disorder ran a behind-the-scenes program in my brain: ruminating on thoughts, images and ideas connected to Nanda. Sleep still fitful, filled with Nanda ruminations. The biggest dilemma: holding memories. I was permeable.

Any hour, day or night, anything I could think of related to him I'd jot down on pieces of paper. I placed a pen and pad in every room of our house, in my daypack, car glovebox and school office. The minute I committed a memory to paper, it changed, my first recollection irretrievable; words replaced the memory and corrupted the original raw memory-data.

Words rode in my pocket. Words scribbled on crumpled bits of paper piled up on the dresser, bookcase, file cabinet, and my work table. Word shrapnel would blow through a room when I opened a window or door. Organising these word-bits seemed impossible, so I emptied a file drawer in the studio, collected the pieces of writing and fluttered them in. The potpourri of sentences flowed in layers each time I slid the drawer open or shut. *The Nanda Drawer.* When it reached half full, I logged the bits and pieces of him into phrases, then forgot what those words meant. I inventoried notes into topics: conversations we had, looks on his face, the way he said things, his body language, lucid dreams. Desperation grew as I harvested and preserved what I tried to remember, most of which diminished into a property thinner than space. I was still losing him.

'Ephemeral' popped out of the word layers. Such a lovely word. A spiritual word. A new mantra. I wanted to understand how to accept impermanence. Life is transitory. Everything changes, everything changing, everything changed.

A few weeks passed. Multiple piles had been dumped into the Nanda Drawer. I tugged the drawer open and words collided. Some stinging words. Triggering words. Nonsense. One-liners. 'I love death' slid next to 'Death knows what I love.' To shuffle again, I slammed the drawer shut, and reopened it. 'What was he thinking?' connected to 'I don't know what to think.' Words flew in swarms. Passages joined. Some phrases fell apart, some held hands. Whole pages revealed themselves.

Perhaps my story will write itself.

Seated at the computer, after logging in random sentences from the Nanda Drawer, I felt compelled to search Nanda's computer and found another curious document titled *Dark and Light*. What followed was one continuous line of type, some sort of poem.

'*In the dark I see images dark takes light into itself if all was dark there would be nothing if all was light there would be nothing.*'

Words much like my own. *Dark takes light into itself.*

I imagined Nanda standing on the railroad tracks, moonlight penetrating his skin, moon in the man, in his blood, riding the rhythm of his heart muscles, churning in his stomach, illuminating his brain, filling his lungs, exhaled as his last breath.

The moon, a camera, captured Nanda beams, absorbed him, a man in the moon, and ricocheted an endless projected loop. *I want to stand in that loop.*

Earlier, I had pinned Nanda's blanket to the ceiling like a curtain, a couple of feet from the wall. I left it there to dry following the Viking boat photo shoot and didn't get around to taking it down. When I swivelled the chair to stare into the red weave, I envisioned a screen, an invitation to project my son's face. *To project is to give light to something.* From my photo archives, I found a slide of Nanda's smiling face, a transparent image the size of a postage stamp, a copy of the Polaroid that once lived in Carmen's pocket. I slid the transparency into a projector, hit the on-switch, and adjusted the lens until light filled his blanket, then enlarged the image of his head to the size of mine. Some of him remained on the surface of the blanket, while the rest of him filtered through the weave to the wall. For a moment, gravity suspended. I didn't expect to find an illuminated pocket of

Nanda between wall and blanket. His blanket. A flag. A dreamcatcher. Both of us caught in its fibrous net. Our secret meeting place. A wish. A prayer. Another attempt to bring him into being. In that glowing space, I let the gleam of Nanda's face mask mine, seep into my eyes, into my skin, into my brain. I thought I could not resurrect him, but I had. The forever Nanda. His projection, as colourful as life, suggested he existed, yet I questioned whether I saw him alive or just the reflection of his body.

What is the physical I am so attached to?

With camera aimed, I recorded the projection of Nanda falling through the blanket onto my face. Our shared illumination, another endless loop of light secured into a photograph. If the camera did not catch the light, our collaged reflection, our latent image would dissipate exponentially until it could not be perceived visually. Lost. But not gone. Like the moonlight reflected off Nanda, still travelling into the universe.

Practising madness didn't make me mad; it made me an artist. I was art, darkness taking light into itself. My psyche exploring and seeking expression. A mother loving her son.

Self-imposed

Sharing Nanda's Blanket

Grief is when you mistake a blanket for your loved one.

The sky, slate grey. A hovering mist. At the back of our house, under the feathered canopy of the pine tree, droplets hung and fell from branches. I listened to the yard drip. As I flattened the small of my back to a cool, stucco wall, my boots slid across moss into mud until the tension in my legs wedged me in place. Behind closed eyes, I imagined the blanket wrapped around Nanda. Then the blanket alone, like the skin of a pomegranate once ripened in spring faded to winter. The blanket a wound. A poultice. A prayer-cloth saturated with his light. Light years of Nanda. Even the shadow of the blanket—full of him.

I bit an edge of fingernail, peeled it off and spat the sliver to the ground. *What if I photographed family and friends with Nanda's blanket? What would they say? What would they do?* I inspected my hands. The moons in my fingernails had slid down beneath the nail folds. I bulldozed the cuticles with my two front teeth until the skin split. Still no moons. Next to me, the camellia wept. I shoved myself off the wall and extracted my feet from the suction of soggy earth.

Blanket Share Number One:
Flora Shows Me the Future

Grief vision is learning to see in the dark.

Therapy with Flora involved sitting across from her in an overstuffed floral armchair with her polka-dotted dog, Lilly, lying over my feet. Anytime I looked at Flora, the shape of her mouth, her eyes, her lunar face, I imagined her to be my older-self. She served me hot chocolate in a handcrafted mug. Offered me a bright blue Fiesta plate piled with home-baked cookies. We discussed creativity, resilience, and loss. I showed her my art; she showed me hers. Large colourful oil paintings of spirits and flowers. I read her my poems. She suggested I apply to Ellen Bass's writers' group. I did. Although the wait to get in could have been two years, Ellen accepted me that week. My grief story birthed as prose poetry. Ellen Bass, my midwife.

Flora left the room and shortly returned carrying a crystal ball like a baby in her arms.

'Look what I have. I love these,' she said as she gazed at me through the fortune-teller's globe. 'Did you bring Nanda?'

I loved how she considered Nanda present. I collected the blanket and my camera from my tote and joined her on the veranda in search of light. She sat the glass ball on a table, then arranged the blanket into several different shapes until balanced on the wrought iron fence. Relaxed into a chaise lounge, she grasped the clear sphere with both hands, turned to me and smiled.

'Tell me what you see?' she asked.

Camera to eye, I zoomed in on the crystal ball, bringing its inside scene into focus. My breath skipped.

'Oh weird, I see Nanda, cloaked in red, standing in your garden.' I adjusted the lens, brought Flora into view and took a photograph.

'He isn't completely gone?' she asked.

She held the ball still. I lowered my camera, moved in closer to savour the vision—beyond imagination—my future included Nanda.

A couple of years later, Flora revealed she had Alzheimer's and stopped seeing clients. I suspected it when she began asking me to share things I already had and reacted as if hearing them for the first time.

'I will forget everything we've shared,' she said, tearful.

'I won't.'

Tell Me What You See

Blanket Share Number Two: Arian and a Swing for Nanda

Another's grief is not yours to express.

Within weeks after Nanda's death, Arian's girlfriend, Claire, left him. Couch surfing, he rarely answered his cell phone. I often drove to Davis to search for him and usually could find him. He wasn't just grieving. I suspected his problems were complicated, ones only he could solve. I suggested programs.

'Fuck programs,' he said.

I feared I'd lose another son.

When I could find him, he'd spend the day with me. I'd feed him, give him information about various resources he might find helpful, careful not to trigger him into disappearing.

Arian, a natural artist, never refused to help me create art. I felt reluctant to ask him, afraid Nanda's blanket might rip open his tender heart, but I asked anyway, knowing he'd be honest with me.

'I guess,' he said. He yawned, laced his fingers together and stretched his arms to his knees.

Arian was staying at a friend's house. We walked through a dim, closed-curtained living room to the backyard, mostly dirt, dried weeds, the fences covered in ivy. It must have been above one hundred degrees, both of us baking. The glare of noon sun reflected off bare ground; I could hardly open my eyes.

'Well, what do you want me to do?' he asked, avoiding eye contact.

'This might be asking too much,' I said.

'No, it's fine, really.' He glanced at me with a half-smile.

'You're sure?'

'Absolutely. I need to.' He sighed.

'How would you pose with Nanda's blanket?' I asked.

Arian grimaced, sucked in, expelled a loud breath and extended his hand. I gave him the folded blanket. He grabbed a corner, raised his arm and let the fabric hang. Walked past an empty fire pit over to a metal garden swing under the shade of a tree and laid the blanket on the seat. From the back of the yard, he retrieved a wooden chair, placed it in the sun next to the swing and sat.

I brought the camera to my eye and just before the shutter clicked, he dropped his head. After that, I couldn't bear to make him do any more.

Arian and the Nanda Swing

Blanket Share Number Three: Robin on Leave

Right beside grief is love.

Robin joined the Coast Guard soon after Nanda's death. On his first leave, he visited Santa Cruz to see me, both of us grief-heads. In a sun-filled backyard, I set Nanda's blanket, folded in a square, onto Robin's outstretched hands. Camera readied, I clicked away as he pondered the blanket.

'I kinda wanna fold it like a flag, the one you get at a military funeral, but that'd be flipadoodle,' he said.

He paged the folds of the blanket like a book, then placed it on the table, pressed his hands on top and leaned in hard.

'I'm not getting a read.' The sides of his dimpled face twitched. 'I'm going to climb the tree with Nanda.'

The second time someone referred to the blanket as Nanda. Robin wore the blanket over his shoulders like a giant kid playing superhero. Halfway up the pine tree, about fifteen feet, he wedged himself into the crotch of a fat limb, hands clutched to branches, and chuckled.

'Unfortunately, I don't have the same nerve as Nanda. He would've gone much higher, all the way.'

Later he gave the Nanda blanket a ride around the yard in our Radio Flyer kiddie wagon. He paused every few steps and glanced into the lens, faster than I could click the shutter.

'Remember the Polaroids?' I asked.

'Sure do.'

In the places where Nanda had posed for the Polaroids, Robin posed wrapped in the blanket.

'Are there railroad tracks close by?' he asked.

'On the other side of that fence,' I said.

He made a classic Robin face: eyes bulged, mouth sucked in so tight his dimples formed parentheses.

When we arrived at the railroad, Robin tucked the blanket under his arm and sprinted down the tracks, shrunk to a dot, then pivoted on one foot and ran towards me. I imagined Nanda until he was Robin again, but then he lay down across the ties. If it hadn't been daylight, I would have collapsed. Robin matched the image I had embedded in memory—my son splayed across the Nanda Junction. Robin readjusted himself, placed the wadded blanket like a pillow between his head and the rail. He pulled a cigarette from a pocket, lit it, inhaled slowly, then cracked his lips and let the smoke seep from his body. I sat next to him, relaxed, as the sun sank out of view. Being connected to Robin felt almost like being connected to Nanda.

'Okay, I'm done,' he said. 'Ice Cream?'

Robin on the Tracks

Blanket Share Number Four:
Bill Holds Nanda

Grief knows your shame.

I thought I made progress, found a means of expression, but anger set in. Anger, I didn't do anger. That fury was hardwired to never surface, yet I had enough rage to run a power plant. Daily two-to-three-hour workouts at the gym seemed to inhibit the urge to boil over, but of all the emotions grief produced, shame buried me alive. I continually had to talk myself out of blame; the roots of guilt penetrated deep.

The night filled with condemnation instead of sleep, I racked my brain to find the logical equation, again, and again, various combinations of what I said, and didn't say, did and didn't do, determined to make a case against myself. Set on repeat, thrashing and wallowing, the Nanda freight train would take a rampaging detour through my head. The Nanda train had been running alongside me, and for the most part I managed to avoid its path with the occasional reminder tap or forceful whirlwind, but nothing like that knock-down, drag-out pillage. Eventually, I'd crash, but reawaken at 2:08 a.m., nose touching the ceiling, then 5:30 a.m., suffering a lack-of-sleep-anxiety hangover.

Each morning offered the challenge of determining the priorities for the day, but I'd forget them. I'd write them down and lose the list. I remembered to brush my teeth, but so hard my gums bled. And, without thinking, I collected hair from my hairbrush to roll into balls. Repetition was a friend. Too tired to make a decent breakfast, I'd buy a latte and a pastry at the local café to start the day. On the drive to work, my fingernails served two rounds of chewing, almost three, which included cuticles.

After a few years of grief, out of the blue, loud and clear, I said to myself, 'You will never be able to have a conversation with Nanda ever again.'

I'd never be able to tell him what a jerk I had been, how insensitive and inappropriate. Cinched in regret, my whole being soaked in shame. I made a trip to Davis to talk to my former therapist, Bill. Told him how I had carelessly revealed my suicidal tendencies to Nanda. His face dropped. So did mine. We both agreed that even though Nanda did not take his life, he put his life in danger.

'The thing is, guilt is like a rocking chair,' seated on a plush chair, Bill rocked as best he could, 'you keep rocking, but you get nowhere.'

Bill could shape his eyes, two lit beacons, into sweet-sorrow homing devices.

'You don't want to keep carrying this, right?' he asked.

'Right.' My eyes burned, but I could feel some ground beneath me. 'Accidents happen.'

Bill bent forward with his elbows on his knees, his head askew with wide eyes, his chin rested on his clasped-in-prayer hands. 'Nanda was highly intoxicated, his judgement and decision making dangerously impaired.'

We looked at each other, into a circular space that people gaze into when they are one unit.

'I brought his blanket,' I said.

Bill relaxed back into his chair with his legs stretched in front of him. He lifted his hands above his head and smiled. A whole-face smile. I gave him the blanket. He wrapped his arms around the folded blanket and hugged it to his chest.

'I know he was nineteen, and I respect him as a man, but for you, he is your child. So, I am going to get on the floor to meet eyes with your child.'

My child. Nineteen years young. I wanted to accept Nanda's death as an accident. He made a mistake. I could have made the same mistake, inebriated, .20 blood alcohol. I could have waited on those tracks for thirty seconds thinking I wasn't in the path of the train. And drunk, I might not have moved.

Bill Holds Nanda

Blanket Share Number Five:
Dad and the Nanda Sash

An open conversation about death facilitates an open conversation about grief.

I got Dad on the phone a few days after Nanda died to inform him what had happened. I listened for a reply. I heard my throat gulp and my breath distort. Birds twittered outside the window. A car drove by. Roger walked through the hallway. Rachel's TV mumbled in her bedroom. *Ah jeez*. I twisted and stretched my back.

'Dad? Are you still there?'

He cleared his throat and lowered his voice to a bass tone. 'Yes.' A sigh escaped him, the length of me hoping it would stop. Then, in slow enunciation using the Queen's English, he said, 'If you could be so kind as to bring the boy's cap.'

A week later, I offered him Nanda's baseball hat. Dad hesitated, then took it and turned away.

'Bloody son of a bitch,' he said.

After placing the hat on a bookcase shelf, he went to the living room window and cracked the blinds, slid his hands into his trousers pockets and peeked through to a clouded sky. His bottom lip protruded, military shoulders went limp. With closed eyes, he waved his head side to side.

'If you'll excuse me,' he said, about faced and swift-stepped to his bedroom.

I assumed he went to change his clothes for our photo shoot. And indeed, minutes later, he sported Scottish attire: a Gordon Highlander kilt, a country tweed jacket, wool knee-socks, a sporran at his waist and a sgian-dubh—a sharp dagger—strapped to his calf. He topped his head with a Balmoral cap. Dad loved to be photographed and looked forward to our session with Nanda's blanket. He suggested a hike in a nearby park with a view of the Pacific Ocean, a short drive from his home.

Sun blasted through stratocumulus clouds, brisk wind danced in all directions, whipping my hair into my face. Dad pleated the blanket lengthwise and draped it over one shoulder. We walked briskly along

Avila Beach to the start of a trail, where a rocky path zigzagged up jagged bluffs. *Oh, of course, he meant a cliff with a view.* At that time in my life, Dad wouldn't have been able to lower me into a cave. I'd grown. I looked at my hiking boots and then at Dad's Ghillie brogue shoes, high polished leather tops with slick polished leather bottoms, and made a face he recognized as disapproving.

'Don't worry about me, worry about yourself,' he said as he headed onto the cliff.

Dad, fit but almost seventy, staggered across rocks and clambered over boulders in those slippery shoes. He precariously balanced in his heavy woollen skirt with the Nanda blanket enfolded to a shoulder and climbed higher.

I lagged and watched through the eye of my camera as he stretched his arms across a slab of brittle geology, scoria and tuff, chips of rock loosening under his weight. He managed to hoist his chest and the blanket onto a crumbling shelf, legs struggling for a foothold. A gust of wind lifted his kilt over his head and the family jewels were displayed for all to see. Yes, I took the photo. Bottom in the ocean breeze, shoes without traction, his legs bicycling in air, muscles taut, he shook as he shimmied and then scrambled up the cliff face, muttering 'Damn it,' and 'Jesus Christ.'

'Oh shit, oh shit,' I yelled and started to climb.

By the time I reached Dad, he had brought both knees, scuffed in the process, onto the ledge, righted his kilt and stood with shoulders proud.

'Bloody hell! Did you get that?' he asked, grabbing my shoulder.

'Get what?' I answered.

'Right then, tally-ho,' he said.

He climbed five hundred feet, almost to the top. I followed but stopped at an escarpment below him and aimed the camera upward. The crescendo of our relationship.

He refolded the blanket into a sash, positioned it across one shoulder, and stared into the ocean.

'How do I look?' he asked.

'Amazing.'

Dad had the best posture I had ever seen, and funny enough, people would say the same about me. Dad tried various heroic stances, his gaze stuck to the sea.

'What do you think happens to us when we die?' I asked.

He scoffed and straightened his tie. 'I'm not one for mumbo-jumbo reincarnation nonsense. Your heart and brain stop, your cells collapse, and you are no more.' He ran a flat hand over the Nanda blanket against his chest. 'Like a battery, you fail. That's it, nothing else.'

I admired Dad for leading me to the top of the cliff, dressed in full regalia to honour his grandson, how he stood at attention with his eyes fixed on the coastal waters where I last left Nanda. We lingered with the sounds of breaking waves, gulls overhead, and wind whistling through rock formations. When Dad relaxed, spread his feet apart, and clasped his hands behind his back, I imagined him saying, 'At ease soldier.'

Dad clutched the blanket and skied in his slippery shoes as we descended from the rockface to the gravely trail. Along the beach headed to the parking lot we strolled wordless. He sat on a curb, blanket intact, removed his shoes, dagger, and socks, poured out sand and brushed his feet clean with his hand.

He looked at me and said, 'Sometimes I see Bibby.'

'Say what?'

'I still hear her.' He stuffed his socks into a pocket, shoved the dagger into the waistband of his kilt and slipped his shoes onto his feet.

I noticed a silver glint of tear at the edge of his eyes.

I could soften.

Dad rolled the Nanda blanket into a neat bundle and secured it under his arm.

I might love him.

He nodded, stood, and marched past me to the car.

Dad and the Nanda Sash

Blanket Share Number Six:
Mum's Heaven

What you believe might not be true; what is true you might not believe.

During one of Mum's week-long mid-year visits, she came knowing she'd be posing with Nanda's red blanket. All gussied up, she wore her hair in perfect waves, shimmery blue eyeshadow, coral lipstick, painted arched eyebrows, cheeks rouged angular. I brought her to work with me. Mum, always eye-catching, wore a shimmering silk blouse of pale pinks and blues, tucked into white linen trousers. Before my thirty students entered the photography classroom, she nabbed a chair at the front, crossed her legs at the ankle, placed her handbag on her lap, and clasped her hands on top of her bag.

I lectured about the frame of the photograph, the window that defines what comes in and out of the edge, and what is and is not included in the final image. In context and out of context, and how that changes the content and ultimately, the meaning. How the photographer defines that edge between the viewer and the world. The photograph no more than a split second of a minuscule perspective of the world.

Mum sat quiet for the entire three hours of class. After the students left, she handed me a scallop-edged pink piece of folded paper, dainty flowers printed around the border.

'Oh, thank you, Jane. I had no idea what you do. I thoroughly enjoyed myself.'

I opened the note to her lacey handwriting.

This multi-talented young lady took me to college. I needed to learn, and so I did. It was there I realised how very proud I am to have a daughter who has brought me great joy with her magical moments in the art world. Taking me away from reality, from a world so stale, in comparison to her vivid imagination.

I love you, Jane. Love Mum

I loved hearing that she loved me.

That night, after Roger went to bed, Mum and I sat together on the living room couch to share a bottle of wine. I asked Mum what she thought happened to people when they died.

'Are you talking about Nanda?' She drank the last sip of wine from her glass. 'I think of Nanda, not as a grown man, but as a little boy in heaven with cute animals.'

My brain did a three-sixty. For a minute, I thought it could be true. I felt comforted; then I felt like throwing up. My face must have morphed soft to stunned to horrified in one motion. She smiled, her lips pearly-pink-perfect, while her eyes darted around looking for something to land on as she refilled her glass.

'Is that okay?' she asked.

'Uh, well, I mean, sure,' I answered.

Thinking back to my lecture about framing imagery, I wondered if the concepts worked for framing what people say. *How do I frame what Mum said? What's missing? What's included? What does she mean?* I swigged some wine.

'But really, I don't even think of him as gone. I think of him away on vacation,' she said and laughed.

After the initial shock, as if the truth didn't matter, I believed her. I also believed she had reimagined some of the traumatic events in our past as having never happened, that she had brilliantly remastered her narrative to maintain her bliss.

The next day we ventured to the Elkhorn Slough, a long tidal wash of brine water rivered inland from the sea. She thought it would be nice to have her picture taken with nature as a backdrop. Sporting a Robin's-egg blue workout ensemble with matching plimsolls—tennis shoes—we hiked along a dirt trail to an overlook. Mum lived life in vogue, as evidenced in sixty-plus years' worth of family photo albums. Every Marilyn Monroe and pin-up girl pose perfected. We settled on the wood deck at the edge of the slough, which offered the best views of water and sky. She swathed the blanket about her shoulders like a stole. I attached the camera to a tripod and focused on her closed eyes. Click.

She lifted her chin, and said, 'I miss him.'

Mum Missing Nanda

Blanket Share Number Seven:
Rachel Waits

Love heals grief.

Rachel and I relaxed on the back steps of the house. Her face expressionless. She was sixteen when Nanda died, and I had not witnessed any apparent signs of grief. Any trouble she experienced would have been impossible to process given that both Roger and I were riddled with the torment of loss—emotionally unavailable. Her brother, Arian, was hard to find, and the move from Davis to Santa Cruz, her friends unreachable, promised a grief-warp. I feared the grief-path for Rachel would be a lifelong puzzle. Through the viewfinder of my camera, bright sunlight segued with the palm frond shadows dissecting her face. In a split second I saw her delicate and fractured.

Rachel attended my college full-time, enrolled in videography and attended my art classes. We spent every weekday together, almost every hour, until she met Justin at school, a sturdy nineteen-year-old with a face like Apollo. He didn't give me much eye contact and kept twice the distance I'd considered normal, but he had been a Boy Scout, his dad a troop leader. He could fix anything, speak on any topic. He loved nature and took Rachel camping. He showed her how to rebuild a truck engine and drive a stick shift. He could draw, really well. And he was a darn good cook. What was not to like? His face softened when he looked at her. Wide-eyed, her cheeks flushed pink when she looked at him. I felt relieved.

They spent hours at the video lab with the filmmaking nerds. Rachel took to creating documentaries, one about drug use in her hometown, another about releasing Nanda's ashes titled, *One Mile Out*.

A few months later, Rachel and I were in the Art Department office, I on the computer and she at a desk behind me doing homework. I heard her chair scuff across the floor and a shuffle as she turned to me.

'Mom.'

I stopped typing and spun around.

'I've been wanting to tell you ...'

273

My teeth started to grind.

'... I really want a baby.'

My daughter shifted from woman to child, child to woman, woman-child, child-woman. She scanned me for a signal then shrank to the head of a pin. I morphed into a pair of tweezers and mentally tried to grab hold of her. *Now what do I do?* I shook my head.

'I'm telling you what I want, not that I am actually going to get pregnant.'

My head spun like a tilt-a-whirl, probably a giveaway. I believed having a baby at seventeen, almost eighteen, might not be a wise choice. With a panic brewing, the only words I could dredge were, 'Wait. Please wait.'

A year later, Rachel and Justin rented a two-bedroom apartment near the college. They both worked at Best Buy and enjoyed being homemakers, decorating their new abode. I was elated, even relieved, when they adopted an orange kitten. The doting fur-baby parents named him Zeus. I rented a room from them and stayed on the long days when I taught night classes, so I didn't have to drive home through dim winding canyons. They cooked, we watched TV, and I lapped up all the attention those two could give me.

One night when Justin had to work, I cooked dinner for Rachel. We sat on the couch with our food. I popped open a beer and leaned back to relax, sighed and smiled at her. She smiled, a smile I had never seen before.

'I have something to tell you.' A dewy glow radiated on her cheeks.

'Okay,' I said. Lips pursed. Eyes closed. I knew.

'Ummm.'

I opened my eyes. Her smile appeared again, a mature smile, a smile that said, 'I've got this.' A womanly smile, confident, eager.

'I'm pregnant, and I wanted you to be the first to know.'

'Oh my. I pleaded with you to wait,' I said.

'I did.'

'That's true, you did.'

Rachel's shoulders widened, back straightened, her face her own. She grew into a woman, a woman I had just met, full-breasted, hips ready. My kid having a baby. A child she would love, a child she could lose.

I have a grandbaby on the way, oh my God.

274

Instead of jumping for joy and hooting and hollering yahoo, I folded my arms into my belly and sobbed. Tumbling inside, my brain kaleidoscoped. Rachel sat beside me, her hand on my back as I drifted far away, helpless.

'What's going on?' she asked.

'I can't,' I answered.

She repositioned herself to face me. 'What do you mean, you can't?'

I couldn't feel her, I couldn't see her, I couldn't free myself from the overload. *My grandchild will need to be loved. Oh my God. I cannot love another soul.* Right next to love, sorrow. Right next to life, death. I dove into the grief well.

She asked again, 'What are you doing?'

'I don't know if I can love one more person. I am afraid I can't.'

'You're serious?' Her jaw tightened. She sighed and laughed a sweet daughter laugh. 'Weird, I thought you'd be happy for me, but I get it.'

'I'm so sorry,' I wailed. 'I don't know what to do.'

I wallowed and sputter-breathed until snot clogged my throat enough to hack.

'I know you, Mom, and you will fall deeply in love with this baby as you have done with us.'

I wanted to run away to an ashram in India. I wanted to get hit by a train.

Five months into her pregnancy, she placed my hand on the dome of her belly and I felt the baby kick. By nine months, my heart ached differently, the Nanda space opened as the baby's lavender body slid from Rachel's womb onto the blanket between her legs. The baby's arms flung wide open with tight fists. Her face brightened red as she cried into the world. Lilly was bathed, measured, wrapped and given to Rachel and Justin, and then the nurse placed her into my arms. I had no choice; she fit inside the Nanda hole, bittersweet. Gazing into her face, the size of a peach, those new eyes seeing me, cured my fear-of-loving. I knew I could break again, but holding my grandchild, flooded with new love, so good, so right, so needed, I couldn't help but take the risk to love again.

Rachel Waits

Holding Hands

You will feel more alive having held hands with death.

By 2001, Arian had procured a job he liked and rented a room in Sacramento. Roger and I had a new address as well; we bought a house in Monterey near the beach. I was thrilled to get a call from Arian. His voice sturdy. I asked him to visit; he seemed eager. I avoided too many personal questions. I didn't want him to clam up. However, in my Jane of Art style, I did ask if he would assist me with another art project. He agreed to participate before even knowing what it entailed. No surprise, he'd never refused to help me make art.

'Absolutely,' he said.

I explained to him how I couldn't get Nanda's hands out of my psyche.

'Huh. I know. Right?' he said.

'Would you be comfortable with me photographing your hands as if they were his?' I asked.

Arian's hands were identical in shape and size to Nanda's.

He laughed. 'Okay. But you'll need to tell me what to do.'

When I got off the phone, I removed the self-portrait of Nanda from our guest room and hung it in the studio. The Arms Wide Open image had become my favourite, and at the same time painfully impossible to view. I wanted to ward off any discomfort Arian might experience sleeping next to a photograph of his brother. I also hung a red Guatemalan tapestry in the bedroom, knowing as soon as Arian walked through the door, I'd sit with him in front of the festive cloth for our portrait in case he disappeared again.

When Arian arrived, he looked good. He wore a new silk shirt and pleated trousers. His shoulders were relaxed, his face not so gaunt, jaw not flinching. He met me with a smile, a sun-kissed face, hair groomed back in waves, his eyes no longer grey, but green, a yellow green, like the colour of a newly formed leaf. He squeeze-embraced me and didn't let go when I did, so I stayed, let myself be loved, both of us alive in each other's arms.

I had purchased some body paint to colourize his skin to dead white. In the studio, I pointed the camera at my work table where Arian and I would join hands. I wanted to create the photographs that I was unable to make at Nanda's viewing. All the other things I wished I had photographed, I processed and visualised in my writing, aside from Nanda's hands—his hands haunted me.

I positioned Arian's arm with palms up onto white gauze. I laid my arm across his, allowing my hand to rest into the curve of his fingers, and waited to be brought back to where I left off with Nanda: trying to hold Nanda's hand, desperately wanting him to grasp mine.

'Kinda creepy, Mom.'

'Holding hands with the dead?' I asked.

'Yeah, except this is forced and fake.' He scrunched his nose.

'Yes, but the grief isn't.'

Arian's pliable hand felt warm and soft. When I looked at his face, I saw a tight-lipped smirk. Arian shut one eye, like when you wait for the needle to enter during a blood-draw. He relaxed when I released the shutter. From a different angle, I shot another couple of frames and sat the camera on the table.

'Were you able to capture what you want?' he asked.

'No. But I can settle for what I got.'

'Right on!'

I could not capture the lost moments of Nanda; instead, the image I created measured the distance between life and death, a chasm too wide to cross.

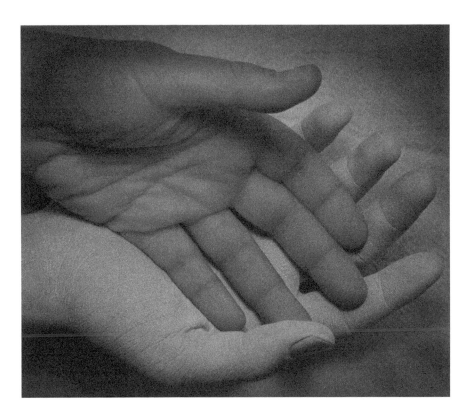

Hand in Hand

To Take a Picture

Grief lurks in the unconscious.

A few days after Arian returned home, I noticed a blank space on the studio wall where I'd hung the Nanda portrait. I scanned the tops of my work table, bookcase, and file cabinet, then scoured the floor.

I yelled, 'Roger!' and walked through the hall to his office. 'Did you happen to take down the Nanda photo I had hanging in the studio?'

He spun around from his desk. 'Nanda photo? No.'

In a panic, I tore apart the studio closet, unpacked boxes, rifled through packages and art supply bins. Roger appeared in the doorway and watched me empty the file cabinet drawers. I opened every folder. Piles accumulated. Stacks avalanched as I stirred the room.

'That's it, someone has taken it,' I grabbed my face to rip it off my skull.

'Who would take it?' he asked.

I released a, 'Uuuuuuuugh!'

Rachel had come over that weekend to visit with Arian, so I called her. Frantic, I asked her if she took it or if she thought Arian might have taken it.

'Are you fricking kidding me, no!' Huge pause.

'How can something just disappear?' I asked.

'Calm down.'

'Someone is messing with me and I ...'

'We've never messed with you or your stuff. Why would we start now?'

When we were done talking, I rang Arian. He picked up after the first ring.

'Did you take the Nanda photo with you?'

'Um, what?' he asked, sounding like he had just woken.

I looked at the clock. 11:00 p.m.

'Oh, sorry for calling so late. The photograph of Nanda, the one I hung on the studio wall.'

'I saw it, but I would never take it. If I wanted a photo of Nanda, I'd just ask you for one.'

For the next three days, I unpacked our bedroom, our guest room, went over the studio a second and third time, and emptied the hallway closets.

The weird thing is, I had the film negative and could have printed another copy. I obsessed for weeks trying to solve the mystery; my family members tired of my obsession, lamenting the Nanda photo.

'You must have misplaced it,' they said. 'It'll turn up.'

Weeks later, inspired to do some watercolour, I walked into the guest room to collect some paper from a stationery box I had wedged between books and magazines in a bookcase. I lifted the lid to find the framed Nanda photo sleeved beneath sheets of watercolour paper. *What the fuck!* I brought the photo to Roger, who was relaxing in bed with a crossword puzzle. I clutched the Nanda image to my chest, my pointer finger pressed to the glass. He removed his reading glasses, stretched his head forward and squinted.

'Is that the photo?'

'Yes. But how did it get hidden away in a box of watercolour paper? In the bookcase! In the guest room!' I asked.

'Oh, you know what,' he said, 'the noise you were just making in the guestroom, just now, is the same noise I have heard several times when you do your late-nighters.' He put his glasses back on.

'What late-nighters?' I sat on the edge of the bed, pressed against his long legs.

'You know! When you can't sleep, you get out of bed in the middle of the night. I don't know what you're doing. Lots of shuffling noise …'

'I know I wake up, but I don't get up.'

'Yes, yes, you definitely get up.' He bunched his pillow to raise his head. 'You get up most nights.'

'Oh my gosh, a restless sleeper, yes, but are you saying I am sleepwalking? Why didn't you say something?'

'I figured you knew what you were doing. Plus, when I did say something, you told me, well, to fuck off.'

'Oh my!'

In grad school, I had attended an art performance about a woman who monitored her sleepwalking. She talcum-powdered the floor around her bed after she retired to sleep, and in the morning, she saw white footprint trails throughout the house. I tried her method, and it worked.

My therapist, who happened to be a sleep specialist, confirmed it. I was a somnambulist. Made sense, given there were other objects misplaced, repositioned, and missing in the house, which I had attributed to grief brain, short-term memory fuckage. I alerted Rachel and Arian and showered them with apologies. They both found somnambulism hilarious. I was horrified. Oddly enough, I stopped the unconscious night walks shortly after the big sleepwalking reveal. Perhaps I finally caught up with my autopilot. Deep down I must have wanted to hide Nanda's portrait, but felt too guilty to disappear it consciously, his face, too fresh for me to view.

To save myself from agitation, I archived the Nanda photograph into the watercolour box for the next few years and hoped someday his image would not make me ache.

Clothes on Fire

Death is inside life, and life is inside death.

After Rachel told me about Carmen taking Nanda's pillow and sheets from his room, we agreed she should have them. But a few weeks later, my need to inventory his linens began to fester. However petty, insensitive, overly sentimental and grief-driven weird it felt, I called to ask her to return his bedding.

She replied, 'I need his bedding to help me sleep. I feel safe in his sheets with my head on his pillow.'

I didn't want to force her, but months later, when she took a new lover, I asked again.

A square box arrived in the mail. Inside, tissue-lined, she had folded his red tartan sheets like gift wrap around his down pillow and crisscross-secured the bundle with a two-inch-wide, sunshine-yellow satin ribbon tied in a perfect bow. I pulled the ribbon loose to find his sheets clean, ironed smooth, evenly folded, and worn holes patched with squares of flannel cloth, the patchwork neatly stitched. She scented his bedding using his favourite cologne. Her love for him sunk deep into the fabric of his pillow.

I held his sheets for a few minutes, then folded them around the pillow and re-tied the bow, placed them into a clean plastic storage box along with ample shame for taking them from Carmen, and marked the top in black sharpie: Nanda's Bedding. Into the studio closet, I stacked it on top of other boxes filled with his clothes, artworks, journals, coin and figurine collections. I knew it would be a while before I breached the bedding box, so I duct-taped the edge of the lid so nothing could get in or—creepy thought—sneak out.

For five years, I had repeatedly unpacked and repacked Nanda's boxes to inspect each of his effects, desperate for insights and reasons. I had pried loose the stories from the lining of his coat, the rim of his hat, his bent wallet, each shirt, all pockets, every hem, with few clues released, and left the bedding box intact until his bedding seemed empty and unusable. I couldn't imagine his sheets and pillow donated to someone or to a thrift store, Carmen and Nanda woven into the fabric. I took the cube of linens to the backyard, dug a hole, squirted in some lighter fluid, and set them into a black flame until they diminished into carbon. Relieved and with no turning back, I filled the hole with dirt and thought his clothing should be next.

Five impossible years. His withered clothes, those cruel reminders, continued to feed my sadness. I chose fire to acknowledge impermanence. I loved the idea of sending Nanda his clothing and sheets through the ether. Fire provided a way for me to make sure nothing was left inside those ageing artefacts. The clothing had to go, but not in a dirt hole in a yard; that had been a spontaneous trial. With Nanda in the sea, the ocean provided a perfect backdrop. I chose the beach for the fiery send-off. My idea was to string his trousers, shirts and hoodie, using safety pins, to a wire stretched between two poles. Roger agreed to assist me.

'How are you going to get the clothing to burn?' he asked.

'By striking a match.'

'I don't think a match will do the job. You want the whole installation to burst into flames, don't you?'

'Absolutely, all at once.'

'We'll need gasoline and a torch.' He grinned.

'Holy shit, oh my God.' I laughed. 'Okay, you are in charge of the pyrotechnics.'

Half a sheer lace moon floated in the sky. Roger and I loaded the car with the medium-format camera gear, fence posts, tent stakes, thirty feet of dog run cable (made of braided wire), a bag of tools, a butane torch and a gallon of gasoline. We drove one whole block to the beach and took turns bringing everything to our location, a secluded stretch of shoreline between the harbour and a dune trail. Roger set the two ten-foot posts twelve feet apart in the sand. We tied the cable to run parallel to the shore from the point of view of the camera, which sat on a tripod facing the ocean. The wind surged, hurling sand towards the lens, so I threw my sweatshirt over the camera. I lined up Nanda's sweats, trousers, shirts, and shorts on the beach weighted with handfuls of sand to keep them from blowing away. Then we pinned his clothing to the cable.

'That should do it,' he said, 'Are you ready?'

'I think so.'

I had loaded the film into the camera and set the aperture and shutter. I pulled the sweatshirt off the lens and gave Roger a thumbs up. Behind the camera, I peered through the viewfinder and focused. He dowsed Nanda's clothes with gasoline emptying the container, the smell of gas just about knocking me out. Torch in hand, he pressed the button to set the flame, jogged past and ignited the trousers, hoodie and shirts, into a blaze. Nanda's clothing whipped with flames.

'Hurry, take the picture,' Roger yelled as he jumped up and down with his arms wide open. 'Take the picture, take the picture!' His sweatshirt inflated with beach wind.

Stunned, I watched Nanda's flaming legs run towards me as his arms, engulfed in flames, waved.

I pressed the shutter release, wound the film, pressed the shutter again, wound the film, pressed, and wound, until the roll was complete, twelve shots, and the fire diminished to smoke. Ember fragments hung from pins; flakes of glowing ash tumbled along the beach. Done!

The sky darkened. The moon peeked through fog, then disappeared. I couldn't talk. When I can't speak, Roger is the perfect person for me, comfortable in silence. My teeth chattered as we packed everything into the bed of his truck. We walked Thorazine-slow.

I crossed the parking lot, headed to a trash receptacle to dump the burnt cable. The brittle, twisted wire smelling of soot looked like an archaeological relic as if someone had dug it out of the earth. Ancient jewellery. The charred fragments of Nanda garments clung like butterflies; the safety pins, fused and melted, resembled calligraphic figures. I couldn't throw the cable away. Returning to the truck, I coiled the blackened wire around my hand, drawing ash lines across my skin, then wiggled the ghost bracelet onto my wrist. I felt Nanda embedded in the wire.

Clothes on Fire

Nanda Wire

The Necklace

Grief is a heavy pendant hung from a chain of loss.

Late one evening, while working in the studio, I heard the familiar squeak of my bathroom vanity drawer sound through the hallway. And then a gasp.

'Everything okay'? I asked.

'What in the world? What are these?'

I could hear him rifle through my drawer.

'Oh, um. Hairballs?' I listened for a response. Nothing. 'Not the gagging-cat variety.'

'I was trying to find some tweezers,' he said.

Roger had never once ventured into my side of the cabinet. I heard the drawer close.

I had managed to pull every hair from my brush since Nanda died. I wound strands into balls, pea to grape size, some browns, a few grey hairs mixed in, and shades of henna red. I saved every ball.

In the nooks and crannies of the vanity drawer there were hairballs tucked away. Groups of them lined and wedged between lipsticks and cream jars, under nail files and dental floss, packed against the edges, crammed in the corners, some stuck to the bristles of my hairbrush.

Although Roger, in general, exhibited a high level of tolerance for my behaviour, whether artistic or psychological, his discovery of hairballs compelled me to do something about the collection. Later in the day, behind a locked bathroom door, not so much a privacy issue, more of a need-for-contemplative-space-not-wanting-any-distractions issue, I sat on the toilet, opened the drawer, and gathered the balls into a heap onto the counter, and counted. Two hundred and fifty-two.

In the palm of my hand, I examined a singular ball. The tangled sphere reminded me of the beads in Bibby's favourite necklace. That necklace once belonged to her great-grandmother, my great-great-grandmother, a graduated strand of red carnelians, the centre bead fat as a thumb. When I was four or five years old, I wanted to bite into that plump bead, thought it would taste like a plum.

Bibby, with spindly arms and legs, stood four feet eleven in heels, each of her breasts larger than her head; she looked as though she could topple. The necklace draped over her shoulders, across the ledge of her chest, hung from the cliff of her bosoms, and the middle bead bobbed as she walked.

When I was seven, Bibby showed me how to restring a strand of amber beads. In a straight line across the kitchen table, she organised the beads by size and divided them evenly to taper to either side of the large centre bead. With a needle and heavy thread, she strung and knotted each bead into place and tied the ends together, then lifted the necklace in both hands like a smiling curve to her smiling face.

I brought the balls of hair into the studio. A necklace seemed like the right thing to do. I had once read how Victorians traditionally wove their lost loved one's hair into jewellery. I considered a necklace made of my hair a modern take. I graduated the various sizes, small to large and back to small, across the studio floor. Bead to bead, the strand measured nine feet long. Needle and thread in hand, I strung and knotted each bead in place. Tied together, I lifted the hairball necklace over my head. Five years of grief floated from my shoulders, over my breasts, past my belly to below my knees, lighter than a dove's wing.

Mourning Necklace

Breathe

Grieve, one breath at a time.

2004. On a Saturday morning, after a sixty-hour workweek, I tried my best to sleep in. Ocean winds ripped inland through open windows, along with the sounds of waves tumble-crashing onto the shoreline. My head replayed my commute to and from work. While driving I had listened to hours of radio news about the brutal details of the Iraq War. Families torn apart. Children lost. Daily death counts climbing. Instead of being thrown into the well of grief, I dipped in, touched what was mine, surfaced, peered outward, thought of humans lying in the desert dust not breathing. I imagined the wind lifting bits of them into the air, up into the atmosphere, circling the world. As sunlight flickered across the walls through breeze-filled curtains, I took a deep breath for those gone, agonised for their families and friends. Nanda, once stuck to Earth, alive, and then heavy and dead. His ashes lifted from my hands by the wind, the same air we all breathe.

We all breathe, we all breathe, we all breathe.

Holding those thoughts, I headed to the studio. With a brush soaked in red ink, I painted the words fire, water, earth and air into a journal. I was a six-year-old-loss-child welcoming a new-self conceived in grief. Those essential elements served as the alchemic art materials I needed to solidify the transformation from lost-self to new-self. I sat with a straight spine, stretched, yawned and felt the impulse to gulp in life.

Air, I needed air. I couldn't ask for a more perfect day to take Nanda's red blanket to the beach, to capture the collective breath in that spinnaker. Sail his billowing flag into the sky. Pray for well-being. Excited, I threw on some clothes and asked Roger if he'd be my cameraman. He looked out the window at our small fruit trees bending sideways and laughed.

'In this crazy gale?'

We walked to the beach, our bodies slanted into the wind, passed agricultural fields, strawberries as far as the eye could see. A pod of pelicans floated overhead like kites pointing to the ocean. We pushed our way over the slough bridge and through coastal dunes where swift air funnelled and sand stung our faces. Gulls swoop-squawked in the gusts. The section of shore where we had once witnessed Nanda's clothes in flames seemed a perfect spot to welcome a wuthering wind full of lost souls into the blanket. Roger, camera in hand, his jeans and sweatshirt rippling, walked a bit further down the beach. He turned and stuffed his dreads into his hoodie.

'Ready?' He adjusted the camera controls and peered through the lens.

I nodded. The second I unfurled the blanket to the ocean, a blast of wind ripped it from my grip. The breath-catcher flew over my head, whipped, twisted and rolled into a ball. One hundred feet behind me, unable to inflate, it collapsed on the sand. Roger exploded with laughter.

Salty lips, misted brow, I trudged through the sand to retrieve the blanket. Facing the ocean, waves lapping over my feet, I opened that fabric against my face and chest, pulled it smooth as it flapped. With arms wide open, I peeked through the weave, waiting for Nanda, somewhere out there at sea. I reached skyward and balanced on my toes.

Lift me up.

I was in the blanket, the whole blanket, not holding on. A blast of wind pulled the fabric skyward, across my torso, over my head, across arms, hands, then leapt from my fingertips. The red sail inhaled open, released all breath and flew into the sky.

My ice-cold toes sank into sand. Roger's dreadlocks escaped his hoodie and waved. I could barely see his eyes through his sea-spray covered glasses. But I could see he was grinning.

'I saw a figure in the blanket when it blew behind you,' he said as he walked towards me, winding the exposed film.

'I have no doubt. I felt it.'

Nanda was in the blanket, the whole blanket.

Inhale

Exhale

Nanda Pond

Death gives birth to grief; love gives birth to Life.

It wasn't enough to float down a river or to stand soaked in torrents of rain. Grief required multiple baptisms. Multiple births. Water, I needed water. I longed to be submerged in a spiritual reservoir, a sacred womb.

I headed to the back garden, blanket in one hand, a shovel in the other, to a spare patch of ground to dig. Fingers of fog dissipated, opening to a canopy of blue. Above me, a white-bright sun and a quarter slice of crescent moon, translucent as milk glass, pinned to the sky like a brooch. Drenched in light, I marked a perimeter six feet long by four feet wide to make room for my body. I shovelled out dirt. Bent over, sweat-soaked, I dug until the basin measured two-feet deep. Not a shallow grave, but a hollow in Earth, the mother body.

Years ago, while attending art school, I dug many holes. One such orifice measured deeper than eight feet and as wide as I could stretch my arms. At the bottom, naked, covered in mud, I looked at Krispy who stood above me. She aimed the camera into the hole and released the shutter. The photograph defied gravity, a bird's eye view of me flying out from the centre of Earth.

I had remembered Bibby saying to me when I was very young, 'Don't be led down the garden path,' so I claimed the path as my own. I dug a trench through the garden walkway. That time Roger assisted me. He stood on a ladder and pointed the camera downward parallel to the ground, a perspective that morphed the trench into a cross-section of tunnel leading to the earth's core. At one end, I curled into a ball—a seed ready to split open.

Those early holes helped me find my way through the life I had. I intended the new hole to assist with the delivery of my new-self into my new-life.

I heard the clank of the gate latch and turned to see Rachel enter the backyard, a camera bag hanging from her shoulder. My three-year-old granddaughter, Lilly, trotted beside her, sweaty wisps of hair around her face, a red-cheeked beacon of joy.

Rachel and Lilly helped me line the pond with a plastic tarp. We stretched Nanda's blanket, a placental weave across the cavity. Rachel prepared her camera as Lilly helped me drag a hose through the yard. Amused, I imagined filling the pond, according to my art mind, with six years of tears—holy amniotic water.

'You know what's funny?' I asked. 'Nanda Pond.' I cracked up.

Rachel nodded and laughed. Lilly looked confused. I explained to the little one, the pool I made was a pond and one of Nanda's nicknames had been Nanda Ponda, often shortened to Nanda Pond. I heard her repeat Nanda Pond and felt a bird swoop in my heart.

The musk of wet dirt permeated the air. Nanda's blanket darkened and glistened. The pool of red mirrored the sun.

I said it again to hear it again. 'Nanda Pond!'

Rachel arranged an orchard ladder to allow her a bird's eye view. I lay on my back into the sun-warmed water, into the mouth of Earth, felt the tug of the umbilical, the reflexive pull of gravity, and bounce-floated like an anchored buoy. Rachel, at the top of the ladder, her face full of love, aimed the camera and rotated the lens. I watched the aperture dilate like a cervix. Her face reddened as she steadied the camera from extended arms to square the frame around the Nanda Pond to catch me. I looked into the eye of the camera as light from my body reflected into the lens. The world tilted. In the cave of that womb, I settled into foetal position as the waters began to recede. The click of the shutter unlocked the gate. In the wishing well of self, the bindings of grief loosened, and the cord attached to an irretrievable old-life severed.

Delivered by the spirit of art, I awakened to a new-life worth living.

Reborn in the Nanda Pond

Buried

Trying to get back to your old self is like trying to bring someone back from the dead.

2005. An urgency, like a siren wailing from inside, alerted me to make more room for an expanding self. Some friends and family members expected me to return to my old-self, the self they knew before Nanda died. Impossible. Only my new-self had survived grief-drowning. I was born when I embraced death. I decided to honour the old-self by putting it to rest. *Time to dig another hole.*

Earth, I needed Earth. A container large enough to hold who I was, not to bury the past, but to relinquish a self that had perished, to let Earth carry the burden. I envisioned the burial centred in a tree circle, like the redwoods surrounding the birthing room where I pushed Nanda out in one squeeze, where the trees waved as the nurse slid him onto my chest. Although a tree circle is technically a ring of new generation trees born from the roots of the dead parent tree, I would be born from the roots of Nanda.

I drove six hours to Faith's property in Mendocino, a forested parcel of land which happened to be a tree circle heaven. Nanda, as a child, spent wild time in the woods there with Faith's kids.

Faith's living space occupied the second floor of her A-frame cabin above her art studio. I hauled the bags and camera gear up the stairs. We sat on her balcony overlooking a grass-filled meadow edged with giant redwoods. Misted in fog, we drank amber ales, munched chips and salsa, and chatted for hours about art and family tribulations. We didn't talk about Nanda, but she knew what I wanted. When the sky darkened, Faith, looking like a modern-day goddess, her hair a waterfall of copper down her back, handed me a flashlight, snubbed the clove cigarette we had shared, tipped her head back and released smoke as she spoke.

298

'You're gonna love this. Follow me.'

I rummaged through bags to collect the camera and blanket. With flashlights in hand, we flicker-walked through the forest to a young tree circle. Tree bodies surrounded a ring of stones, a fire pit. She lit a mound of twigs into a blaze and hefted a log onto the fire. Embers snapped and cracked, scattered and fizzled on the damp ground. A chill ran through my core, but my face and legs were heat-soaked to the bone. I looked into Faith's eyes, the colour of ocean in her oil paintings, cerulean blue. She had tears, tears I couldn't muster. She had cried for me the night Nanda died when I was all cried out, and at his memorial service when I felt numb. She was a waterworks whenever I spoke of him, anytime I choked on grief.

I attached the camera to a tripod next to the fire pit and readied the timer. I joined Faith to face the lens. Gold light from flames bounced across us. A fiery chunk of branch cracked and popped; tiny sparks spiralled and vanished into the night sky. Wearing Nanda's blanket like a cape, she stood behind me, and like a winged woman she swaddled the blanket around us, rested her arms over my shoulders, clasped her hands at my chest and nuzzled her face next to mine. I pressed the remote shutter release. It felt like the three of us standing there.

The next morning after breakfast, we lazed about on the balcony with mugs of coffee as black as grasshopper spit and smoked cigarillos. By noon, sunlight crested the trees. Faith, braless in a camisole, wearing flip flops and tight jean shorts rose abruptly from her chair.

'Let's go,' she said and grabbed my hand.

She collected my camera bag, tossed the blanket over my shoulder, and guided me through the woods, a five-minute walk to an elder circle of trees. Trees as tall as skyscrapers. At the periphery she stopped, set the camera on a tripod, and waved me to the centre. I kicked off my shoes, striped off my trousers and shirt to a leotard, and peered into the treetops. Those giant ambassadors of life formed a ring into the coastal sky. For hundreds of years, they had released bits of self to the ground. I searched for the middle spot. The noon sun squeezed through for a few minutes when the fog blanket lifted from a sea breeze. I tightened every muscle I could, looked at my feet and imagined having a tap root reaching to Earth's core. I dropped to my knees and dug my toes into a mound of redwood needles. I leaned in using my hands as scoops and rhythmically hoisted away damp loam, black matter, full of pungent rootlets, stems, beetles, and leaves. Centipedes scurried. I hollowed out a hole the length and width of my body. With the blanket, I reclined into the trench. Faith knelt to push mounds of soil over me. Dirt sifted through the weave to bare skin.

'Shall I cover your head?' She smiled and made a rascal face. Her fists full of dirt, she scream-laughed.

'Wait! No!' I squeezed my eyes shut.

She loosened her hands and tree litter fluttered; then she opened them all the way. Dirt full of forest debris fell over my face. She scream-laughed louder.

'Just a little,' she said in a baby voice with a cheeky grin.

Trying not to laugh, I spat grit. 'It's not me I am burying, it's my old-self.'

She reached down and brushed dirt from my eyes, then positioned herself behind the camera.

Tucked into Earth, I shallow-breathed, contemplated the calculation of how to separate old from new. The split was simple: measure by loss. Formless forming. I settled into long breathing. My heartbeat, palpable against heavy soil, slowed. Faith invisible. No clicks of shutter. No sounds of birds or rustling trees. Not a flicker. I gyroscoped in that planetary dress. Spun for the moon.

The wind swept through, sounding like applause. In unity, trees waved into the sky. Faith stepped back from the camera, arms soft by her sides, her eyes wide with wonder. In the ground, rested in peace, no need for wake or sorrow, I let go of who I used to be.

Buried in a Circle of Trees

The sun dipped below the treetops splintering through branches to the forest floor, but we still had time for one more round of images. I shook the blanket free of dirt and leaves and offered it to Faith. She donned the blanket as a robe. Her hair fell in waves down the red, her face aglow in the twilight. Feet dark with forest dust, she walked towards a tight ring of infant redwoods, the centre parent tree a dead stump. She pressed an ear to one of the baby trees, then her shoulders, chest, and belly. She stretched a corner of the blanket to wrap a Nanda arm around the trunk, then she reached to join hands and wept. Faith held Nanda, Nanda held the baby tree, the baby trees held the lost mother, they all held me.

I did not succumb to the pang of sorrow. Instead, camera to my eye, I examined the details of the scene before me, like carefully studying the details of a Pre-Raphaelite painting, of love, of loss, but mostly of nature. It struck me, the order in which the trees survived was not my story. I no longer expected to die before my kids.

There is no perfect order in life and death.

I pressed the shutter release with the will to survive nonetheless.

Embrace

Woe Agent

Grab hold of grief and shape it to serve you.

Flora had suggested I introduce myself to her colleague, Coeleen Kiebert, a local psychologist, an artist-mother who had lost her adult son. I took the opportunity to hear Coeleen speak at a local art museum about how she made art to examine that loss. Coeleen, in her late seventies, looked like a priestess in long robes of handwoven linen and silk, flowing trousers. White hair curved to her jaw line framing a wise face. Handcrafted danglies swung from her ears. Living art.

She gestured with her hands, knotted with arthritis, and explained how she created art every day to process her questions about life, death, and self. In pursuit of spiritual insight, she sculpted, fired, and glazed hundreds of pounds of buttery porcelain clay.

'How does anyone cope with the deeper meanings of life without an art form to guide them?' she asked.

The monitor on the wall displayed images of her ceramic statues. First the navigators, the early grievers, chunky, toddleresque beings dressed in helmets and spacesuits. Her ethereal astronauts were equipped with cameras, compasses, barometers, and gauges designed to enter the bardo, the realm between lifetimes, to seek the whereabouts of her dead son. Next on the screen, her Lilliput-sized deep divers, submerged in aqua-coloured tsunami wave-like structures, their stocky bodies descending into that transitional space between death and rebirth, grief-guides in search of wisdom. I had never considered making guides. I felt the pull and imagined who I'd create to plunge in alongside them.

At the end of the presentation, she announced her upcoming workshop focused on the use of clay to feel and process emotional trauma, titled 'Clay as a Way.' I signed up immediately.

Coeleen's home and studio lined the edge of a coastal cliff. I drove onto a gravelled driveway into a courtyard surrounded by trees, and parked. Once out of the car, I discovered a four-foot-tall bronze statue mounted on a pedestal standing at the front of the house, a blindfolded figure reminiscent of the classic Lady of Justice. Not wielding a sword, not with scales in her uplifted hand. Instead, she held a single feather. While grief is heavy, it is also buoyant and delicate. Fragile. I knew from the museum lecture that Coeleen had produced a series of justice statues to assist in solving the mysterious circumstances surrounding the death of her son. She researched for years, unable to uncover exactly what happened to him, so she settled on what she believed to be true. I, too, waded through various forms of how Nanda died, until I conceded to a slim feather of truth.

At the entryway, a fountain trickled into a pond. I saw my reflection break on the surface, then sank my eyes into the algae-green murk. *Some questions will never be answered.*

From the centre of the pond rose an abstract ceramic sculpture, more like a termite mound made from a dizzying mass of undulating blues and greens with sunlit flecks of gold. It morphed into a cliff-face, a wave, a figure, like one of the archangels of the Notre-Dame Cathedral. Coeleen referred to her sculpture as a scholar rock, sometimes called a spirit rock, inspired by an unusual art form she saw in China known as *gongshi*. A stone naturally weathered into an aesthetic shape. Her rock was a contemporary version built from porcelain clay and distressed by hand.

In parts of China, stones of varying sizes, sometimes boulders weighing hundreds of pounds, were unearthed and admired for their natural beauty. Some were placed in a lake or river for centuries, generations, to be carved by the flow of water. Later the eroded stones would be dredged up and displayed indoors or centred in a garden to be revered and contemplated. These found stones released spiritual energy that a scholar might absorb.

On closer observation, her rock-like sculpture revealed lines where her fingertips glided, scratch lines from her fingernails, fist prints pounded in where she struggled, and holes she scraped and chipped away searching for a composition that could balance on the edge of loss. Coeleen, for years, guided by the flow of her muse, carved many spirit rocks with her river of grief.

I walked in slow motion into her studio and found her maquettes displayed on shelves, hand-sized pre-designs of her larger ceramic pieces: navigators and divers and other figures she had made through the years. My eyes jumped to a miniature gold-lustered pieta with enough gesture in the clay to show Mary with Christ lying dead across her lap, her open hand stretched to the sky. Uncanny. I too had pondered Mary many times, another mother questioning why.

Art-soaked, my eyes roamed over her morning work. Clay-doodled figures, still wet and raw, sagging into themselves on circular wooden pallets. Beside bowls of ink, pens, brushes, and stacks of thick paper were her journals splayed open, colours dripping across the pages. I followed the lines in her ink drawings, the calligraphy of paths on how to engineer a grief navigator. I studied her pages of soul-scribbled art notes, similar to mine, describing how to locate one's self, and what is needed for a grief journey.

In the classroom, adjacent to Coeleen's studio, chanting and gongs sounded from speakers. Light poured in through a wood-beamed roof covered with translucent fibreglass panels. Salt air blew in from open sliding glass windows overlooking the Pacific Ocean. Fifteen women sat quietly at workbenches with buckets of water, sponges, rags, jars of carving implements and twenty-five-pound bags of porcelain clay. I joined them, my visceral-hungry art-self raring to create. Coeleen switched off the stereo and rang a bell. She instructed us to each gather a heart-sized ball of clay.

'We rely so much on sight to make art. I want you to close your eyes and make what you feel,' she said.

When my fingers slid into the clay, I felt nothing. After squeezing and pounding and trying to connect to emotional sensations, I succumbed to an impulse. *There are many parts of grief I want to express.* I separated the ball of clay into thumb-sized pieces. I rolled one piece between two palms, like warming a prayer, and sensed a deep aspiration to make something meaningful. In the space of cupped hands, the clay elongated into the body of a serpent, its pointy head protruding past my fingertips, its tail whipping at my wrists. Between thumb and pointer finger, I tapered their tails, balled up their heads, and pinched their faces. Using a pinkie, I poked in howling mouths. Feeling my way, careful not to stick them together, I spaced them apart in rows across the canvas-covered tabletop. I was afraid I'd open my eyes to an army of pathetic worms, instead I discovered organic, sinewy creatures, each unique, fingerprints branded into their faces like the fine details left behind in Nanda's ashes. God was in the clay. Their eyeless faces sage-like, mouths wide open, tunnelled to the core. *Trauma survivors.* With a sharp wood stick I slotted in eyes. *Able to see into the shadows of self.*

For hours, I tooled in facial features, embossed fine patterns and curves into their bodies, twisted and fanned tails. I gave each a pocket to hold a prayer. Grief Ministers, Loss Advocates, and Woe Agents. One hundred sentient beings. Lost in the process, I hadn't noticed the other women and found myself alone in the room. The windows black. Coeleen called from her studio.

'You're on to something, stay as long as you like.'

The clay on my hands dried and crumbled to reddened skin and prune fingers. Chips of clay, bits not intended as art, lay in drifts across the wood floor like shattered bone. Clay dust, the toil of artmaking, packed into the weave of jute rugs. My clothes were covered in clay handprints. Full of art. Breathing art. Being art. Art a mission. A drive. It took me more than seven years to arrive, to feel comfortable enough, to be willing enough, to reveal to others what I knew of loss. I pressed my wrists against my ears and listened to a pulse, rubbed my tongue across my teeth. Clay grit. Felt like ash. Tasted like ash. *Art sometimes tastes like ash.*

What intrigued me most was how Coeleen's art touched humanity. She exhibited in museums and galleries, wrote books, made videos, and gave lectures about the healing qualities of the creative process. My art-eyes opened. And although I hadn't, since Nanda's death, joined the art world, Coeleen reawakened my desire to do so. I intuitively knew that sharing the connection between grieving and the artmaking process was a path I needed to follow.

When I told Krispy about my Woe Agents, she offered to show my work at a gallery where she curated. The group exhibition was titled 'Talisman.' I built a woe wall, like a prayer wall from a twelve-by-twelve-inch square of wood. I drilled one hundred holes and secured one hundred hooks from which I hung one hundred porcelain Woe Agents. Each agent holding a tiny paper scroll.

Instructions on the wall read:

Fragile. Handle With Care.

In honour of the shadow, the dark side of the soul, and those who struggle and suffer, there is knowledge and wisdom in journeying into and exploring the territory of one's being. To feel and follow the pain to its root, excavate and examine what is damaged and lost. To console you, consider adopting a Woe Agent. I am offering you a healing guide, one who has been to the pitch of darkness and back. Souls of woe. Tragedy spirits. Grief-experienced beings for adoption.

There are no fees or costs for the adoption process.

You can take your Woe Agent home after you do the following:

1. Choose a Woe Agent that calls to you.
2. Write your woe on the scroll.
3. Roll the scroll and deposit it into the woe wall.

Your Woe Agent's pocket is ready to accept woes, prayers, and wishes.

Within the first hour of the gallery's reception, the Woe Agents were taken, prayer holes filled. After the exhibition, Krispy mailed the woe wall back to me. Uncurling each note, one by one, I read.

Numerous scrolls depicted childhood trauma. I read about lost babies, dead parents, dismemberment, anguish over loss of self. A woman wrote: 'I lost one of my boobies and now I am bald chemo girl.' A mother wrote: 'Watching in despair as my daughter struggles with meth addiction.' One stated they didn't know why they suffered. One confided: 'My woe is my inability to forgive.' I tugged free another and sobbed to these words, 'Most of my woes are covered by medication.' Another scroll was filled on both sides, the writing overlapped several times, ladened with ink, until illegible. I unrolled one scroll with both sides filled, then scribbled out, except for one word in all caps: INDECISIVENESS.

Woes of anxiety and fear. Pain and torment. Bad luck. Low self-esteem, self-doubt, loneliness, and depression. Too much love. Not enough love. Loveless. Hated. Abandoned. Broken-hearted. No peace. Ill. Irreparably damaged. Dying. Jobless. Immigration worries. Don't know what to do. Stuck in-between. Nowhere to go. Lost. Homeless. Homeless and pregnant. Suicidal.

Snot-faced crying, I continued:

My boyfriend is constantly mad.
I'm going insane.
Living in the wrong universe.
Trying to make it through an amazing string of trials, one after another.
Suffering for all the other sufferers.
Do I stay or go in this wicked world?
Life is a howl into oblivion.

There was one scroll left blank, white space, complicated at best. Unwritten dread too horrible to share? Maybe words could not express their agony? Perhaps they felt the need to protect their privacy, or they just didn't want to commit words to the page. They still adopted a Woe Agent. *Do I need to know why?*

The mound of unfurled woes, as delicate as moth wings, tipped and swayed in the rhythm of my breathing. I stroked each page flat, grateful for the bravery revealed, then rolled them into tight spirals and moored them into the holes of the woe wall.

To honour grief is vital to living, as honouring life is vital to grieving. With a renewed sense of purpose, I vowed to continue making and sharing the fine art of grieving. *When there isn't enough light, I can honour darkness. Be the guide, the agent of woe.*

Woe Agent

Tea Party

Become so familiar with loss that grief loses its teeth.

I arrived at school at 7:00 a.m. and noticed a red light flashing on the office phone. I checked my messages. Rachel, her voice an unfamiliar sombre tone, asked me to call her immediately. Adrenalin surged. She rarely woke at that hour. I envisioned her belly, six months pregnant with her second child whom she had already named Isabella, about to pop too soon, or worse. I rang her back.

'Are you sitting down?' she asked.

'Shit! You know me better than to ask me that. What's going on?' I squeezed the phone receiver.

'Carmen hanged herself,' she said.

The grief monster grabbed me by the jawbone.

'Mom?'

I could see Carmen hanging, her face strained blue, her neck stretched taut from her broad angular shoulders, slender arms and long legs limp, bare feet hovering. My neck tightened. I felt miserable for her family's loss. Imagined Carmen's pain. I also didn't want my new life to go sideways.

'Mom. Say something.'

'I'm glad she didn't do this when Nanda was alive.'

As those bitter words blurted from my mouth, I could feel myself slip.

'I'm sorry. I think I'm, I'm in shock?' I said.

'Same,' Rachel said.

A few months before Rachel called me about Carmen's death, I had been reeling with grief from an unexpected call I received from Wayne. The last time we spoke was at Treehenge, where I floated with Nanda's red blanket in the Bear River.

'Jeannie's gone,' he said, sobbing.

'Oh my God, Wayne, no.'

Forty years of marriage. Jeannie, the love of Wayne's life. Jeannie, who helped me when Nanda died.

'She died December 3rd the day after.' He paused.

'December 2nd, Nanda's deathiversary,' I said.

The last thing Wayne shared was his gratitude. He said my art gave him permission to photograph portraits of his face, to ask the basic questions: What is grief? What does it look like? I promised to share with him what I had learned about loss.

Carmen's last year appeared to be the best year of her life. We wrote each other letters, emails, connected on social media. I had just finished wrapping a Nanda painting to send to her. I had just spoken to her on the phone. She'd purchased tickets to join her girlfriends for a vacation to Hawaii. Enrolled in med school. She had plans to build a new hospital in Kenya with her father.

After finding out about her death I spoke to her family and friends. We were perplexed.

How did I miss her despair?

But Nanda warned us. Carmen wanted out.

Weeks went by. I kept tripping into what losing Carmen meant to me. We cared about each other, but trod softly, both of us easily triggered. I stayed in touch with her, not because I loved her, and I did love her, but mostly because she loved Nanda. I am sure she felt the same way. We were desperate to keep Nanda's memories alive. I wasn't sure I'd miss her, but I'd miss hearing about the details of Nanda's life outside of mine, his quirks, habits, funny gestures. All that I had not asked her. All the things she had not told me. Impossible to hold, yet impossible to let go of. *How do I inventory everything she hasn't shared? How do I carry what can't be measured, the weight unbearable?* I wasn't prepared to lose more of Nanda.

At Carmen's memorial service, her brothers' faces contorted with grief. I melted into projected slide images of her: beautiful, young, tender, bright-eyed. Her smile begged consideration. I cried. Then I remembered: Carmen, laying her head on the railroad tracks, taunting Nanda, and Nanda later standing in the path of an oncoming train. Guilt-stabbed to the bone, a thought I had kept to myself surfaced: I blamed her for his death.

Catapulted into more grief-work, I decided no one was to blame. I reminded myself, however painful, life and death are inseparable. There would be more suffering, but there could also be joy. I had learned it's okay to not be okay, but it's also okay to be okay. I had become strong enough to keep from sliding into the mire of depression. A celebration of life was in order. I needed to trust and engage with the living, with innocence, with my granddaughter, three and a half years old and full of chutzpah. With my daughter's permission, I asked Lilly to help me create a Tea Party photograph to salute life—and death.

'Yes!' Lilly yelled, jumping with her fists in the air.

Yup, I needed that.

Lilly had participated in many photo shoots and was familiar with Nanda's red blanket, but her concepts of life and death were still forming. A year earlier, Rachel and I soaked up sun on the back patio while Lilly played in the yard.

'Gran Mo, come. There's a bird sleeping near the fence. I can't wake it up,' Lilly said.

'Okay. Let's take a look.'

Lilly took our hands and guided us to the bird, and we knelt to see a red-winged blackbird on its back, feathers shiny and smooth, feet curled, eyes closed. Rachel glanced at me sideways and bit the corner of her mouth. Lilly looked confused.

Rachel sad-smiled and rubbed Lilly's back. 'The bird's dead, honey.'

With hands open, Lilly said, 'Well, we need to wake up the bird.'

'The bird has left his body. He's gone,' I said.

She dropped her hands. 'We'll make him come back.'

Her face filled with optimism. My insides twisted.

'It can't come back into its body,' Rachel said.

'But we can keep an eye on him,' I said, hoping to console her. 'Every time you visit, we'll check on him.'

She examined the bird and nodded.

A week later, Lilly walked through my door and beelined for the backyard and headed straight to the blackbird body. Reposed in the shadow of the fence, a slow decomposition. Feathers lost lustre, faded, and began to ruffle. Chest collapsed. Tail feathers had broken away. Bones poked through.

'The bird is gone, and he is not coming back, right?' she asked.

'Yes, you're right. He is gone,' I replied.

'Where did he go?'

'Don't know. It's a mystery.'

Gone, just like my Nanda.

A few months later, Lilly and I were seated together on the couch. We flipped through a photo album until she pointed to a photograph of Nanda.

'I know him. He's my uncle Nanda,' she said. She turned towards me, got up on her knees, and held my face in her hands. She looked into me, her eyes black as a camera lens.

'He is so nice, Gran Mo. He talks to me,' she said.

I believed her.

'He is nice,' I said.

Our tea party took place in Rachel's backyard, next to a wall of bird of paradise in a shade-dappled spot protected from the midday summer sun. My daughter, ripe with her second child, a month from her due date, relaxed in a lounge chair with her camera strapped to her neck and waited for a cue to hit the shutter release. In a summer dress, cheeks hot pink, Lilly helped me set up a kiddie table and two chairs with Nanda's blanket as our tablecloth. I placed an English china cup and saucer, sugar bowl and creamer that belonged to Bibby on top. Lilly collected her miniature porcelain tea set in a wicker basket and arranged the dishes symmetrically across the blanket. We plucked flowers from the garden and gathered them in the creamer for our centrepiece.

'Isn't that beautiful?' Lilly asked.

'Indeed. Do you remember how to make a toast?'

We sat on the kid chairs and practised clanking our tiny cups together.

'Cheers.'

'*L'chaim.*'

'*Skål.*'

'*Sláinte.*'

'Okay, are you ready to be photographed?' I asked.

'I thought we were photographing a tea party,' she replied.

'What do you mean?'

'I mean a real tea party. We don't have tea and cookies.'

I should have known better. I had been creating images to simulate what I wanted to portray: Arian's hand in place of Nanda's, a candy wrapper shaped into a Viking ship. But Lilly was right; the tea party needed to be real, not a facsimile or staged relying on props. She nailed it; she didn't want to pretend, she wanted a genuine tea party with tangible treats, sincere gratitude, and full of love.

'Oh my, Lillykins. Absolutely! What was I thinking?' I turned to Rachel. 'Do you have tea? Biscuits?'

Rachel hoisted herself belly first out of her chair and headed to the back door of the house. 'No tea and definitely no biscuits in this house, but I have fruit, juice, nuts and bread.'

'Excellent! Then we shall drink juice and break bread.'

I raised my palm to Lilly for a high five and she slapped my hand. We loaded the table with snacks, poured juice into the teapot and filled our cups. Rachel lifted her camera.

'Thank you so much, Lilly, for making it real.'

'You're welcome, Gran Mo.'

I flooded with joy. We smiled and lifted our little cups, eyes connected.

'Here's to life,' I said.

'And don't forget Nanda,' Lilly said.

Heart-expanded, I teared up.

Grief is the process of bringing your lost one to life.

'Let's not forget my Nanda Ponda. Cheers!'

Her face emitted love beams.

'Cheers!' she said, pinkie raised.

We tapped our cups together, a sweet clink. Pure joy. Rachel released the shutter.

I witnessed life next to death in the beauty of that courtship and Art more powerful than death. Being in life. Being with death. Grief and love sipped from the same wellspring. Being not okay. Being okay. Being. Just being. Grief softened to being.

A Real Tea Party

Afterdeath

Grief, when the time is right, deserves a purge.

Autumn was once my favourite time of year. The wind came more often, cooling and clearing the air. Clouds performed ballets. Leaves twirled from trees. Pyramids of pumpkins showed up in fields at nearby farms. I looked forward to family gatherings. Then after Nanda's death, instead of enjoying the holidays and birthdays of November and December, I found myself in the elevator shaft plunged into the grief-mine. However, by that eighth year, even though it started with the deaths of Jeannie and Carmen, I managed to stay above ground. I felt motivated to participate in art and kept my spirits high curating and designing an art exhibition for the Gavilan College Fine Arts Gallery, titled 'Passing Through: Life, Love, and Loss.' I invited Coeleen, Faith, Wayne and a new colleague, Diana, to talk about art and grief and showcase their work.

While planning which of my artworks would be best suited for the exhibition, I found myself entrenched in another inventory. Not comfortable showing art I had not yet fully questioned, or realised, I made a list of my grief art projects and placed a checkmark next to work deemed complete. *Is anything ever complete?* No matter how long it would take, I remained determined to keep facing grief until there was nothing left to face or to check off the list. *Grieve until you no longer need to.*

In the gallery layout, I gave myself room to show four photographs. I had chosen three: Clothes on Fire, Nanda Pond, and Tea Party, then I ruminated on how to create the fourth. For months, I daydreamed about Nanda's blanket pouring from my body like blood, spilling from my mouth, and slipping from my womb like afterbirth. The image I had already digested and envisioned just needed a time and place. And, of course, when I shared my ideas with Faith, she knew the perfect location, a remote beach cove where Schooner Gulch Creek poured into the Pacific Ocean. She invited me to Mendocino, agreeing to help me with my art project, and I promised to pack and transport her art back to the gallery for our exhibition.

The day of the photoshoot, she parked her Jeep beside the highway and we hiked through a wooded path, about a mile, toting camera gear, a daypack and Nanda's blanket. Faith's dog, Studly, a hefty golden retriever, led the way. We stepped out of the trees and followed the dirt path into sand. I noticed the creek flowed into ponds next to cliff rocks and driftwood piles tangled in a branch of silvery water veined across the beach to the shoreline.

'You won't believe the skies here, breathtaking opalescent sunsets. And the reflections, fuck, I love painting reflections,' Faith said. She shaded her eyes with her hands, gazed into a horizon of open sea, and exhaled while she spoke. 'Oh my God, breathe that in.'

Both of us, chins up, took long, slow breaths, turned to each other and witch-cackled.

Over driftlettes of sand, we trod to the mouth of the creek, meandered through streamlets to a pool of water beneath a wall of rock.

'I'm going to flow the blanket into that pond. And whatever grief doesn't need to stay inside me can flow to the sea,' I said.

While Faith secured the camera to a tripod and positioned it to view the pond, I stripped down, put on a white dress and tiptoed into the icy water. My new-self intact, a reconstituted art-self crafting a better life, purged what grief no longer needed.

*

November 2, 2006, almost a full moon on the opening night of the art exhibition, 'Passing Through.' The last night of Día de los Muertos, Day of the Dead. The room filled with college students, colleagues, friends, and family, including Dad who drove for two hours to attend. He stood at the rear of the gallery in pleated trousers, white shirt and striped tie, and a navy blazer with a British Army insignia pinned to the lapel. Chin up, back straight as a board, with his arms held behind his back.

I had printed my Fine Art of Grieving photographs like large pages from a book. Dented a crease between image and text and laid them open across fabric the colour of Nanda's red blanket inside glass-box display tables. Faith's Narcissus, life-sized paintings of fates, and portraits of her children as mythological characters hung from walls on one side of the gallery. On the other side, a row of larger-than-life-size images of Wayne looking directly into the camera, looking at the viewer knowing they would be looking back at him, images he photographed over the course of the first nine months after his wife's death. Pedestals throughout the room displayed Coeleen's navigators and divers. Across a centre wall divide, Diana Lynn's installation of lightboxes illuminated family photographs of babies coming into the world next to relatives dying or already gone, representing the cycle of life and death.

Fifty or so people stayed to hear the artists speak. I started our talks with the story of Persephone and how her mother, in deep grief, would not let a wintered Earth thaw until her daughter was returned to her. Faith spoke about losing and finding herself after a friend's suicide. Wayne explained that he documented his face to see what grief looks like. Diana shared her experience of how she came to find those families who allowed her to photograph births and deaths. Coeleen spoke about making peace with what can never be known about the loss of our loved ones. I noticed Dad wiping a tear away when Coeleen spoke about not having any control over what happens in life, that there is such a thing as mean reality.

A journalism student video-recorded the event and documented the work on display. I would use that footage to make a documentary titled *Passing Through: Life, Love, and Loss*. At the close of our show, I thanked everyone for attending and wished them a good night. Dad strolled over to me, his squinty eyes not meeting mine. Little dents formed around his protruding lips before he kissed my cheek. His hands still clasped behind him as if tied together at the wrists. He leaned in again, as if he wanted to tell me a secret.

'This is wrong. Utterly wrong. You should not have done this.' With his face pinched in disapproval, he turned away and headed for the exit door.

Dad must have missed the bit in Coeleen's talk about how we needed to show up with compassion. Having done the work of letting go of the old-self, I catalogued his dismissiveness. I could not go back to being the hard-wired submissive child. My new-self could discern what wasn't mine, what I no longer needed, and knew better than to repeat the work I had already done.

318

Afterdeath 1

Afterdeath 2

Unravel

Grief is a love poem.

In 2007, September's air snapped crisp and leaves fell early. Wayne, in his second year of grief, and I, at almost nine years, sat perched on stools, centre stage in a large lecture hall at Folsom Lake College. A projection screen above our heads read: 'Art and Grief: Learning to See in the Dark.' We had been invited to address how art heals grief. The lecture hall, rated for 150 people, filled with over 200. Many stood in the aisles.

Wayne, dressed in a black suit, white shirt unbuttoned at the collar, rubbed his beard and tapped the remote. A photograph of his loss-weathered face, taken the day his wife died, illuminated the screen. He clicked through a progression of self-portraits, each an incremental step towards his new-self, while he told the story of his wife's death. He explained how death could be beautiful, how she calmed herself and chose her place and time. How her loved ones stayed at her side. He expressed his devastation, shared his thread of hope and how he leaned into his new life.

Wayne shot me a glance, smiled, and handed over the remote. I lifted the script of poems from my lap and scooted forward to the edge of the stool.

Thirty days before our presentation, while organising which artwork and poems to present, I took a break and stepped outside to see the sun disappear and Earth drop her shadow onto the moon. During that lunar eclipse, the moon swelled blood-red, and a memory surfaced; I had once projected a photograph of the moon on Nanda's red blanket.

A poem flowed through me. A moon lullaby.

> Through blood of lunar eclipse
> I spoke

to a dead child
the language of shadow
learning to see in the dark
as memories broke into light.

That was not the first moon poem. The week Nanda died, I wrote a poem called 'Full Moon,' about how the moon had witnessed my son's death, followed me into grief, mute and expressionless, waxing and waning, taunting me into rage. I had saved the poem to a folder on a hard drive for years. Never shared it. Like Earth, I had dropped a shadow on that moon.

Seated at a computer, I searched for the early poem and read it aloud, hoping for enough guts to read it at our presentation. I printed it and stuck it under the stack of poems I knew I could and would read.

On stage, spot lit in a silk dress and high-heeled shoes, lips pomegranate red, I wondered if I'd be ready to moon-speak. Time compressed as I projected photographs of my face coated in ash, the necklace of hair and the Nanda Pond, reading poems about death illuminated by fury, and how a blanket transforms. Sweat trickled down my back as I read the poems born at the start of my grief journey until I reached the last poem in the stack. I stared at the title, 'Full Moon,' and lingered.

Time to thank everyone for coming? Or press to the full moon slide? Am I ready?

I looked out to the audience. Faces alert. Eerie quiet. I needed to face the moon. With a rush of adrenaline, I forced a tense smile.

Oh, what the hell.

Jaw tight, I clicked the remote. An image of me peering over an arms-wide-open-sized moon glowed over our heads, illuminated my page of poetry, reflected into my eyes. Smoothing pages between fingers, my hands trembled. I turned to catch Wayne's eyes. He slight-smiled and patted my shoulder. I took a deep breath, exhaled, relaxed, then forced each word aloud. Before the last line, I choked up and glanced at the audience. *You're okay.* I squeezed my toes and let the last words slide off my tongue.

'No doubt the moon will survive me; so too, the moon will forever remind me of loss.'

In an ah-ha microsecond, that line did not hold as true as when I first wrote it. For the first time, without contempt, I accepted the moon as my forever-loss partner. I wanted to hold the moon, the moon of that night. To hold Nanda, his moon-face smiling. I wanted to appreciate the bead encircling Earth on the necklace strung around my heart. I wanted to dive into the blood-red moon, into the retina of Nanda's eye, and love without anguish.

After an intense question-and-answer session, longer than anticipated, we bowed and thanked our guests. The audience stood, clapped and cheered. Wet eyes, sniffles, handkerchiefs to faces. Upon exiting, weaving through people energised by art, we caught snippets of conversations about grief. No one escapes loss.

We returned to Treehenge still feeling the exhilaration of a performance well done. Wayne's truck rumbled along the dirt driveway beneath giant oak trees, the satisfying crackle of dried leaves beneath the wheels. He parked, turned off the headlights, and we soaked in the quiet of the woods for a few minutes.

'A glass of wine, then a walk?' he asked.

'Perfect,' I replied.

A breeze swept through and the trees clapped. As we entered the house, Wayne's dog, Sam, greeted us; his tail thrashed and thumped against wall and door. I called him Cartoon Dog because he looked like an animated Franz Kline painting, with black and white splashes, and peppered speckles. Wayne lit a fire, which popped and hissed in a potbelly stove. The smell of burnt wood filled the room. He poured a couple of glasses of red wine as I changed shoes.

'What a night,' I said, trying not to relax into the pillowy couch, thinking I'd never get back up.

We clinked our glasses. Guzzled our wine.

'Well, it's not over.' Wayne's face was full of night owl. 'Let's walk to the meadow.' He smiled so big his eyes almost disappeared, then he rose and swooshed his arm at his dog. 'Come on, Sam.'

Almost midnight, we stepped out from the light of the house. Our footsteps crunched; the leaf-littered path barely visible. I followed Sam's white spots and the sound of his breath; the patter of paws trotting in front of me. Wind whistled and pulsed through the hills. Overhead, excited trees waved their arms and branch shadows layered across the ground in frantic riverlettes. Fluttering leaves became schools of frenzied fish. Mesmerised in the dizzying shimmer, I stopped to catch my balance. Sam galloped ahead.

'Oh my goodness, it looks like the ground is cracking open.'

I searched into the trees for something solid. Beyond the mosaic of swaying branches, the sky glowed. Like afterimage, the colour you see after staring at red and then look away, a transparent-neon-indigo.

'No need for psychedelics,' I whispered.

Wayne nudged his elbow into my arm. 'Your eyes will get used to it.'

We walked across the flickering path towards a silhouetted arch, a recess in the trees. Beyond the dusky woods, I could see the meadow and Sam bouncing through a fluorescent carpet of silver grass. Drawn in by light, I walked ahead of Wayne. I stepped out from under the canopy of trees and entered the bowl of the meadow. The moon, as full as the night Nanda died, found me. *How did I not notice the moon tonight and its light falling through trees?*

Sam disappeared into the woods. I turned around to find Wayne morphed into an inky man-shape lingering in the woods. As I walked through meadow grass, I kept my eyes on the moon. Once seen as the headlight on a freight train, the moon transformed into a sweet honeydew melon. My eyes filled with moon-nectar. *I am a moon magnet.* The moon my spotlight, the meadow my stage. I lifted my arms wide open. *You must have heard my poem.*

Eager to set the moon free, the next day before the sun rose, I drove home as fast as I could, two and half hours, not the usual three or four, with the moon captured in my head. As soon as I walked through the front door, I dropped my bags on the living room floor, kissed Roger on the lips and headed to the studio. I opened the door and looked straight at Nanda's red blanket hanging slumped from a coat hanger nailed to the wall, an art object resembling a stripped carcass, a pale umber grid burned across its hide, an ephemeral metre stencilled in from window light marking each day, each year of Nanda's disappearance. The flesh of it, porous, dried up, his scent missing. Body worn, art worn, threads peeking out like broken memories. Nanda's blanket had not found its way to the cupboard of usable things. The thought of his blanket wrapped around another sleeping body stoked my sorrow. I had shaken Nanda loose, wrestled his animal and tried to wring free anything caught in that web. Used up. A collapsed flower.

A tattered sail. A flat balloon. Uninflatable. The blanket once had a life. I couldn't bring myself to set it on fire, but I could undo it.

I pulled the blanket off the hanger and stretched it across my work table. Gathered scissors, tweezers, and a sharp blade. Seated on a stool, I lifted a corner of his blanket into my lap and scrutinised the weave. *How does one unweave the past?* Blade in hand, I severed the hem stitches, unravelled one edge of his blanket to reveal the weft and warp. Each raw thread end a repetition of the tiny red Nanda line on the Nanda Junction map. One by one, I teased and pulled every thread loose. The blanket unmade. Line by line. I laid the threads across the back of a chair and tied the ends together. Not a story left in the fibres. I twisted a strand around my pinkie, wound the yarn into a ball the size of a fist until the spun orb grew larger than my head, then I tucked in the tail. From one continuous line, I made a moon. A moon I could hold.

Holding the Nanda Moon

Epilogue

Accepting the Gift

Grief is in the details, so is the healing.

December 2, 2017, nineteen years had passed since my son took his last breath.

There were two Nandas: nineteen years alive, and nineteen years dead. And two moons: an alive-Nanda moon, and a moon of loss.

Writing at my desk doing memory loop de loops, time escaped me. By 3:00 a.m., I swung like a pendulum from the arc of Nanda's life through the arc of his death. Life is next to death. Death is next to life. *You can't have one without the other.*

I did the maths. Nineteen plus nineteen. Thirty-eight. But totalling Nanda to thirty-eight years was a conceptual error. I had spent nineteen years mothering him and nineteen years grieving him. He'd forever be nineteen.

According to a lunar calendar, the full moon was due to roll into the sky by 7:00 a.m. I wanted to cry, but the tear-gates were stuck. Not grief-cry. I wanted to cry for joy, right beside the sad. I stood to light a candle next to my most loved photograph of Nanda, his arms wide open, and gazed at his beautiful face.

'If I live to be a hundred years old and I am sixty-two now, will I have to repeat nineteen years of grief twice more or is this the threshold at which I ...'

A stone caught in my throat. Back at my desk, I tried to write it. I couldn't even think the words—much less write them. Goodbye. Let Go. After nineteen years of metabolising grief, I had developed a solid sense of self. I wrote: farewell to struggling. The dam at the tear-gates swelled. As far as letting go, I would never let go of Nanda, but I was willing to let go of expecting his return and always needing to make sense of my loss. I was ready to unconditionally welcome any organic bit of him that happened to float by. The more I accepted the reality of his death, the more grateful I felt having gone through that process. I was done with grief. *Can anyone ever be done with grief?*

Art did not save me. Instead, it supported me as I leaned into that grief. It taught me the language of sorrow. Gave me the means to express my loss. Making art in grief was a reVISION of Nanda's life and mine. Rediscovery. Reinvention. Restrengthening. Reorganisation. Resocialization. A massive reBEING. I felt thankful to be alive. Most of my life that had not been true. Grief is a complicated gift, one I had come to appreciate and accept.

I switched off the lights, took another glance at Nanda, and blew out the candle. A wisp of smoke spiralled like a spirit and flew through the open window to our garden silvered with dew. Roses glistened next to twinkling baby's breath in a halo of alyssum. And although the moon could not be seen, I imagined everything bathed in moonglow. A river of love rushed through me and the tear-gates opened.

I missed him, but I wasn't caught in a vice of pining and aching. No more impossible mourning. Rarely longing. *Well, sometimes.* When I wanted to, I could conjure grief, dive into that well. But over time, I needed to visit loss less and less. In truth, Nanda wasn't completely gone. Love remained. Art remained.

After all, love and art transform and outlast grief.

The last entry in Nanda's art journal, drawn
on his train ride home after our last visit.

Acknowledgments

In grief-life, my sense of thankfulness has come to include loss. I needed a thank you willing to shake hands with death and stand willingly in sorrow; a thank you able to resuscitate life, make a clearing for change, and embrace acceptance; a thank you deep enough to dredge despair and reach into the thickest tangle of self-doubt to elicit confidence; to pry loose fear, swaddle anxiety in loving arms; to bring comfort and a sense of belonging; a thank you that acknowledges human fragility and the everyday hero; a thank you that elicits forgiveness; a thank you so bold, it reveals love and compassion in the worst of situations.

The dull, unremarkable, polite gesture—thank you—evolved into a lesson.

Thank you—an incantation.

Thank you—a positive spell.

Thank you—part of the healing.

Thank you to the humans who understood that grief is awkward at best. I want to thank those who accepted my disappearance, the endless inventories, obsession with details, repetitive questions, the agony, blame, guilt, and shame. I am so grateful to those who showed up when I was devastated, anxious, irritable, raw, vacant, disruptive, enraged, and full of woe. Thank you for listening to my long melancholy, for trying to comfort me when nothing could comfort me, and for not placing limits on my grief.

*

I want to extend my deepest gratitude and heartfelt appreciation to these kind humans.

Nanda, my Nandasqualanda Pondi, thank you for showing me how to love.

Lynn Michell—my publisher—thank you for loving my memoir and recognizing it not only as a distinct grief story but also as art. Thank you to her interns, Sri Jonnalagedda, Phoebe Kalid, Aislinn Nolan, and Rosie Pundick, for their discerning eyes and constructive comments that have refined the book's narrative and design.

Roger Edberg, thank you for your unwavering love, for listening to me for hours, days, weeks, months, years, to every detail, and for your discerning eye behind the camera—*River Rituals, Sitting on the Shoulders of the Bear River, Voices in the Mustard Fields, Clothes on Fire, Nanda Wire, Inhale,* and *Exhale.*

Arian Butler, thank you for your willingness to feel vulnerable to art. These photographs are testaments to your love and strength—*Hand in Hand,* and *Arian and the Nanda Swing.*

Rachel Butler, thank you for being authentic, fearless, compassionate, and full of love. You love big! Mostly, thank you for finding me in my loss and pointing me in the direction of transformation and healing. You are also a brilliant subject and photographer—*Rachel Waits, Ashes, Levitation, A Real Tea Party,* and *Nanda Pond.*

Lillian Holloway, from the day you were born you have inspired me to be a better person—excited about living. Thank you for demanding a real tea party—*A Real Tea Party.*

Scarlett and Isabella Holloway, thank you for lending me your creative vision, encouragement, and love.

Mum, Mouse's mum, thank you for bravely answering my questions about life and death, for being the most resilient woman I know, and for posing with Nanda's red blanket—*Mum Missing Nanda.*

Dad, RIP 2010, thank you for inadvertently teaching me how to be brave. Thank you for risking your life to bring Nanda to the top of the mountain—*Dad and the Nanda Sash.*

Robin Alexander, thank you for being there for me, you know you really aren't a Nanda surrogate, but you are one of my favourite men in the world. Thank you for taking Nanda's blanket for a ride—*Robin on the Tracks.*

Dr. Shelly Eyre Graham—writing partner and only-child-universe-spirit-sister—thank you for your powerful observations, insights, and enthusiasm for this project. The gazillions of hours you spent with me brainstorming have made this memoir infinitely more meaningful.

John Brantingham—writing partner—thank you for your infectious passion for storytelling, for being my creative companion and ally, and for being an indispensable part of my memoir journey. Your expert guidance and consistent encouragement have helped me gain confidence as a writer and as a person.

Roxan McDonald—writing partner—thank you for sitting with me for countless hours reading and rereading every version of each segment of my memoir with a fine-toothed brain. Your exceptional editing skills and understanding of nuance significantly enriched the pages of this memoir.

Krispy Mills and Mikivey, thank you for holding me, guiding me, feeding me, singing to me, listening to me, laughing and crying with me, making art with me, and big-loving me.

Wayne and Jeannie (RIP 2005) Olts, thank you for being family, giving me a place to process my grief, and seeing me through all of it. I am so grateful to Jeannie for telling me to face death and lean into grief. Best advice ever.

Dede Plaisted, thank you for reading my memoir in the throes of your own devastating loss, for sharing your home with me, for taking me to spectacular locations to art-process my grief, and for pressing the shutter release without question—*Buried in a Circle of Trees*, *Afterdeath 1*, and *Afterdeath 2*. I am forever moved by how you held the baby tree—*Embrace*.

Rudyard Wallen: thank you for taking care of me while assisting me with my art process.

Ellen Bass, thank you, your mentorship has been the cornerstone of this memoir. For twenty-five years, your relentless pursuit of excellence, patient guidance, and unwavering encouragement have been instrumental to my growth as a writer and the birth of this story.

Marion Roach Smith, you have been my guiding light. Your compassion, creative prowess and keen editorial eye got me to the finishing line with a well-polished, meaningful story.

Coeleen Kiebert, thank you, artist to artist, both mothers of lost children, for mentoring me, bringing me back to life, and reminding me that art is powerful, transformative, and healing.

Sandra Bertman, thank you for coaching me for twenty years and promoting my story because you believed it would bring relief to those experiencing grief.

Abigail Thomas, thank you for showing me how to trust my writing and my voice.

Thomas Moore, thank you for years of encouragement and your help distilling the title.

Nathan Shuherk, thank you for reading this memoir and for writing a rave testimonial. I am grateful for your generous support.

Sherry Holm, thank you for your kindness, for guiding me to my true self, and for asking all the right questions and holding space for me to answer honestly.

Bill Treguboff, thank you for honouring me as an artist and for taking time to lovingly sit with Nanda's red blanket—*Bill Holds Nanda*.

Flora Hansen—RIP 2019, thank you for being curious and reassuring about my most divergent experiences with grief, and for predicting my future—*Tell Me What You See*. By the way, your prediction came true.

George Tarsoudis—Astronomy Photographer—thank you for giving me permission to use your lovely full moon photograph—*Blue Moon*, August 2012. I knew you understood my work when you said, 'I believe, when you look at the moon phase, you can see the face of your son.' I do.

A deep thank you to my beta readers for taking time to read and review my memoir and thank you to my other dear collaborators. I love all of you dearly. Barbara Armstrong—RIP 2006, Tamsen (Vance) Armstrong, Ann Brantingham, Dr. Lorraine Comaner, Kate Flannery, Pat Gardner, Andy Gibbs, Colonel Dick Guthrie, Pat Hanson—RIP 2022, Bonnie Hearn Hill, Justin Holloway, Kathleen Jones—RIP 2017, Kendall Johnson, Avril Joy, Pauline Kirby, Tai Little, Margaret McHugh, Angela Mickelis, Leslie Mikiska—RIP 2021, Susan Orman, Sharon Parsons—RIP, Megan Reis—RIP 2019, Nancy Russell, Debra Ryll, Lee Ellen Shoemaker, Susan Slinger, Patty Spinazze, Deborah Stockdale, Pat Thompson—RIP 2015, Anh Stovall, Zoë Valaoriti, Stuart Vance, Lisa Erbach Vance, Trish Watson, Gretchen Werner, Lidia Yuknavitch, and Maila Zitelli. All your feedback has been an invaluable gift that provided me with profound insights into the impact of my story.

It takes a village to write a book. Full-hearted thank you!

*

Published Excerpts:

'First Full Moon' was first published in *Worthing Flash*, UK, February 2020

'Clothes on Fire' was first published in *Cholla Needles #59*, USA, 2021

'The Necklace' was first published in *Cholla Needles #59*, USA, 2021

'Nanda Finds God' was first published in *Worthing Flash*, UK, March 2022.

'Un' was first published in *The Journal of Radical Wonder*, USA, 2022

'Buried' was first published in *The Journal of Radical Wonder*, USA, 2022

Printed in the USA
CPSIA information can be obtained
at www.ICGtesting.com
CBHW041346030424
6315CB00026B/2486